THE ANXIETY CURE

YOU CAN FIND EMOTIONAL TRANQUILLITY AND WHOLENESS

DR. ARCHIBALD D. HART

Author of *Adrenaline and Stress*

THOMAS NELSON
Since 1798

NASHVILLE DALLAS MEXICO CITY RIO DE JANEIRO BEIJING

Published in Nashville, TN, by Thomas Nelson. Thomas Nelson is a trademark of Thomas Nelson, Inc.

Thomas Nelson, Inc. titles may be purchased in bulk for educational, business, fund-raising, or sales promotional use. For information, please e-mail SpecialMarkets@ThomasNelson.com.

All names have been changed to protect the privacy of the individuals.

Unless otherwise indicated, Scripture quotations used in this book are from the King James Version of the Bible (KJV).

Other Scripture references are from the following sources:

The Holy Bible, New International Version (NIV). Copyright ©1973, 1978, 1984, International Bible Society. Used by permission of Zondervan Bible Publishers.

The New King James Version (NKJV), copyright 1979, 1980, 1982, Thomas Nelson, Inc., Publishers.

New American Standard Bible (NASB), ©1960, 1977 by the Lockman Foundation.

Library of Congress Cataloging-in-Publication Data

Hart, Archibald D.
    The anxiety cure / by Archibald D. Hart.
       p.   cm.
    Includes bibliographical references.
    ISBN 13: 978-0-8499-4296-9 (tradepaper)
    ISBN 13: 978-0-8499-1532-1 (hardcover)
    1. Anxiety—Religious aspects—Christianity. 2. Peace of mind—Religious aspects—Christianity. I. Title.
    BV4908.5.H35 1999
    152.4'6—dc21   99-32884
                                                           CIP

Printed in the United States of America

08 09 10 11 12 RRD 20 19 18

CONTENTS

———∞∞∞———

PREFACE

———◦◦◦———

Anxiety is now the number one emotional problem of our day. Panic anxiety is the number one mental-health problem for women in the United States, and it is second in men only to substance abuse. Many anxious people also suffer from other emotional problems, notably depression. Anxiety and depression go together like Jack and Jill. Clinically, the two are sometimes very difficult to separate.

If you suffer from anxiety or know of someone who is suffering from anxiety, this book is for you. If you are in a high-pressure job and want to prevent anxiety problems from developing, this book is also for you. Prevention is always better than the cure.

I have one fundamental message in this book: *Tranquilizers alone will not cure your anxiety problems.* Is this important? It certainly is.

Why is this important? First, some amazing discoveries have taken place over the last few years that have revolutionized our understanding of what causes anxiety. I don't just mean the rejection of the archaic idea that all anxiety is just in your head. This has been obsolete for some time now. The modern scientific understanding of anxiety has gone beyond this. While a few die-hard psychologists still cling to the idea that all anxiety is purely a mental phenomenon (and therefore anxiety sufferers must spend the rest of their lives in some form of therapy), we now know that a lot of anxiety is biologically based. Notice, I didn't say *all* anxiety is biologically based. For example, the sort of anxiety that the Bible talks about, which is more akin to "worry," is probably a learned behavior that goes back to the earliest part of life. But the anxiety that is rampant in our society today does not necessarily come from excessive worry or bad childhood experiences. In fact, most of the patients I see report a perfectly normal childhood. They are usually extremely competent people.

In recent years, researchers have discovered just how much of our modern-day anxiety is being caused by stress. Stress not only causes headaches, ulcers, and heart disease, it also sets the stage for anxiety by wreaking havoc with the brain's biochemistry. This is why the most frightening increase in anxiety problems has occurred in highly functioning executives, women, pastors, and leaders, the very group who are the most overstressed.

The reason we are seeing such a dramatic rise in stress disease, anxiety, and clinical depression in modern times is not too difficult to discern. Humans were designed for camel travel, but most people are now acting like supersonic jets. In a nutshell, most of us are living at too fast a pace. Our adrenaline is a continuous stream of supercharged, high-octane energy. And, as with any vehicle running on high-octane fuel, we usually burn out quickly. If you really want to know why you are so stressed-out, consider the fact that you, like many others, are too hurried, hassled, and overextended. The pace of modern life is stretching all of us beyond our limits. And we are paying for this abuse in the hard and painful currency of stress and anxiety—plain and simple.

So the formula for understanding this book is simple: *High adrenaline, caused by overextension and stress, depletes the brain's natural tranquilizers and sets the stage for high anxiety.*

The connection between stress and anxiety disorders has been grossly over-looked, which has made it almost impossible for anyone to totally cure their anxiety. Without a proper understanding of the adrenaline-anxiety connection, many people simply rely on medication to control their anxiety. But let me be clear: Overdependence on artificial tranquilizers does not cure anxiety. Medication only relieves the symptoms of anxiety; it does not address the cause.

Perhaps the most important aspect of our recent discoveries is the fact that the brain has its *own* system of natural tranquilizers. But only one of these natural tranquilizers is similar to the benzodiazepines, the most commonly prescribed form of antianxiety medications available to us today. This means we cannot rely solely on artificial tranquilizers to fix our anxiety problems. We have to address the problem at its source, the disruption to these delicate hormones that is caused by roller-coaster, fast-track living.

Although artificial tranquilizers are effective in ameliorating anxiety symptoms in the short term, they don't cure the anxiety permanently. Further, modern tranquilizers are highly addictive. Your brain becomes dependent on them; before you can break this dependency, you have to restore the natural production of your brain's own tranquilizers, else all hell will break loose in your brain. Your brain can be as rebellious as any incorrigible child.

Something else has to change if you are going to cure your anxiety and not depend on artificial tranquilizers the rest of your life. It is this "something else" that you learn all about in the following pages. In fact, from my experience in treating anxiety problems, I am convinced that if you suffer from high anxiety, there is only one long-term answer to your problem: *You have to make some significant life changes.* This is not to say that antianxiety medications don't have their place. They do. I recommend them often. But they are only interim solutions that must be followed by long-term changes if you want to be free of troubling anxiety. So, we have a lot of work to do together in this book.

By the way, lest you think I only know about anxiety secondhand through my patients, think again. I hasten to confess that I am the chief of sinners in this area. That's why I know all about this subject. I was an adrenaline junkie for a long time, and I can easily backslide. I love challenges and thrive on crises. There is never enough time in any day for me to do all I want to. Life is too short, too precious, and full of too many opportunities to be lived half-heartedly, so I pull out all the stops. I have little tolerance for anything that blocks my progress. I know this problem personally, but I also have discovered the answers to overcome anxiety. I have effectively put into practice the advice I offer to you in the following pages.

So read on. This book may save your life. At the very least, it may preserve your sanity.

CHAPTER 1

THE ANXIETY
REVOLUTION

⎯⎯∞∞⎯⎯

An anxious heart weighs a man down.
PROVERBS 12:25 (NIV)

S amantha is a vice president for a large bank group. I must confess some
ignorance about the complexities of banking, but as best I can decipher,
Samantha "sells" money. Surprised? I sure was. I always thought you
bought things with money. Apparently, she shifts money around so as to get
the best return on it. Her work entails quite a bit of travel and takes Samantha
away from home regularly.

She wrote the following entry in her diary a month before she consulted
me:

A strange thing happened to me on a recent plane trip from San
Francisco to Los Angeles. It had been a long, hectic week, and I couldn't
wait to get home to my family. I was restless and irritable at the slowness
of everything. Finally the plane took off. We had no sooner left the ground
when I started to sweat. My heart sped up and felt that it was going to pop
out of my mouth. Then my head felt dizzy and I couldn't get enough air.
It was as if someone had shut off the air supply in the plane. I became
frightened. *What if the plane has no air supply?* I thought. I looked around

to see if others were struggling to breathe too. No such luck. It was me. I didn't know whether to be relieved or scared.

Then the pilot announced we were on our way to L.A. and gave the usual piffle about how high we were going to fly, etc. Now I couldn't swallow, let alone breathe. A tight band around my chest seemed to be getting tighter. *What is going on here?* I thought. My brain was frozen, and my body felt like it had floated off and now belonged to somebody else. I had never, ever felt this weird before. Was I going crazy? Since I couldn't go anywhere, not even leave my seat because of the stupid seatbelt warning, I closed my eyes and tried to relax. But my breathing became even more difficult as I relaxed.

Then just when I thought it couldn't get any worse, I felt a wave of terror sweep over me. *Something terrible is going to happen to me,* I thought. I had to muster up all my courage not to jump up and try to leave the plane. I took a deep breath, shuddered, and discovered that if I slowed down my breathing I felt a little better. Strange. Here I was, feeling that I wasn't getting enough air, yet I felt better if I slowed down my breathing. Later, of course, I discovered that this was a classic sign of panic attack, but at that moment I had no idea what was happening to me.

Because this all happened on an airplane, I intuitively knew that if I didn't get to the bottom of my problem and bring it under control, it could develop into a full-blown fear of flying. This could spell disaster for my job. I finally made it home but felt so fearful that I was quite incoherent and nonfunctional for several days. I stayed home and tried to rest. My husband kept pushing me for an explanation. Finally I told him about the whole episode, and it was then that he insisted I get some help.

THE PERILS OF PURSUING EXCELLENCE

Samantha is not alone in such an experience of panic. Approximately 10 percent of the population, more women than men, have had such a panic attack. Many have had repeated attacks.

But perhaps the most alarming aspect of panic attacks is that they mostly strike the strong. Yes, you read that correctly. Panic anxiety strikes those who seem to be the *strongest* among us.

The common stereotype is that only "weak" or anxiety-riddled people succumb to anxiety, particularly panic anxiety. This is just not true. Because this notion is so widely believed, many who acquire panic anxiety disorder are totally taken by surprise. They say things like:

"Others, yes, but not to me."

"I have always been the one who leads, the one who gets things done."

"In high school and college I was the 'star.' Everyone looked up to me."

"This couldn't possibly be happening to me."

But anxiety is not a disorder that afflicts the weak, the fragile, and the delicate. Often there is not the slightest hint of previous anxiety. This is the disorder of presidents, CEOs, VPs, ladder-climbers, powerhouses, dynamos, live wires, and go-getters. Those in leadership positions are more likely to be candidates for panic anxiety. Reason? *Anxiety is a disease of stress.* High-pressure jobs take their toll more than low-key jobs. People who are caught up in the pursuit of excellence are particularly vulnerable because they can't see the danger signs early enough.

To put it in a nutshell, if the combination of your personality and work makes you an adrenaline junkie, you are at risk for developing panic anxiety disorder. Anxiety is clearly the consequence of too much stress acting on your highly vulnerable brain chemistry. And if you have inherited a weakness in your brain's chemistry, you will have a much lower threshold for tolerating anxiety than others.

CAN WE ESCAPE BEING CAUGHT UP IN A HIGH-STRESS WORLD?

It is unlikely that you can ever escape totally from this high-stress world. We are all on the same train. How can you possibly get off without forfeiting the opportunity to achieve anything meaningful with your life? So the question really becomes: Is a high-pressure life admirable and necessary? To some extent I must say yes. It's the American way. How else can you achieve the American Dream? Success demands that you pay the price of committing yourself to pursuing excellence. I wouldn't really want to live any other way.

But this approach to life has its penalties and pitfalls. So if you want to preserve your sanity and achieve a healthy life, *you have to make some choices and resolve to live a balanced life.* By a "balanced" life, I mean that, like a marathon runner, you must learn how to pace yourself. You give it all you've got going uphill and rest as much as you can going downhill. You try to balance the drain on your energy so that you can "go the distance."

You can't escape the realities of our high-stress world. You certainly can't turn back the clock to simpler times—although, I must confess, this is a wonderful fantasy that I occasionally indulge as a form of escape. I frequently reflect on the many happy childhood times I had with my grandparents. They lived a simple, country life. They were totally self-sufficient, tilling a small piece of land and raising their own food. They saved wisely for their retirement and spent little money during the bleak years of the Second World War. With only a shortwave radio to connect them to the rest of the world, life seemed simple yet luxurious to me as a child. There was a sense of unhurriedness and simple pleasures. All the money in the world couldn't buy such luxury in today's world. It is not for sale; you have to create it.

But we can't go backward, only forward. We must make the most of the present realities of our lives. Frankly, though, seeking to live a balanced life is like trying to find your way through a dangerous minefield. The way to survival is narrow and must be charted with care if you are going to come out the other end intact. You need to understand *all* the dangers and have clearly worked out strategies for avoiding disaster. Likewise, many are falling into stress disease, particularly panic-anxiety disorder, because they do not have a clear strategy to develop the antidotes for the fallout from the pursuit of excellence.

CREATING YOUR OWN TRANQUILLITY

My message in this book is quite unique and, hopefully, simple and easy to apply. It is about creating a tranquil life in the midst of an anxious world. It is about how you can enhance your brain's natural tranquilizers and push back the inroads of stress.

What is revolutionary in this book is understanding the connection between anxiety and the stress hormones produced by the adrenal glands. Anxiety is *not* the presence of some phenomenon in the brain, but the *absence* of something else.

So what is missing when we are anxious? Important brain chemicals called "neurotransmitters." I call them our "happy messengers," and this is an extremely accurate label for them. Our brain is full of these messengers. They help us remember, keep us awake, and in the final analysis, keep us sane. When our brain is robbed of happy messengers, as when our stress is too high and prolonged, it cannot function properly. Anxiety is then the "smoke alarm" alerting us to the chaos. This process is all a very intelligent design of a Master Creator.

Anxiety, therefore, is not the presence of something toxic in the brain; it is the absence of the happy messengers that keep us tranquil. Tranquillity is, after all, the goal your brain is trying to achieve. This book will show you how to restore the tranquillity that has been destroyed by overstress.

The role of stress in producing anxiety, therefore, is foundational to all I have to say. I first explored the connection between stress and anxiety thirteen years ago in my book *Adrenaline and Stress*. Since then, the evidence for a link between the overproduction of adrenaline and emergence of disorders like panic anxiety has expanded immensely.

Indisputably, there is a strong connection between the overuse of our adrenal system and stress disease. But just as living high on adrenaline causes stress disease, it also causes anxiety problems. The mechanism is very simple. To put it simply, *stress depletes our natural brain tranquilizers*. Panic is the main product of this heightened anxiety. In its milder form, this anxiety is simply called a "panic attack." In its more severe form, it becomes an affliction called "panic anxiety disorder," one of the most frightening and debilitating of all the anxiety disorders.

WE ARE ALL ANXIETY PRONE

Before you jump to the conclusion that you don't have a problem with anxiety, let me ask you to continue reading. Many hardworking, driven people (like you and me) don't realize just how close they walk to the precipice of anxiety until one day, out of the blue, a panic attack strikes. Herein lies our greatest danger: Because adrenaline overuse feels so exhilarating and invigorating, we don't consider some of the things that give us an adrenaline rush to be stressful. The purpose of adrenaline is to make us feel excited during a state of emergency, so it is easy to misread that excitement as safe. We don't realize how close we are to the edge of anxiety until we lose our footing and tumble down into the dark abyss of panic.

In this sense, one's first panic attack is really a blessing in disguise. It warns the sufferer that he or she is living too fast, too hassled, and too stressed-out. Losing tranquillity happens because a person's happy messengers are being invaded and destroyed by stress hormones. While they are normally allies, these hormones become enemies in the face of danger and stress.

The early stages of a panic anxiety disorder, then, are really warning signals. If you heed these warning signals and change your ways, as Samantha did, you will be able to overcome your anxiety. But if you ignore these warning signals, you run the risk of creating more suffering than you are bargaining for. Worse yet, you could well end up with an anxiety problem for the rest of your life.

ANXIETY SYMPTOM CHECKLIST

Anxiety symptoms fall into three categories: physiological symptoms, cognitive symptoms, and emotional symptoms. Count the following symptoms that apply to you:

PHYSIOLOGICAL SYMPTOMS
Do you feel:
- ❏ Weak all over?
- ❏ Rapid, pounding heartbeat or palpitations?
- ❏ Tightness around your chest?
- ❏ Hyperventilation (a feeling that you cannot get enough air)?
- ❏ Periodic dizziness and sweating?
- ❏ Muscle tension, aches, or tremors?
- ❏ Chronic fatigue?

COGNITIVE SYMPTOMS
Do you think to yourself:
- ❏ I can't carry on. I've got to get out of here.
- ❏ What if I make a fool of myself?
- ❏ People are looking at me all the time.
- ❏ I'm having a heart attack.
- ❏ I'm going to faint.
- ❏ I'm going crazy.
- ❏ I can't go on alone; no one will help.
- ❏ I can't go out; I will lose control.
- ❏ I feel confused and can't remember things.

EMOTIONAL SYMPTOMS
    Do you think to yourself:
    ❑ I'm full of fears that I can't get out of my mind.
    ❑ I feel like something terrible is going to happen.
    ❑ I worry excessively.
    ❑ I feel uneasy and alone a lot of the time.
    ❑ I often feel isolated, lonely, down in the dumps, and
        depressed.
    ❑ I feel I have no control over what happens to me.
    ❑ I feel embarrassed, rejected, and criticized.
    ❑ I often feel like screaming with anger.

SCORING

This checklist is not designed to be a diagnostic tool so much as it is
intended to communicate the variety of symptoms experienced by
people with high anxiety.

However, if you are experiencing *at least three symptoms* in each
category, then your anxiety level is starting to be a problem, especially if you experience the symptoms often.

If you are experiencing *more than three symptoms* in each category and are not in treatment for an anxiety-related problem, then I
would suggest that you consult a professional right away. It is better
to be safe than regret your failure to take action at a later point.

If taking this inventory causes you anxiety, you probably need to
get some help.

HOW COMMON ARE ANXIETY PROBLEMS?

Since overstress is so common today, you can pretty well predict that anxiety
problems are also common. According to the National Institute of Mental
Health (NIMH), more than twenty-three million Americans suffer from
some form of anxiety disorder, including panic anxiety disorder, obsessive-
compulsive disorder, posttraumatic stress disorder, phobias, and generalized
anxiety disorder. To quote NIMH's Web site on this matter:

[Anxiety sufferers] suffer from symptoms that are chronic, unremitting, and usually grow progressively worse if left untreated. Tormented by panic attacks, irrational thoughts and fears, compulsive behaviors or rituals, flashbacks, nightmares, or countless frightening physical symptoms, people with anxiety disorders are heavy utilizers of emergency rooms and other medical services.

Because of widespread lack of understanding and the stigma associated with such disorders, many people with anxiety problems are not diagnosed and do not receive the treatments that have been proven effective through research. They continue to suffer unnecessarily, and their work, family, and social lives are disrupted. Many become imprisoned in their homes.

And let me emphasize that the stigma I have just alluded to is significantly greater in our Christian subculture. And the lack of understanding, or more accurately, the gross misunderstanding of what causes anxiety is having devastating effects on many Christians and their families. Almost everywhere I travel in the world, I encounter deeply troubled Christians who feel guilty and hopeless just because they do not understand how widespread anxiety problems are in our overstressed lives. I hear it from them in seminars, in letters, and in e-mail messages, pleading for a Christian-based understanding of anxiety.

Many anxiety sufferers believe that God is somehow punishing them or that their anxiety is a sign that they lack adequate faith. At times, I feel like sobbing when I read their pathetic pleas for help.

Their indignity is made even more painful by the condemnation they feel for their so-called failure. Those around them, including spouses, family members, and Christian friends, judge them most cruelly. And this judgment is born of ignorance, even sheer unadulterated stupidity. Believe me, just a little bit of knowledge on this subject could work miracles of recovery. God is not wreaking havoc upon His people like a plague. His own people are condemning helpless sufferers, and their misguided judgments are causing a lot of the misery I see.

DOESN'T EVERYONE HAVE SOME ANXIETY?

Some anxiety goes with being human. It has always been with us and will remain until the end of time. Anxiety can be normal and even necessary in certain instances. Normal anxiety keeps us busy, reminds us to pay our bills, and pushes us forward to succeed. Its presence in human experience throughout history would suggest that in its pure form it serves some useful purpose. And for a long time, psychologists, and philosophers before them saw anxiety as a necessary and normal aspect of life. It was, they thought, the mental equivalent of physical pain that served as a "warning" system to alert us to danger.

But like so many good ideas, they can be taken too far. Anxiety is only normal up to a point. Our happy messengers are designed to fluctuate. We cannot expect to stay in a perpetual state of tranquillity. We all need some anxiety to make our lives meaningful and productive. My concern in this book is the anxiety that is beyond the bounds of normality.

TYPES OF ANXIETY PROBLEMS

Let's look at a brief overview of anxiety problems. Following are the most common types of anxiety:

PANIC ANXIETY DISORDER: This is probably the best studied and understood of all the anxiety disorders. Panic anxiety disorder is characterized by repeated, unprovoked attacks of terror, accompanied by physical symptoms, including chest pain, heart palpitations, shortness of breath, dizziness, weakness, and sweating. A panic attack can resemble a heart attack, and often the first indication of the disorder is when you are rushed to the emergency room with chest pains. It is called a "disorder" when the problem persists for more than a month.

GENERALIZED ANXIETY DISORDER (GAD): This is a free-floating, pervasive anxiety or a constant unrealistic worry. It impacts your ability to complete your daily activities. GAD is often associated with physical anxiety symptoms such as muscle aches, fatigue, sleep disturbances, sweating, dizziness, and nausea.

SPECIFIC PHOBIA: This is a persistent, marked irrational fear of an object or situation that leads to avoidance of the object or situation. Exposure to the stimulus provokes an immediate and extreme response, even a panic attack. To be considered a phobia, the fear has to be excessive and incapacitating.

SOCIAL PHOBIA: Also called "social anxiety disorder," this is a persistent fear of one or more social situations in which you are exposed to possible scrutiny by others and fear that you may do something or act in a way that will be humiliating. Social phobias can also include extreme shyness.

AGORAPHOBIA: This can occur with or without panic attacks and literally means "fear of the marketplace." It is a fear of public places where your panic or anxiety might bring embarrassment. You come to fear leaving home or being trapped in a room or church pew because you could lose control.

OBSESSIVE-COMPULSIVE DISORDER (OCD): This disorder is characterized by repeated, intrusive, and unwanted thoughts (obsessions) that cause anxiety, often accompanied by ritualized behaviors (compulsions) that relieve this anxiety. Common obsessions include fear of contamination or fear of harming someone. Persistent worries, like worrying about whether you turned off the stove and making repeated trips back to check, are also obsessions. Common compulsions are excessive cleaning, counting, double-checking, and hoarding.

POSTTRAUMATIC STRESS DISORDER (PTSD): This is a very special form of anxiety caused when someone experiences a severely distressing or traumatic event; individuals become so preoccupied with the experience that they are unable to lead a normal life. PTSD must involve extreme fear. Generally, it takes repeated traumatic events, not just a single event, to cause this disorder.

ACUTE STRESS DISORDER: This is less serious than PTSD and occurs when severe anxiety symptoms follow exposure to a specific, extreme trauma such as experiencing or observing an accident in which someone was killed. The symptoms of acute stress disorder include detachment, numbing, repeated dreams, and marked symptoms of anxiety including inability to sleep, poor concentration, and an exaggerated startle response. The problem usually doesn't last longer than a month.

SEPARATION ANXIETY DISORDER: Usually associated with childhood or adolescence (although some cases occur in adulthood), this is the feeling of extreme anxiety when you are separated from home or loved ones. In its severe forms, separation anxiety can be quite incapacitating.

HOW ARE ANXIETY DISORDERS TREATED?

The most common stereotype in most people's minds is that tranquilizers are the only treatment for anxiety disorders. Since many people fear that tranquilizers are addictive and can "control" your mind, they intentionally fail to get treatment that could help them.

While it is true that artificial tranquilizers are *sometimes* used in anxiety treatment, they play a temporary and minor role overall. Other medications that are not addictive play a more important role in the long term. Furthermore, artificial tranquilizers only work because your brain has its own tranquilizers. Since your brain's tranquilizers, or "happy messengers," are being systematically destroyed by stress, it only stands to reason that the artificial equivalent must be supplied in treatment under some conditions.

Seldom, however, are medications used on their own. Usually, professional treatment of anxiety disorders requires a combination of medication and cognitive-behavioral therapy. Treatment is usually individualized for each patient, depending on the severity of the symptoms and level of function. I will discuss these treatments in more detail in chapter 4.

IS MEDICATION ALWAYS NECESSARY?

One of the difficult tasks I have in this book is to present the right balance between when to use antianxiety medication and when to avoid it. Obviously, some medications must be taken to provide an effective result. But anxiety sufferers have many questions about these medications. Here are just a few short answers to the more important questions I get asked by patients whom I recommend for medication treatment. (More detailed answers will come later.)

ARE ANTIANXIETY MEDICATIONS ABSOLUTELY NECESSARY? Is it possible, for instance, to cure repeated anxiety attacks without them?

ANSWER: If you are determined and self-reliant and the attacks are in their early stages, you may be able to overcome them without medication. Some anxiety problems definitely need medication; others don't. However, you will need to make some urgent and lifelong changes. In the long term, curing your anxiety is a matter of changing your susceptibility to stress. Without medication, it will take longer for you to achieve a cure, and you will run a greater risk of relapsing.

ARE SOME MEDICATIONS SAFER THAN OTHERS? Many are rightly concerned about the safety of medications. And this should be so for all medications, not just those used to treat anxiety.

ANSWER: If you avoid alcohol and stick closely to the recommended dosages, all antianxiety medications are safe. Your doctor will see to it.

ARE SOME MEDICATIONS LESS ADDICTIVE THAN OTHERS? The matter of addiction should always be a concern.

ANSWER: Absolutely. Not all medications are equally addictive, and sometimes it is the person who is prone to addiction, not the medication that causes addiction. In any event, not everyone is susceptible to developing a dependence on a tranquilizer. (I prefer to call it "dependence" rather than addiction because the word *dependence* more accurately describes what happens.) Furthermore, if your clinician is competent, you will have no trouble coming off your medication when you are ready to do so. I will tell you how to do this in chapter 6.

DO ANTIANXIETY MEDICATIONS HAVE TO BE TAKEN FOREVER? Many are concerned about how long they have to take the medication, especially if it has to be for the rest of their lives.

ANSWER: Absolutely not. They are taken for a limited period of time only. Provided you are addressing the other changes that must also be made, notably learning stress management, a time will come when you can taper off all medications. It may take longer than you would like, but that is up to you and the diligence with which you follow the larger treatment plan. But you are not the best judge of how and when to stop. Your clinician will know how long you will need the medication for your particular problem.

The bottom line boils down to deciding which forms of anxiety should be treated with medications and which should only be treated with good counseling. In any case, you should always be getting some form of counseling, even when you are taking antianxiety medication.

A SPECIAL MESSAGE TO CHRISTIAN READERS

My message is important whatever your faith—or lack of it. However, many of my readers consider themselves to be Christians so I want to address some of my remarks in this first chapter to these readers.

For Christians, my message in this book is particularly important. Primarily, because many of you have such a strong antidrug mind-set, you may be doing yourself a lot of harm by *not* considering a short-term trial on an appropriate antianxiety medication. Not all medications are addictive. Antidepressants are frequently the preferred medication for anxiety disorders, and they are absolutely *not addictive.*

Why should you consider getting professional treatment? Because serious anxiety problems only get worse if you don't treat them early enough. A lot of evidence now indicates that untreated anxiety becomes "encoded" in the brain. In other words, it becomes a permanent problem.

But there is a second important reason why my message here is important to Christians. We Christians are probably *more* prone to developing a high level of stress, and we need to pay particular attention to the connection between adrenaline and stress. Just as we are ignorant of how the "good" stress in our lives can produce "bad" stress disease, so we are also ignorant about how the pressure we feel trying to live good lives can cause severe anxiety problems. Being good by relying on our own resources is a lost cause. The harder we try in our own strength, the more our lives become stressful. That is not what God wants from us.

THE TEN MOST RIDICULOUS THINGS YOU CAN SAY
TO A PERSON WITH ANXIETY
(or to yourself, for that matter)

1. "We all get anxious, so just pull yourself together."
2. "If you would just relax more, your anxiety will go away."
3. "Have you committed some sin that God is punishing you for?"

---

4. "You worry too much, and worry never changes anything."
5. "If you just try harder you wouldn't feel so stressed-out."
6. "Just ignore your problems and they will go away."
7. "Anxiety can't kill you, so just snap out of it."
8. "If you had more faith, you would stop worrying."
9. "Take a holiday and all your problems will go away."
10. "If I can cope with my life, you should be able to cope with yours."

DOES SCRIPTURE CONDEMN ANXIETY?

Before doing anything constructive about their anxiety, many Christians must resolve the issue of whether Scripture condemns anxiety, and by implication, those who suffer from it.

There is no doubt in my mind that Scripture clearly condemns a particular form of anxiety. Jesus said: "Let not your heart be troubled" (John 14:1). But as we have already established, there are many different *forms* of anxiety. Are they all condemned? Before we rush in to condemn *all* anxiety as bad, therefore, we should first examine each of these forms and determine *which* of them Scripture condemns.

It is unfortunate that we have only one word for anxiety in English. Often this restricts our understanding of the many facets of anxiety. A good analogy would be the concept of love. In English, we only have one word for love. We refer to the "love of a mother for a child," "the love of a brother for a brother," and "the love of a lover for a lover" in almost the same breath. But each use of the word *love* means something quite different. This is the same for the word *anxiety.*

Furthermore, many of the anxiety problems we suffer from today were not common in biblical times. Take panic attacks, for instance. I doubt whether the pace of life in New Testament times was hectic enough to cause the conditions needed for panic anxiety disorder. I see no such evidence for its existence in biblical times. In fact, a hundred years ago, panic anxiety disorder was very rare. But with industrialization and urbanization, it has become increasingly common. Remember, there were no jets, electric lights, or concrete jungles until recent times. The pace of life was slow. Camel speed was about as fast as you could travel for long distances. Lots of recovery time was built into the natural cycle of life. No late-night TV or football games could eat up your leisure time. Why, I can vaguely remember times of such boredom even in my own lifetime.

Not only were there likely no panic attacks in New Testament times, there were probably no phobias, obsessive-compulsive disorders, or even posttraumatic stress disorders. These are the products of urbanization, industrialization, and depersonalization. But there is one form of anxiety that transcends time and culture—the form of anxiety we call "worry." And I believe that whenever Scripture refers to anxiety, it means primarily "worrying" or "fretting." *Worry anxiety,* therefore, is that form of anxiety uniformly condemned in Scripture—and it is the *only* condemned form of anxiety.

Jesus sometimes used the expression "taking thought" to refer to this form of anxiety. In the Sermon on the Mount, for example, Jesus clearly draws attention to the destructiveness of taking thought for the future or for what will happen (see Matt. 6:25–34 NIV). And His teaching here is startlingly clear: Worrying doesn't help birds get their food nor does it help lilies grow. And worrying about tomorrow is about as useless as trying to increase your height just by thinking about it. There are plenty of things to be concerned about *right now,* and worrying about tomorrow will not keep tomorrow's evils away.

The apostle Paul, obviously a very intense person who at times experienced "fear" and "trembling" (1 Cor. 2:3), also had a lot to say about worrying. In Philippians 4:6, Paul tells us to "be anxious for nothing," reminding us to pray "with thanksgiving" (NKJV). The apostle Peter also tells us to cast "all [our] care upon him; for he careth for [us]" (1 Pet. 5:7).

Worry anxiety is also portrayed in Scripture as an evil that chokes God's Word: "He also that received seed among the thorns is he that heareth the word; and the care of this world, and the deceitfulness of riches, choke the word, and he becometh unfruitful" (Matt. 13:22). The "care of this world" in this verse could also be translated as "the worry of the world" (NASB). This clearly implies that excessive preoccupation with life's uncertainties is like a bed of thorns that chokes God's Word and constricts the development of faith.

Worry anxiety is also seen as a hindrance that keeps us from doing God's work. Second Timothy 2:4 suggests that soldiers of Jesus Christ should not get overly entangled in or become worried about the affairs of everyday life.

Worrying about daily problems distracts and detracts from the battles we must fight spiritually.

Finally, Luke 21:34 proposes that worry anxiety is a problem that gluts our souls and weighs us down so that we cannot be alert to impending real perils.

Worry anxiety, therefore, is rightly characterized in Scripture as a lack of trust in God and a failure to fully understand His plan and provision for us. It is clearly harmful to us and, therefore, *displeasing to God.*

But this does not mean we should not be concerned about our lives, neither does it mean that we have committed the unpardonable sin just because we spent a sleepless night worrying about a wayward child or an unhappy friend. Paul clarifies this distinction when he tells us to stop *perpetually* worrying about even one thing (Phil. 4:6; emphasis mine). That word *perpetually* is the key word. Worry anxiety is only a problem if it is perpetual—if it goes on and on and on. And then he gives us the prescription for curing our worry: We are to bring our requests to God, with an attitude of thanksgiving, expecting that what awaits us is the "peace of God, which surpasses all comprehension" (Phil. 4:7 NASB).

Worry anxiety, then, is what happens when God's people try to live their lives independently from God. When we refuse to be joined to our Creator, even when He has provided a way back to Himself through Jesus Christ, we settle down into the bog of our own anxiety.

Intimacy with Jesus, furthermore, must inevitably lead to an inner quietness that is foundational to tranquillity. Still, it is hard for believers to stop perpetually worrying and to reach out for the resources God makes available. I have met very few Christian believers who are so perfect in their walk with God that they are free of worry anxiety. Because of our human weaknesses, the Great Physician has prescribed scriptural antidotes for anxiety. These include reliance upon God's Spirit (see Mark 13:11), appropriating God's provisions (see Luke 12:22–30), and resting in God's care (see 1 Pet. 5:6–7). What medicine could be more complete?

THE CONSEQUENCES OF NEGLECTING GOD'S PROVISIONS

The problem, of course, is not with the medicine but with the patients—you and me. We are rebellious children by nature and gag at God's "medicine." We are disobedient, and we love to run away when God calls. So we shouldn't be surprised if, while wallowing in the pigpen like true prodigals, we also suffer from incapacitating anxiety. The responsibility for getting up and leaving the pigpen of disobedience lies with us, as we will see shortly.

Every day of my professional life, I encounter exceptionally fine Christian people who are experiencing incapacitating anxiety that robs them of peace and tranquillity. They have aggravating sleep disturbances, aching ulcers, throbbing headaches, persistent high blood pressure, intractable pain, overwhelming tiredness, and worry that drives them into early graves. The problem is that anxiety itself doesn't kill you; it just makes you wish you were dead. And such suffering is totally unnecessary. It *can* be prevented.

Tranquillity. How do you get it, and how do you keep it? These two questions sum up our quest in this book. There is no doubt in my mind that God intends us to be calm, serene, peaceful, composed, and good-natured—all qualities of tranquillity. According to Oswald Chambers, author of the bestselling devotional *My Utmost for His Highest,* a life of intimacy with Christ leads to a "strong, calm serenity"—as good a definition of *tranquillity* as I could possibly come up with.

As Jesus says in John 16:33: "These things I have spoken unto you, that in me ye might have peace."

CHAPTER 2

THE GABA-ANXIETY
CONNECTION

———— ∞∞∞ ————

Master, carest thou not that we perish?
. . . And [Jesus] said unto the sea, Peace, be still.
And the wind ceased, and there was a great calm.

MARK 4:38–39

Before we can talk of answers, we need to have a basic understanding of the physical causes of anxiety. Let me walk you through the essentials you should know.

A new era dawned for brain research in the spring of 1977, when scientists discovered tools that would enable them to penetrate the very interior of single nerve cells. Since then, new discoveries have been made almost daily about the inner workings of God's greatest miracle of creation—the human brain. These tools, and many that have been added since, help unlock the mystery and intricacy of how tiny cells in the brain go about their business in a world all their own. Most importantly, scientists have discovered how these cells communicate with each other.

Knowing how brain cells "talk" to each other is crucial to your understanding of anxiety. You need to understand a little of this mystery if you are going to formulate a "natural" way to cure yourself of an anxiety problem. The reason so many people feel helpless in the face of emotional turmoil is that they don't know enough about what is going on in their brains; to them, the process seems too mysterious, too enigmatic.

But it's not all that complicated. You will feel more in control of your destiny if you know what is going on in your brain. This understanding, at the very least, will help you to choose the treatment you should pursue as well as help you to avoid those mistakes that are likely to aggravate your anxiety problem. Knowing the basics of what causes anxiety is crucial to becoming the master of your emotions.

Conversations are going on between your brain cells all the time. The vital group of chemicals I mentioned earlier called "neurotransmitters" are the messengers, and their language consists of minute reactions that "fire" nerve cells. Neurotransmitters carry messages between different parts of the brain. Not only do they transport information, but they spur some nerve cells to be more activated and responsive while calming and forcing others to slow down and remain quiet.

These chemical messengers pick up, transport, and then deposit their instructions all over the brain, like the pony-express riders of early western times. As a child, I remember being quite enthralled by movies showing these riders as they leaped from one tired horse to a fresh pony at the pony-express stations spread across the country. I actually considered becoming a pony-express rider when I grew up, but in far-off South Africa, where I lived. Imagine my disappointment when my father told me they no longer existed.

But pony-express riders are a good analogy for the messengers that travel through our brain. Nerves are their pathways, and synapses are the pony-express stations that refresh them. Messages carried by neurotransmitters are often life-giving. They tell different parts of the brain whether to be happy or sad, anxious or tranquil. They help the brain decide whether there is a state of emergency or a danger to be avoided. Likewise, they also tell the brain when to relax because all is safe.

I am truly amazed by this process. Proper communication between our brain cells is all wonderfully complex and vitally essential to our sanity. Normal human emotions are determined by whether these neurotransmitters are successful in communicating their messages to your brain cells. On a typical day in the life of your brain, literally trillions of messages are sent and received by these neurotransmitters.

Some of these messages are upbeat and happy and carried by that group of messengers called "happy messengers." Technically, these neurotransmitters are known as "biogenic amines." They don't just help us to be happy, they also help us to cope with pain and remain tranquil. They energize us and make us feel vital and optimistic. Some examples of these happy messengers include serotonin, noradrenaline (produced in the brain, not by the adrenals), dopamine, and a group of natural tranquilizers that are found in abundance in the brain.

Other messages are communicated around the brain by "sad messengers." These neurotransmitters carry bleak and somber messages. They tell the brain to be downhearted, cautious, and dispirited. An excess of sad messengers makes us depressed, anxious, sleepless, and fatigued. They are the messengers that dominate when we feel overwhelmed by life's demands. Examples of sad messengers are cortisol and a group of enzymes that rob us of happy messengers.

Now let's be realistic here. We are never totally without happy or sad messengers. Both are always present in our brains. *What determines our mood is the balance between the two.* As long as these neurotransmitters are in balance, we are tranquil and happy. But when something happens that upsets the balance and causes the sad messengers to dominate, our sea of tranquillity can become a raging ocean of turmoil. Happiness gives way to misery and emotional pain. Tranquillity (the natural state of the human brain) gives way to anxiety.

WHAT UPSETS THE BALANCE OF HAPPY AND SAD MESSENGERS?

What upsets this balance? Serious illness, for starters. It stands to reason that when your body is fighting a serious illness, it must focus on this battle. Everything else, therefore, must take a back seat. Sad messengers are essential to fighting disease. For instance, have you noticed that when you have the flu you also feel a little depressed? That mild depression occurs because your body needs you to slow down and even disengage from normal activities so it can reserve its strength to fight the invading bacteria or viruses. If you cooperate with these sad messengers, you will recover sooner.

Substances such as alcohol, recreational drugs, and even some prescription drugs also upset the balance between happy and sad messengers. These "substances of abuse" upset your brain's biochemistry by falsely elevating happy messengers for a short period of time, promising tranquillity and bliss, and then letting the system down. You pay for this temporary bliss with more unhappiness afterward.

Also, your brain system can become unbalanced when something goes wrong with your genes. Examples of this type of imbalance include genetically determined mental disorders such as schizophrenia and bipolar depression. Under the influence of certain genes, a very profound unbalancing of the happy and sad messengers can occur. Fortunately, however, we now have medications that can correct these genetic problems. In fact, these apparently more serious emotional problems are a lot easier to cure than some of the psychologically determined neurotic conditions. Brain chemistry is a lot easier to put right than a lifetime of bad influences.

And finally, but most importantly, the balance between the happy and sad messengers is determined by *stress.*

IT'S THE STRESS, DUMMY!

Did I get your attention? No disrespect intended—it's just that this message is so hard to get across to highly intelligent, highly driven, triple–Type A people. So let me say it again: *Too much stress is bad for everything.*

Stress makes you feel thunderstruck by life. The battle of the chemical messengers swings in favor of the sad messengers, overwhelming the happy messengers and causing them to struggle to keep up with the battle. When you begin to run out of happy messengers, you experience negative consequences, such as sleep disturbances, lack of enjoyment about life (called "anhedonia"), and, of course, panic attacks.

IS THERE SUCH A THING AS "GOOD" STRESS?

Stress upsets the balance of every hormone in your body and brain, which is why the only form of "good" stress is "short-lived" stress.

I need to emphasize this point here because Hans Selye (the grandfather of all stress research) is often misunderstood. Selye introduced the concept of "eustress," that form of good stress that we all need for a rich and fulfilling life.

Unfortunately, many have latched on to this concept as a way of rationalizing their overstressed lives. I hear it all the time: "I don't feel stressed-out. This just feels too good to be stress."

Of course, we all need a bit of stress to keep us going. But overstress is *never* eustress. Prolonged stress, whether it is good or bad, will kill you as surely as stepping in front of a fast-moving train. So stop kidding yourself into believing that your stress is "good" stress.

All stress causes problems with the brain's happy messengers. When the brain senses stress, it assumes that there is an emergency. It also assumes that there is danger of some sort and activates the fight-or-flight response. This is hardly a friendly or welcoming condition for keeping happy messengers at home. So in its intelligent way, our brain's sad messengers kick in and take control because they have to ensure survival, not bliss. They mobilize the body's resources to deal with the emergency. And this gives the sad messengers a role to play that they readily jump to. This is the moment they live for. Like fighter pilots who train all their lives for battle, sad messengers relish the moment they are finally called into action.

THE BATTLE OF THE MESSENGERS

As the level of stress escalates, the upper hand in the battle of the messengers shifts from the tranquil and happy to the anxious and unhappy side. You will have noticed this shift in your own emotions from time to time. Soon the whole brain is in a state of chemical unbalance.

Why is this important to know? First, you should learn to read the signs of this shift of balance as a warning signal. If you intervene quickly, you can stop the shift of power, assuming, of course, that it is not a matter of life or death. (If it is, don't interfere. Let the sad messengers do what they are designed to do.)

Second, you need to learn the limits of your own brain chemistry. By paying attention to this shift of power, you will discover just how much stress you can tolerate. You then set up a stress-tolerance boundary and do everything in your power not to trespass this boundary. This means setting limits and telling everyone, even loved ones, to back off when they try to push you past your limits.

So, overstress, not ordinary short-lived stress, is bad for everything. It results in your whole brain being in a state of distress and unbalance. How does this make you feel? Terrible. Your brain's normal state of tranquillity is vanquished. Anxiety dominates. In severe cases a period of panic anxiety sets in. And panic anxiety is itself a stressor, so it feeds more stress into your already weakened system, creating more unbalance. This state of unhappiness can become self-perpetuating and cause a "spiraling down" effect, in which you feel totally overwhelmed by unhappiness and misery. Extreme fatigue, sleep disturbances, deep depression, aches and pains, and an inability to cope with even the simplest demands of life ensue.

RESTORING THE BALANCE OF THE MESSENGERS

"My first thought was *I'm going crazy.* Everyone I've ever talked to about anxiety has referred to it as a form of 'craziness.' It scared the heck out of me. I thought I was losing my mind."

This quotation comes from a letter I received from a reader of my book *Adrenaline and Stress,* describing her first experience of a severe anxiety attack. Her fear that she was going crazy is a very common one, based mainly on the erroneous but widely held belief that all anxiety is purely psychological—"in the mind." Most people still think that anxiety, the absence of tranquillity, is just "in your head." What they mean, of course, is that they believe anxiety is an imbalance of some sort in your mind, your thinking, and your feelings. This is why some people resist taking medication for severe anxiety disturbances. They believe that they are only compounding their "failure" or that they are "emotionally weak."

Nothing is further from the truth. Anxiety is *not* just in the mind. It is in the *brain,* and the brain is more than the mind with its thoughts.

The distinction between the *mind* (what makes you think) and the *brain* (the vast array of ongoing chemical reactions) is very important: The more serious anxiety problems are not just thoughts that have gone wrong, but biochemical events out of control. True, thoughts can trigger stress and hence anxiety, but the thoughts themselves do not constitute the anxiety. For anxiety to exist, a biochemical change must occur in the brain. And sometimes, perhaps more often than we realize, the change in biochemistry can result in anxiety *without* any "mind" component. You can go crazy with anxiety just because your brain is missing an important happy messenger. It can have nothing to do with whether you are mentally troubled. In fact, most sufferers of panic attacks are perfectly normal, highly functioning individuals.

So how can we restore the dominance of the happy messengers? That is what the rest of this book is about.

The first way to restore your happy messengers is to restore a measure of balance to your brain messengers, which may mean taking some antianxiety medication temporarily. Then you have to address the stress in your life and discover what life changes you need to make. (I will offer some important strategies for relieving stress in chapter 10.) Then you need to develop ways for increasing your brain's natural happy messengers—those tranquilizers that are naturally produced in the brain to serve their own receptors.

But before I can jump to discussing practical ways for you to cure your anxiety, there are two messengers I want you to know. These two hormones perform a fascinating but complex dance in creating anxiety. You should memorize them because you will be hearing a lot more about them in the future.

THE DANCE OF THE HORMONES

An understanding of these two messengers is central to understanding how stress creates many of our anxiety problems.

The first messenger I want you to become acquainted with is *GABA* (gamma-aminobutyric acid.) GABA is a neurotransmitter found in abundance in the brain. The presence or absence of this "happy messenger" can make or break your peace of mind. It is the essential messenger that calms your overzealous nerves. It also plays a role in helping you remember. GABA is important because it is the key that unlocks the stress-anxiety connection.

The second messenger you need to know is *cortisol,* a close cousin to adrenaline. Cortisol and adrenaline are partners—they always go together when there is stress. Cortisol is a "sad messenger" that releases sugar from fats to help you in the fight-or-flight response. It gives you the energy for survival. For example, have you ever noticed that when you have an emergency to cope with or a deadline you have to meet, food becomes less important? Your appetite decreases because cortisol kicks in to take care of your needs as it retrieves stored energy. When the crisis is over, however, you become ravishingly hungry because your level of cortisol drops and your appetite returns. You crave carbohydrates as your body demands that you redeposit what you have overdrawn at the energy bank.

You need cortisol for life; you can't live without it. But excessive and prolonged stress depletes your GABA, and this makes you unhappy. More specifically, the stress-activated cortisol disrupts the happy messengers and prevents them from communicating their message to your brain. The result? Severe anxiety, especially panic attacks.

Cortisol, like adrenaline, is good for you when you are stressed—up to a point. In normal stress, cortisol helps to make you more efficient and feel good. You feel energized and productive. But during overstress conditions it turns, intentionally, to making stress uncomfortable for you. If it didn't, you would self-destruct.

Think about this for a moment: If we were designed so that the more stress we were under, the better we would feel, we would seek out more and more stress. Stress would reinforce your feeling good, and the happy messengers in your brain would have a field day. Only without anything to set limits, you would eventually mushroom like an atomic bomb. So, a better plan is to allow your stress response system to help you initially but to work against you if it gets out of hand. This is how God created you.

WHAT IS YOUR STRESS TOLERANCE?

We each have a unique capacity to tolerate a certain amount of the sad messengers before our happy messengers are depleted. This capacity is called your "stress tolerance."

What determines your stress tolerance? First, your *genetic inheritance*. Low tolerance for stress often runs in families. In particular, the tendency to overproduce adrenaline and cortisol in response to stress (the Type A personality) is common among family members. I know because I come from such a family. My grandmother had it (it's not always males), my father and my uncle had it, and my brother has it. I can also see it in some of my grandchildren. Not that low stress tolerance is all bad. But you have to control stress, not let it control you.

Fortunately, we all start out life with a pretty high stress tolerance. When your happy messengers dominated, you found life to be fun, exciting, enjoyable, and challenging. This is how it should be. But then that big test at school came, or you were chosen to participate in some school activity. That night you couldn't get to sleep. You tossed and turned, your body raging with adrenaline, telling you to get going. Welcome to the real world. Then some years later came your first interview, maybe for a job or admission to graduate school. Chest pains or headaches, depending on your personality, come first. Migraines. Acid stomach. The list is long.

We have all experienced brief periods of happy messenger malfunction. But more than 10 percent will go on to feel this way *all the time.* They will either have a low tolerance for stress or their stressors will appear so big that they overwhelm their normal tolerance. Either way, unhappiness wins out, and these people are at greater risk either to become addicted to substances that will temporarily relieve their physical and emotional pain or to become lifelong anxiety sufferers. The majority of us suffer more from overstress than from a low stress tolerance.

This is why our understanding of adrenaline and its impact on stress is so important to understanding anxiety. The biochemical change that starts an anxiety attack is set up by prolonged stress.

ENDOGENOUS ANXIETY

The form of anxiety I am discussing in this book can best be described as "endogenous anxiety," meaning that it is "from within" the brain. This form of anxiety is essentially biological and *not* psychological, at least in its symptoms. Worry anxiety, on the other hand, is purely psychological. There is nothing wrong with our GABAs. We learn to worry if life dishes up a lot for us to worry about. This means you can stop thinking that you are going crazy. Your brain is only doing what it is designed to do.

The term "endogenous anxiety" is one that I have borrowed from the field of depression because it so accurately describes what we are up against. The equivalent term "endogenous depression" is often used to differentiate biological depressions from purely psychological or reactive ones. So why not use the same distinction between psychological and biological anxiety? I believe "endogenous" accurately describes this common, biological form of anxiety.

But not only do depression and anxiety have a common link in the endogenous label, they often occur together as well. It is often very difficult to separate depression from anxiety, so they have to be treated together. We will see in chapter 12 how the common bond of stress connects them both.

THE GABA-CORTISOL CONNECTION

While everything I have said this far is extremely important, what follows is *doubly important.*

I have told you about GABA and about cortisol. Now, let's put them together and complete our understanding of endogenous anxiety. What I will present here is the most up-to-date understanding of endogenous anxiety available to us. It makes perfect sense and explains exactly what you have to do to recover from an anxiety problem.

I know how easily technical jargon can disinterest a reader, so I will restrict myself to the barest minimum. But stay with me here. If you are going to win over your anxiety, you must know its inner workings. If what I am about to describe does nothing else, it should at least fill you with awe at God's wonderful creation.

First, a little background about tranquilizers. The reason why Valium, Librium, Xanax, Ativan, and a host of other tranquilizer medications (called "benzodiazepines" or just simply "benzos") relieve anxiety symptoms is very simple: *The brain has its own system of natural tranquilizers.* Artificial tranquilizers only mimic what the brain is already doing for itself. We didn't know this when tranquilizers were first discovered; scientists figured it out much later. What this means is that when you take a tranquilizer, you are not really taking something foreign to the brain. Tranquilizers work because the brain is designed for them to work. The brain's natural tranquilizers are part of the brain's "happy messenger" system mentioned earlier.

Yes, the brain was actually manufacturing its own tranquilizers, the equivalent of benzos, long before their artificial substitutes were invented. There are literally millions of special receptors for these tranquilizers in the brain. When there is an adequate supply of these natural tranquilizers, we remain calm and happy. But when they are depleted, we become anxious and sad. Later in the book, I will describe ways in which these natural tranquilizers can be restored, thus reducing our dependence on the artificial ones.

For us to be peaceful, our brains must manufacture an adequate supply of these natural tranquilizers. But there is more to tranquillity than manufacturing natural tranquilizers. Not only must there be an adequate supply, but they must be able to reach their "docking stations," called "benzo receptors."

And herein lies the secret to understanding endogenous anxiety. Too much stress, stress that hangs around too long, or a stress-response system that has too low a threshold raises the level of cortisol (sad messengers) being released from the adrenal glands. This increased cortisol finds its way to the brain and blocks the natural tranquilizers from reaching their receptor sites.

Think of the story of Goldilocks. GABAs know where the bedroom is, but they can't get to bed because Goldilocks (cortisol) is already sleeping in their bed. Until Goldilocks leaves, you will suffer from troubled sleep and a lot of anxiety.

What is the solution? After whatever help artificial tranquilizers give you, you must learn to lower your stress and enhance your natural tranquilizers. Lowering your stress gets rid of the sad messengers (cortisol) and restores your natural tranquilizers, putting the happy messengers back in control.

But where does GABA fit into this picture? After all, I earlier heralded the importance of GABA, but what does it have to do with tranquilizers and our tranquillity?

Take a look at the illustration on the next page that shows how GABA works. This is a simplified, though accurate, depiction of how GABA operates in conjunction with the benzo tranquilizers to keep us tranquil.

As I stated earlier, GABA is the most important "calming" neurotransmitter in your brain. About half of the cells in the brain contain something called a "GABA receptor complex." Its function is to control the level of excitability of the cells in your brain. As you see in the diagram, there are *three receptor sites* where three different brain chemicals control a channel through which a calming influence passes. The three receptors are sedative-convulsant receptors, GABA receptors, and benzo receptors. This last site is where the benzodiazepine tranquilizers operate. Each of these receptors has some control over the "calming" channel that controls our tranquillity.

Notice in the diagram that each receptor site has a different shape. This is because each of the chemicals has a different molecular shape. A chemical can only dock in the correctly shaped receptor—nowhere else. Think of them as keys fitting in a lock. If the key fits, it can turn the lock. If it doesn't fit, the

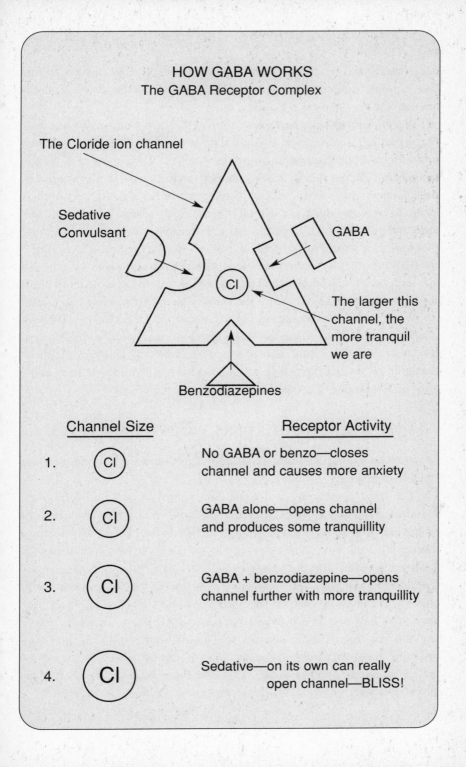

HOW GABA WORKS
The GABA Receptor Complex

The Cloride ion channel

Sedative
Convulsant

GABA

Cl

The larger this
channel, the
more tranquil
we are

Benzodiazepines

Channel Size	Receptor Activity
1. Cl	No GABA or benzo—closes channel and causes more anxiety
2. Cl	GABA alone—opens channel and produces some tranquillity
3. Cl	GABA + benzodiazepine—opens channel further with more tranquillity
4. Cl	Sedative—on its own can really open channel—BLISS!

door stays locked. And only when the key turns is the door opened. In this case, a proper molecular fit opens up the "channel" to calm down the nerve cell and not allow it to be too active.

When all three locks have keys in place, the channel opens to its maximum, putting us at our most tranquil state of mind. Get that? This is shown to the right of the diagram as condition four with the channel at its largest opening. Of course, this state of tranquillity, marvelous as it may seem, will probably put you to sleep because there are too many sedative keys in their locks. To be alert, your brain will pull some of the sedative keys out of their locks and put you in condition three. If your benzos are depleted (say, because of stress) then condition two prevails, and you start to become anxious. But if the GABAs now also become deficient, a state of real panic begins to set in and you experience condition one. The channel is just about closed and shuts down the "calming" effect. This is the worst anxiety state you can experience.

What causes this blockage of GABA? The culprit is *excessive cortisol created by too much stress.* These sad messengers block access to the GABA receptor site so that your natural GABAs cannot reach their docking sites. Artificial tranquilizers (benzos) may help you a little, but until you lower your stress, you will not be able to completely restore your tranquillity.

HOW TRANQUILIZERS WORK—AND FAIL

So, you should now understand how tranquilizers work and why they don't do the job adequately.

The most commonly used tranquilizers are benzos (Xanax, Librium, Valium, Ativan, and the like). They are wonderful medications and a real gift from God, believe me. When properly used, benzos have restored life to many a miserable soul. *But their action is very broad.* They not only fit in their own locks but are able to fit in others as well. That's why benzos can be sedating. They overflow and block the sedation receptor site as well. Sometimes we want this, say, to go to sleep or in surgery—but not all the time. And too many benzos can be dangerous. Barbiturates that act on the sedation-convulsant receptor site can open up the channel too dramatically, producing profound sedation. Taken with alcohol, this oversedation can be dangerous, even causing the person to stop breathing. Many have committed suicide by an intentional overdose of artificial tranquilizers, so you need to be very careful.

Artificial tranquilizers displace your natural benzos and tell your brain to shut down the production of natural benzos. So after a while, you can't stop taking the artificial tranquilizers because the natural ones aren't there. This is why you must stop tranquilizers *very slowly* to allow your brain much-needed time to begin manufacturing its natural benzos. We will discuss the very important topic of how and when to stop taking a tranquilizer in chapter 6.

What about GABA messengers? Stress blocks their receptors, so taking artificial GABA isn't going to help relieve your anxiety very much; the stress-activated cortisol is blocking the passage and GABA cannot reach its receptors.

But if you lower your stress level, you will restore your GABAs. That is what the rest of the book is all about. Believe me, the realization that a reduced level of stress will restore your natural tranquilizers unlocks the key to recovery from anxiety problems. You cannot take artificial tranquilizers the rest of your life unless you have a disease condition that requires it. You have to find a way to restore your natural tranquilizers.

So, this is good news, and it is bad news. The bad news is that you have to take responsibility for lowering your stress level in order to cure your anxiety. There is no magic cure. But the good news is that you have to take responsibility for lowering your stress level in order to cure your anxiety. You don't have to convince anyone else to do anything for you. You can do it for yourself. Surely, this is a message of hope.

CHAPTER 3

POWER OVER PANIC

———❧———

That he would grant you, according to the riches of his glory,
to be strengthened with might by his Spirit in the inner man.

EPHESIANS 3:16

The Reverend Michael Cummings didn't see it coming. It struck like a bolt of lightning out of a clear blue sky. He certainly wasn't expecting it, sitting there in his cozy home study surrounded by the books he loves. His walls are adorned with photographs of his earlier years, especially his college successes—photos of him making football tackles, holding trophies, and shaking hands with important people. No doubt, he was the sports jock of his college. His study also proudly displays academic awards, diplomas, and honors that he has received since college. He is an all-around capable guy.

At thirty-nine, Pastor Michael is self-reliant, strong, assertive, and competent. He exercises regularly, eats healthy foods, and gets regular physicals. He was born to be a leader, and now, as the youngest senior pastor ever of a large suburban church, he is making his mark on the community. That is why the sudden pain in his chest that Saturday morning as he was putting the final touches to his sermon was so alarming.

But it wasn't just the pain that was horrifying. It was the fear that something terrible was about to happen. A feeling of impending doom came over him as he had never experienced in his life.

He tried to shake off the feeling and ignore the pain. But he couldn't get rid of it. What was happening? Had he eaten something that didn't agree with him? It felt like a tight band was restricting his breathing, so it couldn't be indigestion. He needed air, so he got up and opened the window to admit the brisk early morning air. It was an autumn sky, blue and clear.

Pastor Michael stood at the window and took in a few deep breaths. *Could this be a heart attack?* he wondered. Surely not. He was too young for that. He had seen parishioners have heart attacks, and this seemed different. He closed the window and paced around his study for a while, hoping that the strange feelings he was experiencing would go away. His Saturday schedule was full. He had sermons to be finished, a wedding to officiate, and some hospital visits to make. He couldn't afford to get sick now.

Soon the fear became unbearable. Sweating profusely, he felt a slight tremor in his hands, so he decided to call to his wife. Maybe she would be able to reassure him. But she wasn't reassuring. She insisted that they immediately go to the emergency room of their local hospital. "Better safe than sorry" had always been her motto. She packed him, now shaking uncontrollably from the pain in his chest, into their Suburban and rushed him to their local hospital's emergency room.

The doctors did the usual tests for someone with chest pains. But they found nothing wrong with his heart. He certainly was not having a heart attack, so they prescribed a few days' supply of an artificial tranquilizer and advised him to see his private doctor, making some vague reference to the experience as possibly being a "panic attack."

Pastor Michael went home somewhat relieved. The "attack" had already passed and he had become himself again, strong and confident. He felt fine later that day and fulfilled all his Sunday pastoral duties without a hitch. His sermon seemed unusually better than it had been for a long time, no doubt due to his sense of having just escaped a terrible calamity.

Quickly, he decided to put the incident behind him as if it hadn't even happened. He flushed the tranquilizers down the toilet, muttering under his breath something about "not being seen alive with this junk." The next morning his wife reminded him that he needed to see his private doctor to figure out what caused the episode of panic. Pastor Michael shrugged it off.

"I'm feeling great now. It must have been my stomach. There's nothing wrong with me."

Three days later, it happened again. This time it was even more frightening. He was driving to his church office when it struck. The pain in his chest was so severe that he continued past the church and drove himself directly to the emergency room. This time he was convinced he was having a heart attack. Maybe the doctors had missed something the last time.

The outcome was the same. Many tests but nothing wrong with his heart. This time the doctor insisted that he take the tranquilizers and get help right away.

This time Pastor Michael didn't feel relieved when it was all over. Now he knew there was something wrong. He became despondent. He wished it had been a heart attack. At least that would be a sort of status symbol. After all, all the big shots in his church had had heart attacks. But a panic attack? What on earth was that? It sounded like something that happened only to weak people, not strong leaders like him.

But panic attacks do not discriminate the weak from the strong. If anything, they favor the strong and mighty. And the stronger people are, the harder they fall.

FAMOUS PEOPLE WHO SUFFERED FROM ANXIETY DISORDERS

One of the most tragic consequences of anxiety is that it undermines your very sense of self. Your self-esteem plummets; you feel like you are inferior to everyone else. You are overcome by shame and envy those not troubled like you are. But not only does 12 percent of the population feel like you, several famous people also suffered from an anxiety disorder and have lived to make a difference.

Who are these famous people who have touched the lives of others despite their affliction—at a time when there was absolutely no help for this type of problem? Here are just a few:

- ALFRED LORD TENNYSON (1809–1892), the famous poet, had a "nervous illness" so severe that he despaired of his life at times when he couldn't even write.

- CHARLOTTE BRONTË (1816–1855), the gifted writer and one of the Brontë sisters, developed a state of anxiety and depression in 1852. She portrayed her condition in the character of Lucy in *Villette*. At one point, she makes Lucy say: "Sleepless, I lay awake night after night, weak and unable to occupy myself." This is a classic case of anxiety insomnia.
- SIGMUND FREUD (1865–1939), the developer of psychoanalysis, suffered from panic anxiety disorder at the time he wrote his famous papers on anxiety neuroses. He worried a great deal about his "spells."
- SIR ISAAC NEWTON (1642–1727), the famous physicist and mathematician, had a nervous breakdown in 1677 and again in 1693, suffering from severe insomnia, loss of concentration, and extreme sensitivity. He was housebound until 1684, a classic case of agoraphobia.

I could keep going and relate stories of many celebrities, ancient and modern, who have experienced some form of anxiety disorder, but I think I've made my point: You are not alone nor inferior just because you suffer from a high level of anxiety. You are certainly not crazy nor are you imagining your feelings. And, more importantly, your problem is treatable even without spending the rest of your life taking artificial tranquilizers.

WHAT IS PANIC ANXIETY DISORDER?

While I am trying to touch on several of the more important anxiety problems, much of my discussion will focus on panic anxiety disorder simply because it is the more serious of the common disorders. However, panic anxiety disorder has many features in common with other anxieties, so my discussion will generalize to all anxiety problems.

Because the symptoms are so very similar, the first experience of a panic anxiety attack is often mistaken for a heart attack. This is one of the reasons why it is so frightening. You feel like your very life is at stake. Invariably, therefore, the first professional to see a panic sufferer will be the emergency-room physician.

What are the symptoms of a panic attack?

People with panic disorder experience frequent, unprovoked panic attacks that involve some or all of the following symptoms:

- Racing heartbeat
- Heart palpitations
- Chest pains
- Feeling of a tight band around the chest
- Fear of dizziness or lightheadedness
- Weakness all over
- Sweating all over
- Dizziness
- Nausea
- Flushes or chills
- Difficulty breathing
- Tingling, numbness, or tremors
- Sped-up thoughts and confusion
- Feelings of unreality
- Confusion
- Fear of losing control or doing something embarrassing

There are a few very important features of a panic attack, and everyone should be aware of them. First, panic attacks occur without any warning. They often strike at the most inopportune times, catching you off guard. Your heart pounds, you feel that there is a tight band around your chest, your breathing becomes shallow, and you may become dizzy. Second, you are overcome with feelings of terror, losing control, or even dying.

Panic anxiety disorder, as opposed to just one or two panic attacks, is characterized by unexpected and repeated episodes of intense fear accompanied by physical symptoms that may include chest pain, heart palpitations, shortness of breath, dizziness, or abdominal distress, often mimicking the symptoms of a heart attack. As a result, a panic disorder is frequently not diagnosed until extensive and costly medical procedures fail to provide an alternative diagnosis.

How long does a panic attack last? Fortunately for the sufferer, most attacks last only a few minutes, usually no more than ten or fifteen. That is the good news. The bad news is that a panic attack can leave you so exhausted and frightened that you can hardly continue with your regular duties afterward.

Does panic anxiety disorder only occur at certain ages? No. Panic disorder can appear at any age, although it is more likely to begin in young adulthood.

Does it strike both sexes? Yes, but as I mentioned, current trends show that twice as many women as men suffer from panic. Why is that? We don't really know, though I suspect that it is due to the greater stress that women experience in our world today having both to be breadwinners and mothers. Single moms are particularly vulnerable to panic anxiety disorder. And, as we will see, panic anxiety is clearly a stress-related problem.

Can you just ignore your panic attacks and continue living a normal life? Not really. I know that many do "grin and bear" their panic attacks, but when left untreated, panic anxiety disorder can lead to an even more serious problem: a form of phobia discussed earlier, called agoraphobia. The term *agoraphobia* literally means "fear of the marketplace" because its main characteristic is a fear of being in a public place. About one-third of all people with untreated panic anxiety disorder suffer from some degree of agoraphobia.

"I have a fear when I go out that I will be unable to return home or get back to a safe place or person. Is this agoraphobia?" a panic sufferer asked me once. Yes it is. The fear of agoraphobia is not so much a fear of a strange place as it is a fear that you cannot get back to your place of safety. You also develop a particular fear of places where you have had an attack. For example, if you have an attack while shopping in a supermarket or in a mall, you may begin to avoid going to that supermarket or mall. If it occurs while you are driving over a bridge, you may start avoiding that bridge or stop driving altogether. The association between the place and the panic attack becomes cemented together.

HOW COMMON ARE PANIC DISORDERS?

What is alarming about panic attacks is that they are clearly on the increase. Panic anxiety disorder strikes between three and six million Americans. No one really knows how common minor panic attacks are because they generally go untreated.

As already stated, panic disorders can appear at any age. They are seen in children and in the elderly, and anyone in between. But most often they begin in young adults in their twenties and thirties. One comprehensive Australian study found the following characteristics in panic sufferers seeking treatment:

- 73 percent were female
- 65 percent were married
- Mean age was thirty-seven
- Mean age for first panic attack was twenty-six
- Mean length of time that the participants experienced ongoing symptoms of panic was ten years.[1]

Yes, you read that correctly. The mean length of time for experiencing ongoing symptoms was ten years in this study. And that was the *mean,* so that means that while some had it for fewer than ten years, others had it for longer. I have had patients who started having panic attacks in their late twenties and still have a propensity for panic twenty years later.

There were some other very interesting findings in this study:

Who first diagnosed the problem?
- General practitioner—53 percent
- Psychiatrist—29 percent
- Psychologist—21 percent
- *Diagnosed themselves*—35 percent

What secondary condition did they suffer from?
- Agoraphobia—65 percent
- Major depression—54 percent

How long did it take to diagnose their problem?
- One week—25 percent
- One month—12 percent
- More than six months—55 percent

That's right. More than half the sufferers from panic anxiety did not know what they suffered from for more than six months. And while this study was undertaken in Australia, I can assure you that it is not that different in the U.S.

The important point I am making here is this: Freedom from panic can only be achieved by taking control of the problem yourself, making a sustained effort on several fronts (including finding the right balance of medications that best suit you), altering your lifestyle (especially lowering stress below your threshold), changing your thinking habits, and learning how to relax as well as use some form of Christian meditation.

As you will see in chapter 17, I was surprised to see how effective meditation was in altering the course of panic attacks. As Christians, we have an extremely helpful resource that is by and large ignored in modern-day spirituality.

PANIC ATTACKS VERSUS PANIC DISORDER

Not everyone who experiences a panic attack will develop a full-blown panic disorder. For example, many people, usually under high stress, will have one or two attacks and never have another. I have seen several such patients. For some, of course, the first or even the second attack served as a wake-up call alerting them to their high stress. They quickly made changes that I believe aborted any further attacks. For some, the panic was merely situational. They went through a period of intense difficulty in their life, but like so many of life's upheavals, the situation eventually passed away.

Some life traumas, however, are known to increase one's risk for panic disorder. These traumas act to lower your "threshold of tolerance" for stress by weakening your system's defenses. No doubt they also "condition" you to experience exaggerated stress. When your ability to cope with stress drops, you experience increased stress. Stress creates more stress when it is not dealt with effectively.

What life traumas or major events can precipitate a panic state? Again, the Australian study I referred to earlier carefully explored the life events that preceded the first panic or anxiety attack of those in their treatment program. I have listed some of these in the accompanying sidebar to help you determine your current vulnerability to panic attacks.

What is important to note in this sidebar is that all the life events listed are known to be "high stressors." It is very possible that many of those suffering from panic attacks with these life events in their background will find some relief after they resolve their life event. However, 36 percent of panic sufferers

EVENTS PRECEDING A FIRST PANIC OR ANXIETY ATTACK

The figures in parentheses are the percentage of people in the study who experienced this particular life event. Some may have had more than one of these experiences at the same time.

- Major life trauma such as a serious accident or abuse (36%)
- Drug or alcohol abuse (28%)
- Death in the family (25%)
- Financial problems (17%)
- Major illness (14%)
- Divorce (11%)
- Childbirth (11%)
- Loss of a job (11%)
- Depression (10%)
- Unemployment (8%)
- Car accident (8%)
- Near-death experience (8%)
- Pregnancy (3%)
- No identifiable preceding life event (36%)[2]

could not identify a single life event that preceded their attacks. Clearly, this group was suffering from general stress produced by a lifestyle that was interacting with their lowered stress threshold.

What effect do childhood events have on the later development of a panic disorder? The next sidebar is a little more startling. There is no doubt that negative childhood experiences can make you vulnerable to high anxiety later in life, but it appears from this data that it can also make you prone to panic attacks.

SPECIFIC CHILDHOOD EVENTS IN PANIC SUFFERERS

- Unwanted or neglected as a child (59%)
- Physical abuse (54%)
- Verbal abuse (45%)
- Violence in the home (37%)
- Parental violence (33%)
- Sexual trauma (31%)
- Left alone (31%)

SECONDARY PHOBIAS

As mentioned earlier, panic anxiety disorder is often accompanied by other conditions, such as depression or alcoholism, and it may spawn more phobias than just agoraphobia. Many of these "secondary" phobias are connected to the places or situations where the panic attacks have occurred. For example, if a panic attack strikes while you're riding an elevator, you may develop a specific fear of elevators. If it attacks in a movie theater during a particularly scary thriller, you may become phobic of movie theaters or scary movies in general. Because of these secondary phobias, panic anxiety disorder causes some people's lives to become very restricted. Many panic sufferers begin to avoid normal, everyday activities such as grocery shopping, driving, or even taking vacations. Life can be pretty miserable if you allow these fears to take control of your life.

Often, the only way many people can continue a normal life and participate in necessary activities (such as going to the doctor or dentist, taking trips to see family members, collecting social security checks, etc.) is to be accompanied by a loved one. They just cannot trust themselves when alone. They feel vulnerable and fear that a panic attack will incapacitate them with no one there to help. Basically, they avoid any situation they fear will provoke an attack that would cause them to feel helpless.

WHEN DO PANIC ATTACKS OCCUR?

Panic attacks can occur at any time of the day or night. They can occur when you are at the height of some aggravating battle at work or when you are quietly relaxing on the beach.

A fairly high percentage of attacks (61 percent) come while going to sleep. Quite a few occur during sleep and wake the sufferer. Since these patterns are quite common, let me comment on them.

Why would a panic attack occur when you are relaxing or sleeping? It is a well-known fact that most stress symptoms don't appear when you are at the height of your stressful situation. Take tension headaches, for example. They don't attack while you are intensely preoccupied with some deadline and rushing to finish up a project. Tension headaches strike *after* the project is over, or more commonly, as you leave the office to go home, drive home, or sit down to unwind. This is how adrenaline works. During the emergency, adrenaline protects us from pain or stress discomfort. *Only after adrenaline has done its job does it demand its penalty.*

I believe that panic attacks follow these stress patterns. They may be precipitated by a highly anxious situation, but they can just as likely occur when the stress drops or when you lie down to rest or go to sleep.

WHAT CAN YOU DO TO PREVENT PANIC ATTACKS?

What can prevent a panic attack? Good preparation. After a stressful situation, allow yourself plenty of time to "unwind," and do your unwinding slowly. In other words, avoid a sudden drop in adrenaline. For instance, when you first get home from work, don't go and crash in front of the boob tube. Take a little walk. Enjoy the slow wind-down. Smell the flowers. Attend to "unfinished business" in your thinking. Do a "mental wash" and clean out any unresolved resentment, anger, or disappointments. Let go of stuff that is not really your responsibility. Listen to the birds. Then go home and putter around for a while. Then sit and read. Finally, relax completely. Such a slow wind-down pattern can avoid the sudden drop in adrenaline that seems to precipitate the onset of the more serious stress symptoms.

CAN YOU PREDICT A PANIC ATTACK?

Sometimes panic attacks just happen out of the blue, without any warning. But sometimes there are signs that an attack is building. If you can learn to recognize these warning signals early enough, you can certainly take steps to abort the attack.

Panic sufferers report that some or many of the following symptoms often *precede* a panic attack:

- Increased sensitivity to light
- Tunnel or diminished vision
- Tight throat
- Indigestion
- Burning sensation in the stomach
- Acute hearing and intolerance to noise
- Missed heartbeats
- Nausea
- Lightheadedness and dizziness
- "Pins and needles" or localized burning sensations
- Cold flashes
- Hyperventilation

The last of these warning signs, hyperventilation, is extremely important. If you can recognize this symptom early enough, you can stop your panic attack.

Not everyone hyperventilates just before a panic attack, and not everyone who hyperventilates is going to have a panic attack. But in my experience, a high percentage of panic sufferers do hyperventilate. They suffer from a form of panic that is caused by insufficient carbon dioxide in their bloodstream.

A brief explanation of how your respiratory system works will help you gain some power over your panic attacks.

Normally, the delicate balance between the level of oxygen and carbon dioxide in your bloodstream is carefully controlled. Your lungs put oxygen into the blood, and later that same blood collects the carbon dioxide (in the form of carbonic acid) produced by your muscles and other metabolic functions and carries it away to be disposed. When you begin to do aerobic exercise, you burn up energy, which produces carbon dioxide. The moment your brain detects an increase in carbon dioxide, it tells your lungs to breathe deeper and faster to take in enough oxygen to counteract the carbonic acid. So you puff and pant, but this puffing and panting is saving your life.

In anxiety-triggered hyperventilation, this normal respiratory process goes wrong. The cycle of events goes something like this: Something in your life, or just your thoughts, causes you to feel anxious. This raised anxiety speeds up your respiration because your body thinks there is an emergency. You begin to take in more oxygen than your body needs, and your carbon dioxide drops. Without enough carbon dioxide, your blood cannot carry waste products away so a state of extreme emergency is created. If you are panic prone, this state of emergency will trigger a panic attack.

COMMON MYTHS ABOUT PANIC ATTACKS

Because panic attacks can be so frightening, you can easily slip into believing some terrible things about them. If you continue believing these self-engendered myths, you will only multiply the intensity of your fear. Here are some common myths that you need to get out of your head as quickly as they pop in:

- *A panic attack will cause me to have a heart attack.* Rapid heartbeat and palpitations are a part of a panic attack, but they are not a form of heart attack. A healthy heart is capable of beating very fast without sustaining any damage. In panic, chest pains pass quickly, unlike the pain of a heart attack, which is continuous, crushing, and pressured. Movement makes the pain of heart attack worse, while resting makes panic pain worse.

- *A panic attack will cause me to stop breathing or suffo-cate.* In panic, you feel as if your chest is shutting down and you can't breathe. This is not due to suffocation but often to too much oxygen. Your brain is forcing you to breathe because it is getting the wrong messages. Feelings of choking or suffocation in panic, however unpleasant, are not dangerous.

- *A panic attack will cause me to lose my balance or faint.* You feel dizzy or think that things around you are spinning, but this sensation passes. If you feel like you are going to faint, sit down and breathe more slowly. Because your heart is beating faster, you are unlikely to faint. Moving about will help to restore your balance.

- *A panic attack will cause me to lose complete control of myself.* It may feel like you are losing control, but actually your body is doing something to protect you, not harm you. You need not fear that you will scream, cry, or jump off the curb. Complete loss of control is simply a myth.

- *A panic attack means I am going crazy.* No one has ever gone "crazy" because of a panic attack. You may feel and experience strange sensations, but this only lasts for the duration that your brain's blood flow is upset because of your rapid breathing.

What can you do to prevent your panic attack? Let me illustrate with an actual case.

Shirley travels to work and back each day on one of Los Angeles's famous freeways. Every afternoon, to fill in the time on the stop-and-go journey home, she turns on the radio and listens to the day's news.

Everything was fine until one day, due to extreme work stress, she began having panic attacks and came to see me for help. I started her treatment, but since it would take a little while before it took effect, I wanted to know when and where her attacks occurred. So I instructed Shirley to keep a record of when they happened. She was as surprised as I was after the first week. Nearly all her attacks began while driving home on the freeway.

Shortly after turning on her radio she began to feel dizzy. Because it is very difficult to tell whether you are hyperventilating, I told Shirley how she could "test" for hyperventilation. Sure enough, she was hyperventilating. The anxiety of all the bad news she heard from all around the world was making her anxious, causing her to hyperventilate and triggering her panic attack. At times, the panic was so bad she had to pull over into the emergency lane and wait a few minutes for it to subside.

What is the test for hyperventilation? It's quite simple. Try holding your breath. The compulsion to breathe during hyperventilation is so strong that the pressure to take in air is unbearably uncomfortable. How did she stop her attack? By cupping her hands over her nose and mouth and rebreathing her exhaled carbon dioxide. After a couple of minutes, the state of emergency subsided. (I'll have more to say about how you can use these warning signals to abort panic attacks later.)

By the way, there was one other suggestion I gave to Shirley: Don't listen to the news while driving home.

CAN PANIC SUFFERERS ALSO HAVE OTHER PHYSICAL AND EMOTIONAL ILLNESSES?

People with panic anxiety disorder often have other physical and emotional illnesses. This often complicates both the diagnosis and the treatment. Research shows that while panic disorder can coexist with many other disorders; most often, as mentioned, it is associated with depression and substance abuse.

Why these two? Clearly, there is a powerful biological link between anxiety and depression, but the link goes further than this. Those who suffer from panic attacks easily become disillusioned over recovery and feel like total failures. This can cause reactive depression. Those who don't get treatment may try to "self-medicate," and the most readily available escape from the pain of panic is either alcohol or some other mind-altering drug. About 30 percent of people with panic anxiety disorder use alcohol and 17 percent use mind-altering drugs in unsuccessful attempts to alleviate the anguish and distress caused by their conditions. An indication of just how frustrating this disorder can become is shown in the statistic that approximately 20 percent of people with panic anxiety disorder have attempted suicide.

What other problems are associated with panic? People with panic anxiety disorder may also have "irritable bowel syndrome," a classic anxiety problem characterized by intermittent bouts of gastrointestinal cramps and diarrhea or constipation. A relatively minor heart problem called mitral valve prolapse (MVP) is also found in panic sufferers. In fact, panic anxiety disorder often coexists with unexplained medical problems, such as chest pain that is not associated with a heart attack or chronic fatigue.

One further complicating factor in understanding panic anxiety is that one form of it occurs regularly in members of the same family, suggesting that at least this form has some genetic linkage. This form of panic anxiety usually starts on or before age twenty. One study of 838 adult first-degree relatives (parents, children, or siblings) found that close relatives of panic sufferers who had started to panic before or about age twenty had a seventeenfold increase in incidence. This is a strikingly elevated risk of panic anxiety disorder. Families who have seen panic emerge in someone of this age range need to be aware of the condition and take steps to prevent others from succumbing. Treatment should be started at the first sign that panic attacks are beginning.

The development of panic anxiety disorder at any other age does not seem to be as strongly connected within the family, except for possible high-stress circumstances common to all members of a family.

TAKING PERSONAL CONTROL OVER YOUR TRANQUILLITY

Anxiety has many faces. It is the "butterflies" you feel in your stomach before you give a speech or take a test, the nervousness you feel when you know you are about to be bawled out, or the heart palpitations you experience when you are in a threatening situation. Because it puts you on your guard and prepares you for what is to come, a little anxiety can be a good thing. However, when normal anxiety seems to spin out of control, disrupting your daily life, you could be suffering from an anxiety disorder.

If there is one message that anxiety experts are shouting from the rooftops, it is this: *Anxiety sufferers must take personal control over their anxiety.* This is especially true for people who suffer panic attacks. No amount of medication, psychotherapy, nutritional supplements, or any other "external" resource is going to completely cure your anxiety problem. You have to get involved and take responsibility for your recovery. In fact, I prefer to use "recovery" with respect to anxiety problems rather than "cure" because the word *recovery* more accurately describes the process one has to go through. It is certainly not something that you can fix in an instant.

In our medicalized world, you can easily fall into the trap of believing that a cure must be "dispensed" to you. For example, suppose you have the flu. You go to the doctor, and she gives you an antibiotic to prevent an infection from taking over your weakened system. You go home and take the medication, as you should, and you feel cured in a day or two. Or, more directly to the point, you develop a pain in the chest that feels like pneumonia. You go to the doctor to have it cured.

Thank God, we have many cures for medical diseases. But anxiety problems are different, even when biological factors are heavily involved. Anxiety medications don't cure anything, though they are a necessary starting point. They only relieve the symptoms of anxiety; they don't take away the cause. *Only you can deal with the cause.* Anxiety sufferers need recovery more than they need a cure.

WE RESIST HELPING OURSELVES

We are living in an age when everyone thinks of themselves as victims. People want to be rescued from what has harmed them. They also want quick fixes to their complex problems. A patient who had suffered from a longstanding anxiety problem once expressed it to me this way: "If no one is going to rescue me from this problem, if I am never going to be totally freed from it, and if there is no magic answer, no miracle pill, then what hope is there? The very thought that I have to take responsibility for recovering myself scares the life out of me. I can barely get out of bed most mornings, let alone think about taking care of myself."

I didn't respond immediately but allowed a long pause. I wanted her to reflect on her frustration and discover the answer for herself. Finally, she said: "I suppose you are right. No one has rescued me thus far. I'll have to take control of getting this problem under control myself. I've been passive about it for too long."

She is absolutely right. Self-empowerment is the key to achieving tranquillity and surviving the long-term ravages of anxiety. This does not mean that God won't help us. Of course He will. He gives us the courage to go on when all feels hopeless. He gives us hope. He provides the power we lack to become effective in our lives. No human suffering can be born without such hope. But at no time does God expect us to surrender control to others and become helpless in the face of anxiety.

Why is it important for me to stress this point here? Because the majority of people with anxiety problems give away their personal power. They surrender it to the disorder, to the doctors who try to help, to the medications that must be used in the interim, and just to plain old helplessness. Whatever you do, don't resign yourself to a "victim mentality." You are to be a victor over anxiety, not a slave to it. This is the attitude that will move you out of the clutches of anxiety.

But more importantly, don't capitulate to ignorance, myths, stigmas, and shame. These cause you to abdicate your right to control what happens to you. Ignorance of the nature of your problem will only make you more afraid, and this fear will breed more anxiety. At all costs you must break the spiral of anxiety causing more anxiety, which, in turn, only causes *more* anxiety. Clinically, this cycle is called the fear-of-fear response, and it is very common in anxiety disorders.

CREATING YOUR OWN HAPPINESS AND TRANQUILLITY

If it seems that this chapter is a rallying call, you are right. Since stress is so dominant as a cause and contaminant of anxiety, it must be reduced. And no pill can take your stress away. You have to deal with it yourself.

This means you must take responsibility for your own life instead of blaming your stress and unhappiness on your loved ones, your boss, the economy—or anything else. We create our own unhappiness. But by assuming responsibility to fix it, we can create our own joy. This is what God desires of us, and He is ready to empower us to achieve a more complete wholeness. God will not do it for us. I say this because many Christians are sitting waiting for God to assume all the responsibility for their unhappiness and to zap them straight. God doesn't work this way. He waits for us to invite Him to help us, and then He guides us along the path of recovery.

This means you will have to learn new ways of thinking and perceiving. You will also have to change your unbalanced lifestyle and many of your actions. You will have to examine your relationships, your job, your anger, your lack of focus and discipline, your impatience, and your disappointments for signs that you have abdicated your responsibility.

Taking responsibility also means that you stop blaming others, as well as yourself, for your bad feelings. Self-blame doesn't motivate us to change. It merely punishes us without providing any solutions.

So the rest of this chapter will present the twelve steps that I believe are essential to taking control of your anxiety recovery. The only similarity to the twelve steps of addiction recovery is in the number. Anxiety problems are *not* addictions as such, but the remedy is a form of recovery.

"Work the steps" as consistently and as seriously as you would if you were an addict in recovery. This means that you should consider each step in turn, devote attention to the suggestions given for that step, and "work" that step until it becomes second nature. Then move on to the next step.

TWELVE STEPS TO PERSONAL EMPOWERMENT FOR ANXIETY SUFFERERS

1. CLAIM YOUR STRENGTH IN CHRIST. Claim promises from God's Word.

2. FEEL THE POWER THAT CHRIST GIVES YOU. Move beyond the cognitive. Let Christ's power seep into your bones and lift your courage.

3. TAKE CONTROL OF YOUR FEAR. The difference between panic and recovery is that recovered sufferers have overcome their fear of panic.

4. DROP THE "WHAT-IFS" IN YOUR LIFE. Change your attitude to "So what?"

5. OVERCOME YOUR PERSONAL PASSIVITY. Anxiety doesn't take your control away; you surrender it.

6. INCREASE YOUR POWER BY FINDING OUT ALL YOU CAN ABOUT YOUR DISORDER. Knowledge and understanding are your allies.

This is true of medications too. You know your body better than anyone. Don't let "experts" push you around. You be the expert.

7. DON'T BE DEMORALIZED BY HELPLESSNESS. Remember, knowledge is the key to overcoming feelings of helplessness, so learn all you can about anxiety disorder.

8. BE COMPASSIONATE TOWARD YOURSELF. Too many sufferers are their own worst enemies. Don't self-accuse ("I'm stupid," etc.).

9. DON'T LET YOUR PROBLEM DOMINATE YOUR LIFE. Relegate it to a secondary position and give priority to living.

10. BEWARE THE PITFALLS OF SELF-PITY. Instead of saying, "Woe is me!" try saying, "What can I do about it?"

11. FIND A GOOD SUPPORT GROUP. A group of understanding peers can help build your personal power. Isolation frets.

12. NEVER, NEVER, NEVER, NEVER GIVE UP. Remember Sir Winston Churchill's call to the people of Britain at the height of their despair under Hitler's air attacks: "Never give in, never give in, never, never, never, never."

CHAPTER 4

THE TREATMENT OF PANIC ANXIETY DISORDER

———— ∞∞ ————

Then touched he their eyes, saying,
According to your faith be it unto you.
And their eyes were opened.

MATTHEW 9:29–30

S ince her earliest years, Susan can recall feeling anxious about one thing
or another. Even as a young girl, she worried about her mother, a rather
helpless soul, being left alone at home while Susan was in school. When
she bought a new dress or new shoes, she worried for days that she had
bought the wrong style or that she had spent too much money. When she
went out of the house, she worried about whether all the doors were locked
or whether she had left a window open. Susan worried about her pets, her
school grades, her reputation, and her future. There wasn't much she didn't
worry about.

At nineteen years of age, Susan became a Christian, mainly through the
influence of a college friend. For a period of about three months, she felt a
newfound freedom from her tendency toward worry anxiety. She learned how
to pray and study Scripture, and she found much hope and reassurance in
these spiritual disciplines. It seemed that her anxious tendencies were now
behind her.

Then one day Susan woke up to find that her new sense of peace had simply vanished. All her old anxieties returned, greatly intensified. "What's happening to me?" she implored shortly after starting therapy. "Why has the anxiety come back? I believed that God had freed me from all that pain. Have I failed God somewhere? Has He abandoned me? Am I doomed to be a failure all my life?"

Susan's experience is a common one. Conversion often brings a wonderful sense of comfort and release from anxiety. It is the honeymoon phase of faith, and new believers often experience great excitement over a newfound prayer life and fresh insights from Scripture. God's Spirit seems very close and His comfort very real, which they are.

But anxiety can become deeply rooted in our personalities, and while God *sometimes* provides a miraculous removal of these roots, more often He calls upon us to begin and then continue the process of sanctification that has been opened to us through salvation. God expects us to continue and maintain our spiritual growth. He provides the tools from which to shape our maturity, the power to use these tools, and the courage to be determined, but we have to learn how to use them. God seldom provides a shortcut to sainthood.

"God has not abandoned you," I reassured Susan. "He is now calling you to put all He has promised into action and to continue your walk with Him. You have to learn how His resources are sufficient for all your anxieties. If you feel guilty because you are afraid you've failed God, then confess that guilt and use it to turn yourself back to Him. Don't ever let your guilt feelings drive you away from God."

Susan and I then spent the next few sessions exploring the idea that times of anxiety are not necessarily times when we have no faith. Feelings of anxiety certainly don't cancel out our salvation. In fact, some of the greatest saints have known the deepest darkness and have had to fight through to overcome their dread. Even Jesus once felt deserted by God, and His experience in Gethsemane was as full of abandonment as anyone has ever experienced. Nevertheless, Jesus remained faithful to His Father's plan.

Severe anxiety disorders have their roots so far back that many years of "faith building," and perhaps professional therapy, may be required before the problem can be brought under control. It is important, therefore, that we not reproach ourselves for being slow learners. That kind of attitude only adds to our misery and stands in the way of our growth. We have to empower ourselves, with God's help, to deal with our deep-rooted anxiety.

TAKING CONTROL OF YOUR ANXIETY

In the previous chapter, I strongly emphasized how crucial it is for anxiety sufferers to take control of their own therapeutic destiny. As an anxiety sufferer, no one is going to look out for you and "manage" your case as well as yourself, for obvious reasons: It is *your* tranquillity that is at stake, and no one knows your mind and body better than you do.

As part of this "self-empowerment," you should know what causes panic attacks, how panic is correctly diagnosed, and what your treatment options are.

AVOIDING HELPLESSNESS

Knowledge puts and keeps you in control. It is the best antidote for feelings of helplessness.

This principle is now well established in several difficult areas of treatment in which you have several options. For instance, a friend of mine recently discovered that he had prostate cancer. For a few days, he felt absolutely helpless. He received so much conflicting advice that he thought he would go crazy. His depression over the discovery got really bad, so he decided that he needed to do his own homework and take control himself.

He set about discovering all he could about the treatment of prostate cancer, the options available to a man of his age, and the possible outcomes. The change in his outlook was dramatic. No amount of therapy could have transformed his helpless depression into an optimistic outlook as much as improving his knowledge of his options.

I don't want to imply that even the severest of anxiety disorders is as serious as cancer, but the feelings of helplessness are very comparable. The treatment options are not always that clear for anxiety sufferers, and they have many questions: *Should I take medication? If I do, what are my chances of getting better? How long must I stay on them? Aren't tranquilizers addictive? What do I do if I can't ever get off them?* I would respectfully suggest that the confusion caused by questions like this is due entirely to a lack of adequate knowledge. We've discussed already a few of the essentials at length, but now let's look at all of the important basics.

WHAT CAUSES PANIC ANXIETY DISORDER?

While the exact cause of panic anxiety disorder is under intense scientific investigation, quite a few pieces of the puzzle are now fitting into place. The main key is the connection between GABA and stress-induced cortisol elevation, as discussed in chapter 2.

Other related causes include heredity, biological factors, and an overreaction to normal bodily sensations. Some research suggests that panic attacks occur when a "suffocation alarm mechanism" in the brain erroneously fires, falsely reporting that death is imminent. This idea, while accurately describing the sensation of the panic attack, doesn't really explain its origin. For me, the key to understanding the cause of panic anxiety disorder lies in understanding just how upsetting stress is to many areas of the body and brain.

However, there is an interactive effect with how a person's body *tolerates* stress. As we've discussed, genetic factors play a part in determining how reactive our stress response mechanisms are. This explains why some people become more excited than others by exactly the same actions. So the influence of the genes passed on to us from our parents may have a greater effect on *how we handle stress* than on how prone we are to panic itself. Type A people (those who are driven, "hot reactors," and always in a hurry) inherit a large part of this tendency rather than develop it later in life. And, in my experience, they are at greatest risk for panic attacks.

ENSURING CORRECT DIAGNOSIS

There are several physical disorders that either mimic or complicate the diagnosis of panic anxiety disorder. It is very important that these physical disorders are either ruled out as alternative explanations for your panic or treated. In some cases, the symptoms of panic may not reflect true panic anxiety at all but some other disorder that requires treatment. Misdiagnosis can lead to serious errors. Here are some of the more important disorders that complicate the diagnosis of panic disorder:

MITRAL VALVE PROLAPSE

Mitral valve prolapse, known simply as MVP, is perhaps the most important physical condition that complicates panic disorder. In this condition, usually present from birth, a valve in the heart (the mitral valve) prolapses, or slips out of place when it is supposed to close. The result is that some blood leaks past the valve. For most, MVP is a harmless condition, except for the discomfort that arises in a panic attack. Listen to one person's description of MVP:

> I had my first panic attack a few weeks ago. I, too, thought I was having a heart attack or a stroke. I went to a neurologist and my family doctor, and I had an MRI and an echocardiogram [a test that uses sound waves to take a video of your heart]. My attack consisted of my whole left side going numb, with heart racing and a hot flash. Since then, I have been experiencing numbness in my left side at different times. My foot will be okay and my face will act up or vice versa. The neurologist was concerned with a possible tumor in the brain causing the numbness or the possibility of multiple sclerosis, along with a few other things.
>
> My MRI, thank God, came back normal. The echo was used to see if the heart was functioning as it should. That showed that I have mitral valve prolapse. It is a valve in the heart that should close so blood can't flow backward but it doesn't close all the way. It's very common in women my age [twenty-seven]. It doesn't go away but usually doesn't amount to anything else. However, it is aggravated by stress. This is what made my panic attack more intense.

This story could be repeated many times. She was fortunate that an alert doctor looked for MVP. Most cases go undiagnosed.

WHAT SYMPTOMS DO PATIENTS WITH MVP EXPERIENCE?

Because the association between MVP and panic anxiety disorder is so common, I would like to devote a little more space to its discussion.

Most patients with MVP are unaware that they have the condition. Some patients will develop symptoms later in life, even though the condition has been present for many years. Furthermore, symptoms of MVP also occur commonly in the population without MVP as well. All of this, combined with the fact that MVP symptoms are difficult to treat, leads to the potential friction in the patient-physician relationship. Often, patients with MVP are simply viewed as "too worried."

With this in mind, a patient with MVP has the following general symptoms:

CHEST PAIN is very common in the population at large and is most frequently due to causes other than pain from the heart. The pains associated with MVP often are short, sharp, or stabbing, and, unlike heart disease pain, they occur predominantly at rest and only occasionally with exercise. This is precisely the type of pain experienced by most people without MVP or cardiac disease. Some physicians feel that this type of pain is secondary to the "stretching" of the supporting structures of the valve as it slips out of place with each heartbeat. These pains may be responsive to medications such as beta blockers (used to block adrenaline and therefore help to lower stress) or certain calcium blockers (used to lower blood pressure).

PALPITATIONS (awareness of the heart beating) are also very common in MVP. Since this condition is very similar to what is experienced in panic, it can often be misunderstood. Palpitations respond to exactly the same medications as those used for chest pains.

FATIGUE may also be present in MVP sufferers. This is certainly one of the most common complaints in our society as a whole, and it is by far the most frequent complaint not associated with any obvious medical problem. Due to its high incidence, fatigue is common with MVP and panic anxiety.

CAN MVP BE SERIOUS?

I have emphasized so far that MVP is really a benign problem for most people. However, you need to talk about the seriousness of your particular condition with your cardiologist so as to know what you may or may not do.

There are two possible complications of MVP you need to keep in mind:

First, the mitral valve may undergo some progressive deterioration. This condition is extremely rare (estimated to occur in about one in every ten thousand cases), but you need to face up to this if you have MVP.

Second, the heart valve can become infected, resulting in endocarditis, the infection of a structure on the inside of the heart, in this case, the mitral valve. This infection can occur because of old abnormalities of the valve structure, allowing bacteria or other organisms to "set up shop" on the valve. There is no clear evidence that all patients with MVP should receive preventative medications (called "prophylactic antibiotics"), but most cardiologists advise at least some of their patients to take medications prior to some dental or other surgical procedures with a higher risk of infection.

While I think it is only fair that people with MVP are aware of these two serious possibilities, I also urge them not to dwell on them since these complications are so very rare. Talk to your doctor about the risks of MVP.

WHAT IS THE TREATMENT FOR MVP?

There is really no treatment for MVP, only for its symptoms. Most cardiologists feel that a good exercise program, a healthy diet, and the ability to deal with the stresses in a patient's life can lead to improvement in his or her sense of well-being and thus the associated symptoms. Some of my patients have reported that eating several smaller meals a day rather than three large ones works best for them. They also find that reducing the consumption of red meat, egg products, and fats makes their digestive system work better.

Most often, the symptoms of MVP disappear as mysteriously as they appeared. Having a good and trusting relationship with your doctor is very important, as the following story illustrates:

> I have found it difficult to find a good doctor. As a child, I often had "wondering pains" and other symptoms the doctors couldn't explain, so they told my parents that I was making up symptoms to get attention. When I was twenty, I was rushed to the emergency room with chest pains, difficulty breathing, and an irregular heart rhythm; every fourth beat was irregular and I was feeling weak and extremely anxious. In the chest-pain section of the ER, the first doctor started screaming at me that the only thing that could cause my irregular heartbeat was heavy cocaine use. Even then I knew that caffeine made me feel poorly. I was not about to experiment with recreational drugs.
>
> From there I was sent to a cardiologist who gave me an echocardiogram and determined that I had mitral valve prolapse. He then decided that this was probably the cause of my other symptoms and called it "panic attack," but he said that I should not worry because it can be treated.

Years later I changed jobs and, therefore, health plans. I went to my new doctor with a written list of symptoms and a stack of my previous medical history. This doctor had no need for any of that; he wanted to know about my one main symptom. When I mentioned "panic anxiety disorder," he walked out of the room, grabbed a sample medication sent to him from a pharmaceutical company, and told me to follow the instructions on the package. He made me feel that I was imagining all my symptoms and that my problem wasn't serious. I never went back to him and I have had real difficulty trying to find a doctor to take my case seriously.

ASTHMA

One of the major symptoms of panic is "air hunger," a feeling that you are not getting enough air to breathe. You feel claustrophobic and need to get out of the place you are in or reach an open window. The feeling of "air hunger" is misleading in the panic response because, in fact, you are taking in too much oxygen due to hyperventilation. A similar response occurs in an asthmatic attack, except asthmatics are not getting enough oxygen due to an airway obstruction.

A recent study compared asthma attacks with panic attacks so as to identify discriminating symptoms.[1] The researchers compared seventy-one patients with panic disorder, with or without agoraphobia, with seventy-one patients with asthma. While there were many similarities between the two groups in the way they experienced breathing difficulties, there were three symptoms that differentiated the panic group from the asthmatic group: The asthmatics experienced wheezing, mucous congestion, and coughing; the panic sufferers didn't.

This is not to say that a patient must have only one or the other disorder. Obviously, if you are an asthmatic, you may also develop panic anxiety symptoms. You will need to be treated for both conditions. But if you experience wheezing, mucous congestion, and coughing during an apparent panic attack, you should report this to your physician for follow-up.

PAROXYSMAL SUPRAVENTRICULAR TACHYCARDIA

This one is a mouthful, but it is known simply as PSVT, a special form of rapid heartbeat that is often indistinguishable from the rapid heartbeat of panic. Here again we have a disorder whose symptoms overlap considerably with panic anxiety disorder. Unrecognized PSVT symptoms are often misdiagnosed as panic anxiety disorder. In fact, they are often ascribed to various psychiatric conditions. In one study, prior to eventual diagnosis of PSVT, physicians (nonpsychiatrists) ascribed the symptoms of 54 percent of these patients to panic, anxiety, or stress.[2] Women were more likely than men to have their symptoms erroneously ascribed to one of these disorders.

There is no simple way to rule out PSVT; it can occur in people with perfectly normal hearts. PSVT is characterized by a rapid heartbeat, or tachycardia (150 to 230 beats per minute), that starts abruptly and causes palpitations in the chest. It can also stop abruptly. Sometimes coughing or a sudden movement stops the tachycardia. If you experience any of these signs during a panic attack, tell your doctor. There is treatment for PVST, but its diagnosis requires that you wear a Holter monitor to record your heart rate patterns for a while.

HYPOGLYCEMIA

Hypoglycemia (low blood sugar) is the experience of uncomfortable physical symptoms during times when the bloodstream has a lower than normal level of glucose. Hypoglycemia is relatively rare and found mostly in people with diabetes mellitus. It appears that some people can suffer from hypoglycemia without having a fully developed diabetes—this is called "reactive" hypoglycemia.

The problem here is an insufficiency of insulin, a hormone used to break down and store sugar in the body. Too much exercise, a change in diet, or just a drop in the sugar level, say, shortly before the next meal, can lead to symptoms of hypoglycemia.

When the symptoms of hypoglycemia are severe, they are indistinguishable from those of a panic attack: trembling, lightheadedness, perspiration, anxiety, irritability, rapid heartbeat, unsteadiness, and weakness. The similarities are not coincidental. To combat the low blood sugar, the adrenal gland secretes adrenaline, which helps release extra sugar into the bloodstream; this is also a form of stress response that triggers panic anxiety attacks.

How can you tell if hypoglycemia is aggravating or causing your panic? Pay careful attention to when you have an attack. Are you hungry? Is it just before mealtimes? Does sugar in some form relieve your anxiety? Do you wake up in the early hours of the morning with a panic attack? If any of these is true, you may want to alert your treating professional to the fact that low blood sugar, and possibly hypoglycemia, should be eliminated as a cause. This diagnosis may not eliminate your panic attacks altogether, but it may reduce their severity and give you increased control over when you have them.

HOW ARE PANIC DISORDERS USUALLY TREATED?

A tendency toward panic anxiety disorder and agoraphobia runs in families. Nevertheless, *early* treatment of panic disorder can often stop the progression to agoraphobia.

Cognitive-behavioral approaches, sometimes referred to as "cognitive therapy," are clearly superior to other forms of therapy in treating panic anxiety.[3] In this form of therapy, patients learn how to view the panic situations as controllable and how to reduce anxiety through breathing exercises or refocusing attention away from anxiety-triggering situations. Another approach is called "exposure therapy," in which a patient is gradually exposed to a threatening situation. This gradual exposure can often help alleviate the phobias that may result from panic disorder. In exposure therapy, people are very slowly exposed to the fearful situation until they become desensitized to it.

Why is the cognitive-behavioral approach so effective? There is no doubt that individuals with panic disorder often have distortions in their thinking of which they may be unaware, and these distortions give rise to a cycle of fear that raises the stress level and triggers the panic attack.

In cognitive-behavioral therapy, patients are taught that typical reactions such as, *That terrible feeling is getting worse, I'm going to have a panic attack*, or *I'm going to have a heart attack* can be replaced with substitutes such as, *It's only uneasiness—it will pass*. These alternative self-statements help to reduce anxiety and ward off a panic attack. By modifying thought patterns in this way, the patient gains more control over his or her anxiety problem.

Although cognitive therapy in combination with medication is generally considered standard treatment for panic anxiety disorder, other forms of therapy are sometimes also necessary. Many panic sufferers have some residual underlying vulnerability that keeps them at risk. They can benefit from a more broad-faced psychotherapy focusing on their negative emotions and themes of fear of separation, constriction, or the need for interpersonal control.

What forms of therapy would be used here? One would be a psychodynamic form of psychotherapy, a form of "talk therapy" in which the therapist and the patient, working together, seek to uncover emotional conflicts that may underlie the patient's problems. Although psychodynamic approaches may help to relieve the stress that contributes to panic attacks, they do not seem to stop the attacks directly. In fact, there is no scientific evidence that this form of therapy by itself is effective in helping people to overcome panic anxiety disorder. However, if a patient's panic disorder occurs along with some broader and preexisting emotional disturbance, psychodynamic treatment may be a helpful addition to the overall treatment program.

MEDICATIONS IN THE TREATMENT OF PANIC ANXIETY DISORDER

Some people find the greatest relief from panic symptoms when they take certain prescription medications. I happen to believe that it is absolutely essential to stop the actual panic attacks as soon as possible to break the buildup of the fear-of-fear response. Even the most effective therapy will take some time to kick in, whereas medication can control the panic attacks immediately.

Several types of medications have been shown to be safe and effective in the treatment of panic disorder, and I will describe exactly how they should be taken in the next chapter. Let me just give a broad overview with a brief description of each so that the reader will know where a particular medication fits into the larger treatment picture. The advantage of having a broad array of medications is that the clinician can balance out the side effects against the treatment effects. (Please note that the use of lower case for a drug name indicates the generic name, while upper case signifies the trade name.)

The major medications used in the treatment of panic attacks or panic anxiety disorder are:

BENZODIAZEPINES (BENZOS): Over the past fifteen years, benzos have been used successfully in treating panic anxiety disorder with agoraphobia, but not without some controversy. In the early days, clinicians were not very adept at limiting the development of dependency on these medications. That has now changed considerably with the advent of newer benzos that are easier to manage. Outcome studies of panic disorder treatment have demonstrated that alprazolam (Xanax), lorazepam (Ativan), and clonazepam (Klonopin) are all clinically effective. I prefer Xanax at first, switching to Ativan later because it is very fast-acting. All benzos can be maintained without the need to increase the dose over a period of seven to eight months, unlike earlier tranquilizers.

Tricyclic antidepressants (TCAs): Tricyclic antidepressants were the first to be used in treating a broad range of anxiety disorders. Results are somewhat varied. TCAs take longer to kick in (two to three weeks) and can have some very uncomfortable side effects. TCAs are now used only when other forms of treatment are not more effective or when a high level of sedation is required. The most commonly used TCAs are imipramine (Tofranil) and clomipramine (Anafranil). Anafranil is helpful when there is a high level of obsessive thinking.

Monoamine Oxidase Inhibitors (MAOIs): MAOIs are antidepressants used for treating "atypical" depressions. They are, however, proving to be very effective in treating panic anxiety disorder. Some clinicians believe that MAOIs are the most potent antianxiety medications available, but their considerable side effects and diet restrictions limit them to later use if other forms of treatment are not so effective.

Selective Serotonin Reuptake Inhibitors (SSRIs): The most commonly used medications today for the treatment of panic disorders are SSRIs, another form of antidepressant. The side-effect profiles of SSRIs are better, and they are safe, nonaddictive, and highly effective. Data supporting their clinical effectiveness is growing by leaps and bounds.

THE IMPORTANCE OF STARTING TREATMENT EARLY

As I mentioned earlier, a predisposition toward panic anxiety disorder and agoraphobia runs in families. Stress, however, is the crucial trigger that starts the panic process, both in those with this family predisposition as well as in others. The predisposition for panic disorders is nothing more than a lower stress threshold or a greater tendency to pump adrenaline and cortisol under stress. Whatever the factors causing panic, *early* treatment of panic anxiety disorder is absolutely essential. The sooner panic is treated, the less likely it will persist and the greater chance that you can prevent it from progressing to agoraphobia.

Studies have shown that proper and early treatment consisting of a combination of cognitive-behavioral therapy and medications helps 70 to 90 percent of people with panic disorder. Significant improvement is usually seen within six to eight weeks.

WHAT KIND OF DOCTOR SHOULD I SEE?

Where you start in your search for help is not as important as where you end up. It is vital that you find a competent professional who has the proper credentials and training in treating anxiety disorders. Pure psychotherapists are not adequate without conjunctive treatment by someone knowledgeable in psychopharmacology (treatment with appropriate medications). So you could start by talking to a pastor, counselor, psychologist, social worker, or psychiatrist, depending on your financial resources. If the professional you are seeing is competent, he or she will inform you of their level of expertise and their willingness to collaborate with other professionals. One thing I have learned about treating panic and other severe anxiety disorders is that a team approach is best.

Let me address a delicate matter. Many Christians are fearful of going to a psychologist or a psychiatrist because of the stereotypes associated with these professionals. They would much prefer just to see their pastor or local counselor.

Now let me stick my neck out here and risk the ire of my clinical psychologist and psychiatrist colleagues. *Many counselors are very competent.* They could easily provide you with all the cognitive therapy and counsel you will need for your full recovery. And the proof they are competent will depend on whether they invoke a team approach and collaborate with their clinical psychologist and psychiatrist colleagues, especially when it comes to adjunctive medication or more specialized diagnostic testing.

Why is such collaboration necessary? Psychiatrists are trained in medicine and have the expertise not only to prescribe medications for anxiety, but also to rule out serious medical conditions that your family physician may overlook. Clinical psychologists are trained to perform sophisticated psychological tests that could also help to rule out severe psychological conditions that may underlie your anxiety. You could either go to see these professionals first or raise the issue with your pastor or counselor.

Wherever you begin seeking treatment for your anxiety, you should also plan to see your family doctor for a full medical checkup; any competent nonmedical professional will, or should, call for this. Many psychiatrists do not perform routine medical examinations, so they may ask you to see your family physician or other specialist.

In this day of lawsuit-happy Americans, physicians often feel compelled out of legal fears to order expensive tests to rule out a physical cause of your symptoms before declaring that it is an anxiety problem. Still, it is absolutely imperative that you start with a medical checkup, even if you are seeing a counselor or psychologist.

Here is a very helpful point: When you see your medical doctor, make sure that you mention that you suspect that you have an anxiety problem. Telling your doctor this will let him or her know that you have an open mind about this possibility. If, after talking with you, examining you, and calling for some routine tests of your blood chemistry and vital organ functioning, your physician is confident that you have no physical disease and that an anxiety disorder is probable, he or she knows that you are open to that possibility. Then he or she won't feel compelled to have to prove it to you by ordering additional, needless tests.

RESISTING YOUR PANIC INSTEAD OF FIGHTING IT

Don't *fight* your feelings of panic; instead, work at *resisting* them. There is a difference. Fighting your panic symptoms is likely to make them worse. It increases the fight-or-flight response that is responsible for the anxiety in the first place. You are helping to feed the enemy. So here are some suggestions for how to stop fighting your panic:

- *Don't run away from your symptoms.* Face up to them squarely, as you would any bully or enemy. Say to yourself: *I'm just going to wait until these feelings have passed, then I will be in control again.*

- *Accept that what your body is doing for you is right for the moment.* I happen to believe that a lot of what happens to us is the body doing what it was designed to do. It may seem uncomfortable, but, like all pain, it is serving a purpose. So just watch and accept your body's reaction, without creating further fear.

- *Give your panic a wide berth and allow it to pass.* Many, in the moment of panic, think they should be doing something to stop the attack. Other than taking control of your breathing, there is nothing you can do. Wait it out. Let it pass. The attack will pass more quickly if you don't react with more fear.

- *Keep reminding yourself that the attack is only a temporary interruption.* All panic attacks are time limited. No one has ever gone into a permanent state of panic. Just accept the interruption for that moment in time.

TREATMENT OF PANIC DISORDER

Now we come to the matter of treatment. If you saw a psychiatrist for evaluation, depending upon the diagnosis, your psychiatrist will either handle your treatment or refer you to a psychologist or counselor. The distinction between these professionals often confuses many laypersons. The important point to remember, as explained previously, is that a psychiatrist is also a medical doctor.

Here my bias will show again. Collaboration with a medically trained professional is imperative at the outset if medications are to be used, and medications are usually essential in the early stages of the treatment of severe anxiety problems. However, the long-term work that is necessary to change the thinking habits, attitudes, and lifestyle associated with panic is better undertaken by a competent psychologist or counselor. It takes time to turn these habits around permanently, and this ongoing therapy needs to be guided by someone who has been trained more like a coach than a healer.

MORE DETAILS ABOUT COGNITIVE-BEHAVIORAL THERAPY

Cognitive-behavioral therapy is such an important form of treatment that I want to provide a little more information for you.

In cognitive therapy, discussions between the patient and the therapist are

not usually focused on the patient's past, as is the case with some forms of psychotherapy. Instead, conversations focus on the difficulties and successes the
patient is having at the present time and on the mental skills the patient needs
to learn.

The behavioral portion of cognitive-behavioral therapy may involve
learning a relaxation technique. By learning to relax, the patient may acquire
the ability to reduce the generalized anxiety and stress that often sets the stage
for his or her panic attacks. Behavioral therapy often includes breathing exercises designed to help the patient learn how to control his or her breathing and
avoid hyperventilation, which can exacerbate some people's panic attacks.
(Effective relaxation is such an important part of gaining mastery over panic
that I am offering a relaxation tape that outlines several strategies for coping
with anxiety, including progressive muscle relaxation, thought stopping,
Christian meditation, and sensory enhancement exercises. You will find details
of how you can obtain this tape in Appendix A.)

Another important aspect of behavioral therapy is exposure to internal
sensations, called "interoceptive exposure." During interoceptive exposure, the
therapist compiles an individual assessment of internal sensations associated
with panic. Depending on the assessment, the therapist may then encourage
the patient to trigger some of the sensations of a panic attack by, for example,
exercising to increase heart rate, breathing rapidly to trigger lightheadedness
and respiratory symptoms, or spinning around to trigger dizziness. The therapist may also use exercises to produce feelings of unreality. Then the therapist teaches the patient to cope effectively with these sensations, such as
learning how to cup your hands over your mouth and nose so as to rebreathe
your carbon dioxide and thus lower your oxygen intake. The patient also
learns to replace alarmist or panic thoughts, such as *I am going to die,* with
more appropriate ones, such as *It's just a little dizziness. I can handle it.*

Another important aspect of behavioral therapy is "in vivo" or real-life
exposure. The therapist and the patient determine whether the patient has
been avoiding particular places and situations, and, if so, which patterns of
avoidance are causing the patient problems. They agree to work on the avoidance behaviors that are most seriously interfering with the patient's life. For
example, fear of driving may be of paramount importance for one patient,
while inability to go to the grocery store may be most handicapping for
another. Some therapists will go to an agoraphobic patient's home to conduct

the initial sessions. Often therapists take their patients on excursions to shopping malls and other places the patients have been avoiding. Or they may accompany their patients who are trying to overcome their fear of driving a car.

The patient approaches a feared situation gradually, attempting to stay in spite of rising levels of anxiety. In this way, the patient sees that as frightening as their feelings are, they are not dangerous, and they do pass. On each attempt, the patient faces as much fear as he or she can stand. Patients find that with this step-by-step approach, aided by encouragement and skilled advice from their therapists, they can gradually master their fears and enter situations that had seemed unapproachable. Many therapists assign their patients "homework" to do between sessions. Sometimes patients spend only a few sessions in one-on-one contact with a therapist and continue to work on their own with the aid of a printed manual. Often the patient will join a therapy group with others striving to overcome panic anxiety disorder or phobias, meeting with them weekly to discuss progress, exchange encouragement, and receive guidance from the therapist.

Cognitive-behavioral therapy generally requires at least eight to twelve weeks of work before you really begin to see improvement. Some people may need more time to learn and implement the skills. This kind of therapy, which is reported to have a low relapse rate, is effective in eliminating panic attacks or reducing their frequency. It also reduces anticipatory anxiety and avoidance of feared situations. In my experience, I have found that cognitive-behavioral therapy, when combined with proper medication, is the single most effective way to treat panic disorders.

CHAPTER 5

WHEN AND HOW TO USE ANTIANXIETY MEDICATIONS

————— ∞ —————

I am weary with my groaning; all the night make I my bed to swim;
I water my couch with my tears.

PSALM 6:6

W hat? Are you crazy? Take a tranquilizer? You have got to be out of your gourd. I'd rather die than be seen taking a pill like that. I thought we had stopped using that stuff a long time ago."

I moved the telephone receiver six inches away from my ear. I had met Chuck on a flight from L.A. to Chicago some weeks before and, knowing that I was from Fuller Theological Seminary, he had tracked down my telephone number. He was calling to follow up on a conversation we had on the airplane.

We were strangers as we settled down into our cramped airplane seats. As we started in superficial talk, Chuck told me he was a business lawyer on his way home after a chaotic series of meetings in L.A. Bottom line? His life was out of control. Soon it came out that he was a very active Christian. In fact, I discovered this when he tried to witness to me. I relieved his tension as I assured him that I was also a Christian and on my way to speak at a pastors' conference. We settled down to a more relaxed experience of each other over the next three hours of our flight.

From the outset, Chuck came across as a very outspoken person. He spoke his mind freely and without constraint and, during the few hours we chatted, I really grew to appreciate him for it. I knew where I stood with Chuck.

Then he discovered that I was a clinical psychologist, and his tension returned briefly. Finally, Chuck shared with me that he had recently started having some strange experiences. It seemed clear that the experiences he was describing were panic attacks. In fact, Chuck had had such attacks several times earlier in his life, but he had always stoically ignored them. In fact, he had kept the attacks so secret that even his wife was not aware of them. But the latest bout of attacks seemed more serious, so he asked me what he should do about them. I told him what I thought the problem was and suggested he see a psychologist or psychiatrist. We then moved on to talk about other matters. Deep within, I was left with the impression that Chuck would once again stoically ignore them.

So here he was, some weeks later, venting his frustration over the phone and updating me on his encounter with the psychiatrist he'd seen. As I expected, the psychiatrist had prescribed standard medication treatment, including Xanax, to initially get the panic attacks under control. Chuck wanted to know what Xanax was. I explained that it was a rapid-acting minor tranquilizer. And that was when he went ballistic. The psychiatrist had assumed that Chuck knew all about panic disorders and Xanax, so he didn't bother to explain how the medication worked, what it was supposed to do, and how important it was to his recovery. Absent any real information, Chuck's prejudices kicked in and opposed the treatment.

I calmed him down and finally got him to listen as I clarified what was causing his problem and why he needed to follow his psychiatrist's recommendations. However, it did remind me just how much resistance people have to taking a tranquilizer, especially Christians.

OVERCOMING PREJUDICE AGAINST ANTIANXIETY MEDICATION

While this book will emphasize the natural processes for curing your anxiety, you need to fully grasp the following point: *It is almost always necessary to use medications during the early stages of the treatment of panic disorder.* Why? To prevent any future panic attacks from occurring.

No one should take medication like tranquilizers without knowing something about what they are, how they work, what they do, what you can expect, how soon you can expect them to work, and when you should stop taking them. Knowing when and how to stop your medication is so important that I have devoted an entire chapter to this topic. Nothing is more confusing and even horrifying to a panic sufferer than the issue of when and how to use antianxiety medications, especially tranquilizers.

Our culture has, quite rightly, created a strong antidrug sentiment. We had to. Drug abuse was out of control, including the overuse of prescription drugs. As a result, so much stigma is now attached to the use of tranquilizers that the average person resists the idea of taking them—even when it is absolutely necessary for them to do so. Those who must take tranquilizers just to achieve a modicum of normalcy feel ashamed of it. They deliberately conceal this "secret" for fear that others will judge or condemn them as "weaklings" or "failures." This inappropriate and unnecessary secret only feeds their anxiety with more anxiety. Feelings of shame only make their condition worse.

Many patients are so bothered by the thought of taking a tranquilizer that they have literally turned themselves into worrywarts over the issue. And when a therapist suggests that they take some medication, they fight it with all their might. Only when their anxiety becomes unbearable or starts destroying their lives do they finally relent. "But only if I don't have to tell anyone," they plead.

Of course, you don't have to publicize to your world what medications you are taking. It's no one's business but yours. Whatever treatment you are receiving for *any* problem whatsoever is entirely a private matter. You are not violating friendship with anyone because you keep such information private. However, when my patients have become better informed about the nature of their problem and the purpose of the medication, much of the stigma falls away from their minds and they find that they don't have such a strong need to keep their treatment secret. Unfortunately, many uninformed people still misjudge emotional problems and attach a stigma to any form of psychotropic treatment. When you are with these people, it is better to keep your personal matters to yourself. Just don't feel guilty or inadequate about your treatment.

I hope that the information I will provide here will help you internalize a greater level of self-confidence and a conviction that you are doing the right thing before God in seeking out help.

THE MANY FORMS OF ANXIETY

To understand when and how to use antianxiety medications, especially tranquilizers, let me begin by reminding my readers that *there are many forms of anxiety.* Some forms of anxiety may need medication temporarily, but others may not. Some may need medication for a long period. A few sufferers may only be able to survive if they take medication the rest of their lives.

Which anxiety problems don't generally need medication? One example is *phobias.* Tranquilizers never cure phobias and seldom make them easier to deal with. The treatment of phobias requires good, old-fashioned psychotherapy, preferably the cognitive-behavioral therapy I outlined earlier. It seems strange to be referring to psychotherapy as "old-fashioned," but the use of antianxiety medications has become so dominant in our culture that we sometimes forget that a tranquilizer is not always the cure for every anxiety problem.

Another example of an anxiety problem that doesn't get better with medication is *separation anxiety,* in which you become extremely anxious about being separated from your loved ones. Such anxiety originates within your mind as a result of your thinking patterns and can only be cured by psychotherapy that addresses these patterns.

Anxiety comes in many shades. Some forms of anxiety are quite normal and need nothing more than reassurance or the passage of time to heal them. For instance, I will tell you honestly that I do not enjoy going to the dentist. Does anyone? It all goes back to a few bad experiences with an incompetent dentist when I was a child. To my dentist friends out there, I sincerely apologize. You are all wonderful people doing a necessary job. But count me out of ecstasy on contemplating a dental appointment. So from the time I make an appointment to when I actually am sitting in the dreaded chair I can sense my anxiety, not a lot, but enough to intrude into my awareness and spoil my day. The anxiety all disappears once I hear, "Open your mouth wide." That's the problem with anxiety—it's all about anticipation.

But some forms of anxiety are neither petty nor inconsequential. As we've seen, they are serious enough to be classified as disorders and can imprison you in your home and rob your life of happiness and contentment. These forms are serious and cannot be neglected. They don't just go away on their own.

Another point often overlooked by laypeople who have a strongly negative view of so-called mind-altering drugs is that there are many types of medication used to treat anxiety, *not just tranquilizers*. Sometimes an antidepressant such as Zoloft (a nonaddictive, non-mind-altering drug) is the preferred long-term solution to an anxiety problem. Remember that some medications (tranquilizers) are used to *prevent* immediate anxiety attacks, while others (antidepressants) are used to *reduce the frequency and severity* of panic attacks in the long run.

WHEN DO YOU NEED MEDICATION?

Before undergoing any treatment for panic anxiety disorder, sufferers should always have a thorough medical examination to rule out medical causes of their distressing symptoms, such as mitral valve prolapse (MVP), hyperthyroidism, certain types of epilepsy, or cardiac arrhythmias (disturbances in the rhythm of the heartbeat).

WHICH ANTIANXIETY MEDICATIONS ARE USED FOR WHICH PROBLEMS?

While I will provide as much information about antianxiety medications as is appropriate here, I will intentionally not quote specific dosages outside of just mentioning broad ranges. To do this would be too misleading. Only the clinician treating you should tell you an appropriate dosage, depending on your weight, condition, related medical problems, and the severity of your anxiety. Never compare your dosage with anyone else's. We all differ in our tolerance and need for a certain level of medication.

It is important that you seek out competent help from a professional who is trained to treat anxiety disorders. Many anxiety sufferers have had their hope of being cured dashed to the ground by incompetent treatment. The blanket prescribing of tranquilizers or the inappropriate withholding of them by inadequately trained professionals is not helpful; it is a downright travesty.

HOW CAN I HELP IF A FAMILY MEMBER HAS A PANIC DISORDER?

People who suffer from panic attacks need a lot of support and encouragement. Here are some practical ways you can help:

- Work hard at learning all you can about panic anxiety disorder. The more you know, the fewer mistakes you will make.

- Don't make assumptions about what the panic sufferer needs; ask them. Second-guessing only creates more tension.

- Don't put pressure on the family member to get better quickly. Let the panic sufferer set the pace for his or her recovery.

- Find something positive in every experience to praise and reinforce. If the affected person is only able to go partway to a particular goal, such as a movie theater or party, consider that an achievement rather than a failure.

- Don't enable avoidance. Negotiate with the panic sufferer to take one small step forward when he or she wants to avoid something.

- Don't sacrifice your own life to please the sufferer. This only builds resentment. Make sure that you continue to live your own life fully. Sooner or later, the panic sufferer will begin to improve.

- During an attack, avoid telling the panic sufferer things like: "Relax. Calm down. Don't be anxious. Don't behave like a coward." These reactions only create more anxiety. Instead, calmly reassure the panic sufferer that the attack will pass quickly, and he or she will soon be in control again.

- Don't overreact when the affected person experiences a panic attack. Behave calmly and objectively. Remember, the panic sufferer is not causing the attack nor does he or she have much control over it at the time.

- Give yourself permission to be anxious. It is only natural for you to be concerned and even worried about the family member with the disorder.

- Be patient and accepting, but don't settle for the affected person being permanently disabled. Encourage aggressive treatment of the problem. If one treatment isn't working, suggest he or she try another.

WHAT SIDE EFFECTS CAN I EXPECT FROM ANTIANXIETY MEDICATION?

No medication is free of side effects. While research is constantly seeking to find new medications that have fewer side effects, called "smart bomb medications," and a whole new range of antianxiety medications are now on the horizon, we will always have to contend with the unwanted effects. The most common reason for treatment failure is "noncompliance." In other words, the patient deliberately stops taking the medication. And the most common reason for noncompliance is the discomfort of the side effects.

But first, a word of caution. While it is absolutely essential that anyone taking medication should know its side effects, knowing too much about potential side effects can feed your already anxiety-prone state. If you ever consult a drug reference manual, you will notice that every medication listed has an arm's-length list of possible side effects. While some medications differ, almost every drug has the same list of common effects, such as addiction, blurred vision, confusion and memory problems, constipation, dry mouth, headache, heat intolerance, high blood pressure, low blood pressure, muscle jerks, nausea or vomiting, etc. Drug manufacturers cover all the bases.

I am not saying these side effects are not important. I am saying that it is important not to let your imagination run away with you. You need to know what the *real* effects are for you.

I cannot tell you how many times I have referred a patient for medication only to find that a few weeks later the patient has stopped taking it. Why? Because shortly after starting the medication, the patient heard or read that the medication has a certain side effect. From that moment on, he or she started experiencing that side effect. So keep your imagination under control.

Every medication you take has a small list of *essential side effects* you need to know about. Make sure you ask questions of your doctor so that you are clear about the following four things:

1. What are the most common side effects?

2. What must I do or not do because of these effects?

3. How long will these effects last?

4. What must I do if I experience these effects to a great extent?

Some side effects are temporary and only cause problems during the first few weeks of treatment. If the known temporary effects don't pass, then you may need to change the type of medication you are taking. Many effects are "dose related." This means that if you lower the dose (never do this without your doctor's permission except in an emergency), the side effects will diminish or go away. By gradually increasing the medication a few days later, you may find that the effects are no longer there. Persistence is important if you are going to win over your panic.

Since it is important to distinguish between important and nonimportant side effects, I have listed in the accompanying sidebar the most common side effects of medications used to treat anxiety and suggested ways to manage them. Of course, whenever you experience side effects from *any* medicine, you should consult with the person prescribing or monitoring your medication. It's a good idea to list the side effects that are causing you discomfort and give this to your doctor, keeping a copy for yourself. Your doctor may be able to adjust your dosage schedule in a way that will make you more comfortable or may ask you to tolerate the side effects because many of them will go away on their own. Either way, some of the hints I offer in the upcoming sidebar may help you to stay on target with your treatment.

COMMON SIDE EFFECTS OF ANTIANXIETY MEDICATIONS

Addiction (dependence)

This is a potential problem only with one kind of medication—the minor tranquilizer (Valium, Librium, Xanax, Ativan, Klonopin, and others in that category). Antidepressants and mood stabilizers are not addictive. If you are worried about addiction to a minor tranquilizer, discuss ways to minimize the risk with your therapist. Careful attention to stopping the medication slowly, as I will describe later, can readily break any dependence. However, if you have a history of addiction, you should avoid minor tranquilizers.

Constipation

This can be a chronic problem, but there are many things you can do to help. Make sure you drink at least eight glasses of water during the day, every day. Eat fresh fruits, vegetables, and whole-grain breads and cereals. Get some exercise every day, such as walking, bike riding, jogging, playing sports—any physical exercise will help prevent constipation. If you're following all these suggestions and still have problems with constipation, your doctor may prescribe a stool softener (a tablet or liquid taken daily by mouth) or suggest that you regularly take a medicine made of natural fibers, like Metamucil.

Dry Mouth

This common side effect of antidepressants usually disappears after the first few weeks. In the meantime, it helps to have a bottle of water with you during the day to sip if your mouth feels dry. Some people find it helps to chew gum or suck on hard candies occasionally. Your mouth may also feel better if you brush your teeth at least twice a day.

Headaches

This is most likely to result from the use of the selective serotonin reuptake inhibitor antidepressants (SSRIs). These headaches usually go away on their own after the first few weeks, and in the meantime, Tylenol or similar painkillers may help. Be sure to let your doctor or nurse know at your next visit.

High Blood Pressure (hypertension)

This occurs mainly with antidepressants, and you probably would not be able to detect it on your own. Your doctor or nurse or the staff of your program will periodically check your blood pressure when you first begin taking your medication to make sure your blood pressure is normal.

Low Blood Pressure (orthostatic hypotension)

You may notice this problem as a feeling of dizziness or light-headedness, especially when you stand up suddenly. If you have this problem, it will help to get up slowly from a sitting or lying position (especially first thing in the morning when you're getting out of bed). If you feel dizzy or lightheaded, sit down or hold on to something sturdy until the feeling passes. Increasing the amount of water you drink to at least eight glasses per day will also help.

Problems in Sexual Desire or Performance

This happens with one type of SSRI and can take the form of lack of interest in sex, inability to have orgasm, change in the quality of orgasm, or delay in orgasm. Sometimes it is hard to tell if these sexual problems are being caused by the illness or by the medication since stress, depression, and anxiety can also cause problems with sexual desire and performance. If you have either a decrease in sexual interest or difficulty in sexual performance, let your doctor or therapist know. A decrease in dose or the addition of another medication will usually solve the problem. Sometimes it's necessary to stop the medication and change to another.

Rapid Heartbeat (tachycardia)

You may be unaware of this problem or you may actually feel a rapid heartbeat as palpitations or fluttering in your chest. Rapid heartbeat (faster than 120 beats per minute) is a fairly common problem that occurs in the beginning of treatment with many medications. Most people adjust to it, and the heartbeat gradually slows down to a normal rate. Deep breathing and other relaxation techniques may be helpful. If this problem persists, your doctor or nurse may order another medication to slow your heartbeat.

Sleepiness (somnolence)

It is common to feel sleepy during the first week or two (sometimes longer) when you're taking a new medication. Report this problem to your doctor right away, but in the meantime try to adjust your schedule to allow for short rest periods or naps during the day. Avoid driving or operating any other machinery until the sleepiness passes. Along with this sleepiness, you may notice some problems with coordination (called "ataxia"). This will pass as the sleepiness passes.

Weight Gain

With some medications, people gain weight. This can be due to any combination of the following: fluid retention, increased appetite, lack of physical activity, or a change in the metabolism of carbohydrates. The most effective way to deal with weight gain is to decrease your food intake slightly and, at the same time, increase your level of physical activity. Substitute lower-calorie and lower-fat foods for ones that are high in fat or calories.

WHY CONSIDER MEDICATION?

As I have already indicated, major depression is not the only emotional disorder where medication is sometimes appropriate. As you now know, any anxiety disorder also has a strong underlying biochemical disturbance and responds well to medication. Except in relatively minor cases, the effective use of medication is essential for effective treatment in the early stages of panic and other anxiety disorders. Proper medication, combined with cognitive-behavioral psychotherapy, will ensure a complete cure in most cases. I am confident of this approach since I've been using it for years.

One reason why medication is especially important in treating the early stages of an anxiety problem is that in anxiety, unlike depression, the symptoms themselves become the source of further problems. In other words, when you are depressed, the feelings of depression slow you down and aid your recovery. When you are anxious, the anxious feelings create more anxiety so that the disorder literally feeds off itself. For example, in panic anxiety disorder, the extreme fear of a panic attack creates a spiral of more anxiety and sets up the conditions for further attacks. This is the fear-of-fear response I mentioned earlier. In anxiety, therefore, it is imperative that this vicious cycle is interrupted and the system stabilized, so that the necessary counseling or psychotherapy can be introduced. If you are constantly fighting off your panic attacks, you hardly have the energy to address the life issues that originally gave rise to your anxiety problems.

So medication helps by stabilizing the nervous system so as to reduce the fear of anxiety symptoms, restoring control and confidence by buying time for the underlying issues to be addressed in therapy, and ensuring that the problem will not worsen at the time you start making life changes.

There is some risk in using medication to relieve symptoms, as every professional therapist knows. Once the symptoms are relieved, there is always the strong possibility that the patient will not be motivated to make the necessary life changes or address the underlying conflict that is causing his or her anxiety problem. Some therapists, therefore, may discourage the use of any antianxiety medication at first or at all. Others will allow enough medication to allow the patient mild symptom relief but leave enough anxiety in place to motivate his or her attention to underlying issues. As in any disorder, every case is different; how much medication to use is a matter for the individual therapist or physician to decide in consultation with you.

In all but the mildest panic attacks, however, I believe treatment should definitely include some medication. My experience has been that it is not possible to make progress in therapy while the ogre of panic still hangs over you like the sword of Damocles. The potential for an attack looming over you undermines all your confidence and destroys the results of therapy; months of hard work can be undone by just one new panic attack.

How can you know if you need medication to control your anxiety? Here are some definite indications that your therapist will usually take into account when evaluating your condition:

- Is your anxiety so debilitating that you can make no progress in therapy without medication? If so, medication is necessary.

- Are you making progress without medication? If so, it is likely that you can continue without it.

- Can you function adequately at home and/or work without medication? If so, it is unlikely that you need to take it.

- Do you feel confident that you can control your attacks yourself? If so, try and see how you do.

- Are you suicidal or demoralized, or does the anxiety present any risk to your life or others'? If so, medication is essential.

TYPES OF ANTIANXIETY MEDICATION

The miracle of modern medicine is that we have a large number of effective medications to reduce the pain of people who suffer from mental and emotional disorders. I never cease to thank God that I live in an age when human suffering can be minimized in so many ways. Research is continuing to find more effective medication, especially for panic attacks, agoraphobia, and obsessive-compulsive disorders. I believe that in the next few years, we will see some significant progress in these areas.

In the meantime there are now five kinds of medication that appear to help reduce anxiety symptoms that we briefly discussed earlier: tricyclic antidepressants (TCAs), serotonin reuptake inhibitors (SSRIs), monoamine oxidase inhibitors (MAOIs), benzodiazepines tranquilizers (benzos), and adrenaline blockers. It is important that you understand the difference between these medications and why you are taking a particular one. Allow me to bring them together in an understandable way.

TRICYCLIC ANTIDEPRESSANTS (TCAs)

These agents are traditionally used in the treatment of severe depression or depression mixed with anxiety. The reason why antidepressants work to relieve anxiety in the long run is that the same neurotransmitter deficiencies that cause depression also cause disruption to the system that keeps us in tranquillity.

Almost any of the dozen or more tricyclics will work in reducing anxiety. For instance, the common medication used for panic anxiety, imipramine (Tofranil), is given in very small dosages at first (say, 10 to 25 mg per day) and then gradually increased so that the side effects can be tolerated. The full dosage is usually taken once a day, at bedtime.

COMMON ANTIDEPRESSANTS USED TO TREAT ANXIETY

(This chart is offered only as a guide. Do not change your medication dosages without consulting your physician.)

GENERIC NAME	TRADE NAME	APPROVED INDICATIONS (Besides Depression)	APPROVED ADULT DOSAGES
TRICYCLIC ANTIDEPRESSANTS (TCAs):			
Clomipramine	Anafranil	Obsessive-Compulsive Disorder	100 to 250 mg/day
SELECTIVE SEROTONIN REUPTAKE INHIBITORS (SSRIs):			
Fluoxtine	Prozac	Anxiety, Panic Anxiety	10 to 80 mg/day
MONOAMINE OXIDASE INHIBITORS (MAOIs):			
Phenelzine	Nardil	Panic Anxiety	45 to 90 mg/day
Trancypromine	Parnate	Panic Anxiety	20 to 50 mg/day

Because one in four patients will experience early overstimulation, tricyclic antidepressants are most efficient when the physician "starts low and goes slow." Imipramine, for example, is best prescribed with a low initial dose of 10 mg and gradually increased, as tolerated, by 10 mg every two to four days up to a dose of 150 to 250 mg. In contrast to depression, which may take four to six weeks to respond to tricyclics, panic anxiety disorder *can take up to twelve weeks for a treatment response.* Use of imipramine, desipramine, or nortriptyline is usually best since considerable data and experience have been accumulated with these agents. Doxepin and amitriptyline have side effects that are troublesome to patients already hypersensitive to internal physical sensations.

SELECTIVE SEROTONIN REUPTAKE INHIBITORS (SSRIS)

The newer serotonin reuptake inhibitor drugs have been found to be quite effective in both anecdotal case studies and research. Fluoxetine (Prozac) in low initial doses of 2 to 5 mg can be gradually increased to a 20 mg dose. Paroxetine (Paxil) can be similarly taken. Sertraline (Zoloft) can be started at 50 mg daily and, if no antipanic effect is noted after two to three weeks, can be increased to 50 mg twice daily. The serotonin reuptake blocker clomipramine (Anafranil) has also been shown to be effective in controlled trials but may be associated with more side effects.

A very recent development has shown that the SSRI Zoloft has many advantages in treating anxiety, including panic attacks.[1] Perhaps its greatest advantage is that it is not dependency producing. Other SSRIs, like Prozac, may be just as effective as Zoloft. This study did not compare the two medications. So, you should discuss this option with your prescribing clinician.

MONOAMINE OXIDASE INHIBITORS (MAOIS)

Monoamine oxidase inhibitors (MAOIs) are thought to be superior to tricyclic antidepressants for some patients because of their broader spectrum of action. Phenelzine (Nardil), the most studied drug, must be given ultimately in a dose of 1 mg per kg (of body weight), with initial doses of 15 mg two to three times daily. Problems with staying awake during the daytime and nighttime insomnia may be combated by switching from morning to evening.

Drowsiness, weight gain, and sexual dysfunction can be limiting factors in the use of Nardil. The patient must also avoid alcohol and most other medications and adhere to a diet low in tyramine when taking this medication. This means no processed foods like cheese and wine. However, this is of little practical importance for most patients, unless they are cognitively impaired or have a disorder of impulse control that makes them likely to act out self-destructively or abuse alcohol or other drugs.

BENZODIAZEPINES (BENZOS)

Because of the overstimulation that occurs with tricyclic antidepressants and patient concerns about the possible dietary interactions of MAOIs, about 25 to 30 percent of panic patients may require benzodiazepines as a long-term treatment. Initiating benzos may be necessary to bring panic attacks to a sudden stop. Antidepressants are then started several weeks later after the acute symptoms disappear. The benzos can then be slowly tapered after eight to twelve weeks of antidepressant treatment.

The most commonly used benzos are alprazolam (Xanax), clonazepam (Klonopin), and lorazepam (Ativan). Alprazolam absorbs very rapidly, so some anxiety may return between doses, but it does help to stop an attack if taken immediately. Clonazepam is associated with higher rates of depression and possibly greater sedation.

ANTIANXIETY MEDICATIONS

(This chart is offered only as a guide. Do not change your medication dosages without consulting your physician.)

GENERIC NAME	TRADE NAME	APPROVED INDICATIONS	APPROVED ADULT DOSAGES
BENZODIAZEPINES:			
Alprazolam	Xanax	Anxiety, Anxiety Depression	0.75 to 4 mg/day
		Panic Disorder, Panic Attacks	1.5 to 10 mg/day
Chlordiazepoxide	Librium	Anxiety, Alcohol Withdrawal, Preoperative Sedation	5 to 300 mg/day
Clonazepam	Klonopin	Seizure Disorders, Panic Attacks	1 to 6 mg/day
Clorazepate	Tranxene	Anxiety, Seizure Disorders, Alcohol Withdrawal	7.5 to 90 mg/day
Diazepam	Valium	Anxiety, Alcohol Withdrawal, Muscle Spasm, Preoperative Sedation, Status Epilepticus	2 to 40 mg/day
Halazepam	Paxipam	Anxiety	60 to 160 mg/day
Lorazepam	Ativan	Anxiety, Preoperative Sedation	0.5 to 10 mg/day
Oxazepam	Serax	Anxiety, Anxiety Depression	30 to 120 mg/day
Prazepam	Centrax	Anxiety	20 to 60 mg/day

(Avoid alcohol and other CNS depressants with all these agents. Drowsiness may impair your ability to drive.)

NONBENZODIAZEPINE ANXIOLYTICS
(Including Adrenaline Blockers):

Buspirone	BuSpar	Anxiety	15 to 60 mg/day
Hydroxyzine	Atarax	Anxiety, Preoperative Sedation	50 to 400 mg/day
Meprobamate	Equanil	Anxiety	400 to 600 mg/da
Propranol	Inderal	Anxiety	10 to 40 mg/day

Doses are standardized for alprazolam since far more information is available for this agent. Clonazepam doses are one-half and lorazepam twice those of alprazolam. The starting dose of alprazolam is 0.25 to 0.5 mg four times daily. Many patients will respond to between 2 and 4 mg per day and rarely will a patient require more than 6 mg. Response is rapid and occurs in one to two weeks. Side effects of sedation and ataxia (loss of coordination) are self-limiting. In the first hour or so after dosing, some degree of mild cognitive impairment may occur, especially in older individuals engaged in complicated tasks.

ADRENALINE BLOCKERS

As I have already indicated, Xanax is often used in conjunction with an adrenaline blocker such as Inderal (propranolol). This medication blocks certain receptors in the nervous system that primarily stimulate the cardiovascular system, so they are very effective in anxiety disturbances that cause rapid heartbeat and other cardiac reactions. Used at higher doses than usually used for anxiety, Inderal lowers blood pressure. It should be avoided by patients with asthma or diabetes.

HOW LONG SHOULD A MEDICATION BE TAKEN?

How long you take your medication depends largely on the severity of your anxiety. It is not unusual for medication to continue for at least a year. Thereafter, the medication can be tapered off slowly. If a relapse occurs, the medication is reinstated.

Medications are designed to speed your recovery and prevent relapse so you can return to a productive and satisfying life. Therefore, you must continue to take medication until you achieve these two goals. If side effects from your medication cause you any discomfort, report the problem(s) to your doctor or therapist at your next visit (or immediately if the effects are severe).

The ultimate goal of all treatment is, of course, a medication-free (and less anxious) life. By cooperating with your treating professionals, you should be able to achieve this goal.

CHAPTER 6

WHEN AND HOW TO STOP A TRANQUILIZER

———— ❦ ————

And the whole multitude sought to touch him:
for there went virtue out of him,
and [he] healed them all.

LUKE 6:19

Drug companies must hate Hawaii," were the first words out of Mitch's mouth as he settled his suntanned body into my reclining therapy chair. I hadn't seen him for a month. He'd been on vacation—and guess where he'd been? He'd been to Hawaii, to one of those idyllic, remote Polynesian islands that are wrapped in white sand beaches, coconut trees, and gentle breezes.

It had been his first trip to the islands of paradise. I had recommended it some months before when Mitch, a triple–Type A personality in his late thirties, had had several panic attacks. We had started treatment, including a tranquilizer, and I had advised him to take an extended vacation, not just a perfunctory long weekend, as was his custom. So he splurged and took his family to Hawaii, where he spent three wonderful weeks as a beach bum singly consuming the world's supply of suntan lotion and guava juice.

It took a few days for Mitch to overcome his adrenaline withdrawal, spent pacing up and down and complaining he was bored. Then he found himself

86

lying calmly on the beach appropriately painted with white sunscreen daubed on his face and body, resembling a Hawaiian painted warrior. During those lazy days, he discovered a wonderful sense of peace. His wild business world seemed a starlight nonexpress away. Not a care in the world. Nothing to be responsible for. He even stopped making telephone calls to his business after four or five days. He felt wonderful. So, he decided he didn't need to take his tranquilizer anymore. He stopped it—cold turkey.

"Drug companies must hate Hawaii," he repeated, just in case I hadn't heard him the first time. But I knew exactly what he was doing. He was making the classic mistake that many panic anxiety sufferers make shortly after they start treatment—they feel so good that they stop their medication. They think that just because they've not had any problems for a few weeks they must be cured. In any event, cold turkey is not the way to stop medication as potent as a tranquilizer.

Now I was faced with a dilemma: Should I break the news to him cold turkey or gradually? Since Mitch is a cold-turkey type of guy (most Type A personalities are), I elected to lay it out candidly. How else could I get his attention?

"Mitch, you should not have stopped your treatment without first consulting me or your physician. Hawaii is great, but a three-week beach interlude, albeit on a picturesque Hawaiian island making 'hang loose' signs all day to the natives, isn't going to undo fifteen years of crazy work habits." I went on to explain that panic anxiety disorder doesn't permanently vanish without putting up a fight. I warned him that if he didn't follow through on his treatment, it was just a matter of time before he would come pleading for me to help save him from his terrible anxiety. He left, convinced that he was cured and that he would never allow the panic attacks to return.

Three weeks later, Mitch called—not because his attacks stayed away for three weeks, but because he stubbornly tried to ignore them and convince himself that they wouldn't last. Typically, your attacks start again one or two weeks after stopping the medication if you haven't made the life changes that are necessary for a permanent cure. Mitch cooperated after that.

THE IMPORTANCE OF TREATMENT FOLLOW-THROUGH

Noncompliance with treatment recommendations is the major reason why treatment fails. This is true for all disorders and for all treatments. You know that if you break a leg, you don't just leave that cast on for a few weeks until the leg feels better, then assume that all is cured and remove the cast. The initial growing together of the bone is weak and can easily be fractured again. Complete healing of a broken bone takes time. This is even truer for anxiety disorders.

Another good example: Many patients who have an infection like strep throat do not complete the full course of prescribed antibiotic medications. After a few days, they start to feel better and assume that all is well, so they stop taking the antibiotic. But the organism causing the infection has only just been knocked back, not yet eliminated. It will regain strength and return in a few days, as sure as the sun rises in the east. Only this time the organism takes over with a vengeance because it has gained strength by knowing what it is up against.

These examples come from the physical world. But do they apply to the emotional realm? I would say that the need to follow through on treatment is as applicable, if not more so, to problems like anxiety attacks. Full compliance with treatment recommendations for psychotropic medications like tranquilizers and antidepressants, if needed, is absolutely essential if treatment is going to be successful. In my experience, a good 50 percent of people I see and recommend to a physician for medication do not follow through completely.

For this reason, I go out of my way to convince patients to do exactly what their doctor recommends. No exceptions. The only way your doctor can know whether a recommended treatment is going to work is for you to try it. Then if it doesn't work, he or she can move more intelligently to the next option of treatment. If your doctor skips over the treatment that was the right treatment and didn't know it, you and your doctor could well be wasting time and money in proceeding with other, noneffective treatments.

Stopping before the full course of treatment is completed is sometimes worse than not starting in the first place. And it's not just the "rebound" that makes your condition worse. Some psychotropic medications just don't work as well the second time around. It is as if your body resists the medication because it "remembers" it.

WHEN MEDICATION ISN'T EFFECTIVE

If you have been taking medication for a reasonable amount of time and are sure it isn't working, you need to find out why. What are some of the possible explanations?

- It is possible that the diagnosis of your problem isn't correct. You need to revisit the nature of your problem with your doctor or psychologist and request that some further assessment or testing be done to clarify the real nature of your problem.

- Other medical problems may be interfering with your treatment. For instance, you may have hyperthyroidism, hypoglycemia, or mitral valve prolapse.

- You may not be taking a high enough dose for your particular problem.

- You may be on the wrong sort of medication, so ask to try another.

- You may be taking a generic form of the medication that is not up to par with the original. Some years ago, a generic form of a particular antidepressant came on the market and several of my patients switched to the generic medication. Within the month, they nearly all went back into depression even though the generic medicine was supposedly equivalent. Upon further investigation, researchers found that the generic medication, while identical from a chemical point of view, had been compressed so hard that the tablets did not dissolve in the patients' stomachs appropriately. They were like little rocks and just passed right through their systems.

- Inadvertently, you may be skipping taking your medication at certain times, and this could lower the effective dosage in your bloodstream.

- There may be coexisting conditions such as depression, phobias, or obsessive-compulsive disorder that need to be treated as well as your primary problem.

- Finally, if you are not getting cognitive-behavioral treatment or supportive psychotherapy, you may not be learning to make the necessary thought and life changes that are essential to your cure. Cognitive-behavioral forms of therapy have proven to be more effective than other nonspecific forms of psychotherapy in several controlled studies. Check to see if your therapist is trained in cognitive-behavioral therapy and request a switch if necessary. With the

abundant evidence of the superiority of cognitive-behavioral therapy for panic attacks, it is unethical for any professional to deny you
this treatment unless there is clear evidence that there are other
causes for your problem that require some other form of therapy.

WHEN CAN YOU STOP TAKING A TRANQUILIZER?

The obvious answer to this question is—when the course of treatment is
completed. For all the medications used to treat panic disorder, treatment
should continue for a minimum of six to twelve months. It is better to taper
off the treatment slowly so that it can be reinstated if the problem reemerges.
If your stress levels have not subsided or you feel you have not yet mastered
the other lifestyle changes I recommend in this book, do not stop the medication treatment. Stopping the medication should dovetail with your mastery of your life.

I am serious when I say "Doctor knows best." Yes, I know, not all doctors
know best. This is why second, or even third, opinions may be necessary to
build your confidence. If you don't have confidence in your treating professional, you should stop right away and find someone you can trust.

About one-third to one-half of anxiety patients are able to discontinue
their medication after making changes. If you are only taking benzodiazepines, the relapse rate is higher, especially if you come off the medication
too fast. It is no big deal if you experience some reemergence of mild anxiety
symptoms when coming off your benzos, and you shouldn't rush to restart the
medication. Wait and see if your brain adjusts to the absent benzos and builds
up its own natural tranquilizers in the few weeks after stopping the artificial
tranquilizer.

More practically, there are a few clues to when you should consider stopping your medication. However, *never stop any medication without consulting
a physician,* even if you are under the care of a nonphysician. Here are some
of these clues:

• When you are convinced that the problem has been absent for a
  period of time.

• When the treatment does not seem to be working.

- When the side effects seem unbearable despite a lower dosage.

- When your treating clinician thinks the time to stop has come.

HOW SHOULD YOU STOP YOUR MEDICATION?

The general rule about stopping medication is that you should do it very slowly, lowering the dose by very small amounts every few days. This is true for both tranquilizers and antidepressants, although some antidepressants (like Prozac) have such a long life in your body that they automatically taper themselves. However, if they have a long half-life, you can't start another conflicting type of medication until the first is completely "washed out" of your system.

The greatest complication in stopping medications like this is withdrawal systems. These can be very mild and insignificant or serious like having a seizure if you have been on a high dose of Xanax for a long time. Your prescribing clinician is the one best equipped to tell you what you can expect, which is why you should never stop taking medication on your own.

Withdrawal symptoms (which hardly ever occur if the medication is tapered off *very slowly*) include rebound anxiety (anxiety returns but much intensified), agitation, diarrhea, insomnia, headaches, ringing in the ears, low blood pressure, and blurred vision. Stopping Xanax suddenly can precipitate severe panic attacks because the brain has become dependent on an external supply of tranquilizer to block its receptors; the sudden withdrawal of this agent leaves many receptors raw and exposed. For this reason, I would pay particular attention to how you should come off Xanax. If you follow these rules for other medications as well, you will be on the safe side.

Xanax used in combination with an adrenaline blocker such as Inderal has been very effective in the treatment of panic attacks. The adrenaline blocker, which reduces the body's fight-or-flight reaction, is used in much lower doses than in treating heart disease and takes about two weeks before it is fully effective. In the meantime, Xanax works to control the anxiety. The Xanax is then gradually reduced until only the adrenaline blocker is in place.

A newer tranquilizer called buspirone (BuSpar) has recently been introduced. When used skillfully and with the right type of patient, BuSpar has fewer side effects, is not sedating, and does not create dependency. This is partially because the medication takes longer (up to four weeks) to begin controlling the symptoms; since the patient doesn't feel immediate relief, he or she is less likely to become conditioned to use of the drug. In this respect, BuSpar is more like an antidepressant and thus safer to use. BuSpar is sometimes given with Xanax initially, like an antidepressant. It is long acting and Xanax is short acting, so the Xanax controls the anxiety in the short term until the BuSpar takes effect. The Xanax is then *slowly* withdrawn, leaving the BuSpar to control the anxiety without the same dependency risks.

Another effective tranquilizer is Klonopin (clonazepam). Klonopin has strong antiseizure properties and is preferred for long-duration administration because it is easier to remove. Often your doctor will first transition you to Klonopin if you have been on Xanax for a long time (more than six months) before starting to taper you off all tranquilizers. In this way, the risk of having a seizure is reduced.

Generally speaking, it is easier to come off an antidepressant than a tranquilizer, so you may be left on an antidepressant for a much longer time. Sometimes, depending on the nature of your anxiety problem, you may be asked to stay on the antidepressant for several years. Don't be alarmed by this. Again, "Doctor knows best."

If you have had repeated bouts with panic anxiety disorder, or if your anxiety is generalized and pervasive, it is better to be safe than sorry; prevention is better than cure. There is a lot of evidence to suggest that the long-term use of antidepressants can prevent future attacks of both anxiety and depression. Taking an antidepressant is a small price to pay for not having to worry about whether you are going to have another bout of emotional pain.

WITHDRAWAL FROM XANAX

Let me now specifically address how to come off Xanax. If you master these principles, you never need to fear taking such an effective medication like Xanax. I know many Christians who have to take Xanax to survive with any sense of tranquillity, but they fear that they will never be able to come off it. If you have this fear, I hope my advice here will give you peace of mind.

The seriousness of the symptoms that can attend sudden withdrawal from Xanax highlights the need for competent supervision when using the drug and also when discontinuing its use. Again, let me say: *Never lower your medication without medical supervision.* While only prolonged use at high dosages is likely to cause the major withdrawal symptoms, many users have to cope with the discomfort of lesser symptoms. With proper help, however, even these can be easily avoided.

Severe withdrawal symptoms may have to be treated with two other agents, so let me mention them here so you know what is going on. The first is Tegretol, which can reduce the risk of seizure and help control your pain, and Klonopin, which helps to bridge the gap between Xanax and your brain's natural tranquilizers. The process is a fairly lengthy one that must be closely monitored by a physician. Once the withdrawal is complete, an ongoing antidepressant is often helpful in maintaining improvement and controlling anxiety without having to return to Xanax.

STOPPING A LOW DOSE OF XANAX

For those who have been on a low dose of Xanax (say, below 3 mg per day) or if you have taken a higher dose for a short period of time (a month or two), there is a very effective and almost foolproof way of withdrawing. (Your physician should, of course, approve this or any other method.)

The principle is this: Reduce the dosage of Xanax so slowly that your body adjusts to the change very gradually, almost imperceptibly. This means reducing the dosage in increments far smaller than even a fraction of a tablet at a time. You have to shave off grains of the tablets, not break them into small bits.

Let's take, for example, someone who is taking 2 mg per day in four tablets of 0.5 mg. Dropping one of these tablets is equivalent to 25 percent of the total dose, and for Xanax this is just too much of a sudden drop. You will feel greater anxiety, increased tension, and general discomfort with that drastic a change. It may even precipitate another panic attack.

The secret is to reduce your medication by much less than 25 percent, or one tablet. Make sure, first of all, that your prescription is for the smallest tablet available-0.25 mg. (For example, if you have been taking one 0. 5 mg tablet, substitute two 0.25 mg tablets.) Then, using a clean razor blade or a sharp knife, shave off just a little of one tablet at a time. Maintain this slightly reduced dosage for a few days and then take off a little more of your tablets. By gradually shaving off a little more every few days, you allow the brain to start producing its natural replacement for what you are systematically taking away. Your brain doesn't rebel, and you will feel great.

Continue to *gradually* reduce the size of the tablets until you are at one-half, then one-fourth, and so forth. When you have shaved away the entire tablet, start on the next one until you are down to almost nothing. The moment you notice an increase in anxiety or withdrawal discomfort, hold the dosage constant until the discomfort disappears, then continue to shave away a little more. The discomfort shouldn't last longer than a few days. If it does, up the dose a little and wait until the discomfort ceases, then proceed again. If at any time you have a panic attack, consult your doctor. You may be trying to stop your tranquilizer prematurely.

I know the entire procedure I have described sounds tedious, and it is time-consuming. But this procedure reduces the risk of withdrawal problems to almost nothing.

During and after the removal of Xanax, you need a significant degree of emotional support and constant reassurance. I strongly recommend ongoing counseling or psychotherapy to facilitate this support. It is also important that you refrain from all other stimulants, including coffee and over-the-counter stimulants. Caffeine is a benzodiazepine antagonist and prevents tranquilizers from doing their work. You should also avoid alcohol.

The key to withdrawing from Xanax without the discomfort of withdrawal is *patience.* In the process, your brain's own chemical factory will be trained to do what it does best—keep you tranquil and at peace.

Now, let's look at the more natural resources for curing anxiety problems.

CHAPTER 7

ENHANCING YOUR NATURAL TRANQUILIZERS

———————&roo———————

Thou wilt keep him in perfect peace, whose mind is stayed on thee;
because he [or she] trusteth in thee.

ISAIAH 26:3

The reason why artificial tranquilizers work is that the brain has specific receptors for the molecules of these artificial tranquilizers. As I mentioned in the beginning of the book, this discovery, which took place not too many years ago, has revolutionized both our understanding of how anxiety problems are created in the brain as well as how we can find effective medications to help relieve these problems.

On this latter point, it means that new "designer" medications can be discovered more easily without the old trial-and-error method in which hundreds of drugs are applied, one after another, to see if they can help. All a scientist needs to know about a problem now is the molecular shape of a particular receptor in the brain, and he or she can go to the computer and design a medication to fix the problem. If the shapes match, you have a hit. It is like a key in a lock; if it fits, the tumblers open, and you go free.

But it also means one other important discovery: We can do a lot to enhance our brain's own natural substances, especially tranquilizers, without depending on external substances. In fact, it is precisely because the brain produces its own tranquilizers that artificial tranquilizers work. It stands to reason, therefore, that the more you increase your own internal tranquilizers, the less dependent you become on the artificial ones. This is what this chapter is all about.

KEY STRATEGIES FOR ENHANCING NATURAL TRANQUILIZERS

What are the key strategies for enhancing our natural tranquilizers? They fall into two categories: behaviors that antagonize (or diminish) our natural tranquilizers and behaviors that increase them. Good nutrition can also play a part in ensuring that our natural tranquilizers are on their best behavior and may even help to advance them significantly. I will say something about this at the end of this chapter.

BEHAVIORS THAT DIMINISH NATURAL TRANQUILIZERS

It is just as important to know what behaviors reduce our natural tranquilizers as it is to know what will increase them. Those that reduce natural tranquilizers must be eliminated, while those that increase them should be encouraged.

Which behaviors reduce our natural tranquilizers? Mostly, they are behaviors connected with our fight-or-flight response. My preferred way of understanding these behaviors is that they are the ones that cause us to overuse our adrenaline. And as I have already emphasized, not only do the threatening, dangerous, or catastrophic things of our lives cause our adrenaline to explode as if we were in mortal danger of being destroyed, but the exciting, challenging aspects of our lives can also increase our adrenaline. Whether you are running on high stress or not is all a matter of how persistent your arousal is.

Here are some of the more important behaviors that reduce our natural tranquilizers. If you can reduce or eliminate them, you will automatically be helping your brain to produce more natural tranquilizers.

STRESS

At the top of my list of tranquilizer busters is stress. But the word *stress* means different things to different people. For instance, if you spend all your life on the sidelines of a professional football field, coaching your team to victory, you will be under significantly more stress from the adrenaline ups and downs of each game than just sitting in front of the TV screen shouting your head off at the idiots who are not doing what you think they should be doing. (Of course, being that I am originally from South Africa, I am more aroused by a rugby game, but that's another story.)

My point is this: Your TV-connected adrenal rushes are *temporary* and quickly pass. Your natural tranquilizers may even be enhanced by the short experience of a rush because the game is a distraction from your real stress. But for the professional team manager, it is a different story. *His adrenaline is pure poison.* It is life-or-death stuff to his body, so it is not surprising that people in highly stimulating vocations like coaching succumb easily to stress-related heart disease and anxiety. In chapter 10, I will discuss stress-busting in more detail.

OVERAROUSAL, EXCITEMENT, AND PLEASURE SEEKING

People who constantly seek excitement or pleasure (called Type T personalities) also produce excessive amounts of stress hormones—only they don't know it because the excitement makes them feel good. The pleasure center in the brain sends "happy" signals all right, but not to encourage you to seek more excitement. It is to help you get through whatever activity you are engaging in. Unfortunately, over the long run, prolonged excitement is also destructive because it undermines your natural tranquilizers, which are trying to calm you down. In a nutshell, excessive excitement works against tranquillity.

Ask yourself: Do you feel less or more stimulated when experiencing some thrill or pleasure? The answer is more, the last time I checked. Excitement is a stimulant, and while we need stimulants to add some zest to our lives, too much excitement destroys our happy or tranquilizing systems. I know I am going to sound like a killjoy, but the fact is that we were not designed for perpetual pleasure. Pleasure, like a mountaintop, is only pleasurable when surrounded by valleys of tranquillity, calmness, and peace.

CONFLICT

Next to stress, conflict is the next most common destroyer of our natural tranquilizers. The reason is that conflict is a powerful trigger of the fight-or-flight response.

Conflict can take many forms. We can be in conflict with others (interpersonal conflict) or we can be in conflict with our values or goals that cannot be achieved (internal conflicts).

I went through a period of a year or so when neighbors behind where we live acquired a large dog to protect their property. I have no objection to neighbors having large dogs to protect their personal possessions. Though I've seen no need for such protection, I don't object to neighbors having it.

The problem was not the dog, but the neighbors. It just so happens that they were frequently away for long periods at a time. And that wasn't a problem either, as they had someone come in to feed and check on the dog. No, the problem was that the dog lived outside, day and night—especially night. And that wouldn't have been such a problem if it didn't sleep all day and stay awake all night barking at the stars, crickets, and shadows.

Well, my sleep was really upset, and I found myself becoming very angry. We complained about the barking dogs, but to no avail. My happy messengers vanished, and I was miserable and became extremely anxious. Finally, my wife came up with a solution: Sleep with earplugs. It worked, and soon afterward the dog and its owners moved to another state, presumably because there was such an outcry from so many neighbors. And I learned my lesson. Conflict can kill your peace, so you must either find a solution that gets rid of the conflict or move yourself out of the conflict situation.

UNDERASSERTIVENESS

Underassertiveness is a unique type of tranquillity destroyer because we often think that if we just keep our mouths shut, "grin and bear it," and "turn the other cheek," we will be better off. True? Absolutely not. Underassertiveness breeds hostility and frustration.

Christians, in particular, have problems with underassertiveness. First, they confuse assertiveness with selfishness. Second, they confuse assertiveness with aggressiveness. They think of assertiveness as a form of anger, which it is when you don't do it properly. Most people have difficulty being assertive in a loving, kind way. They get angry as a way of overcoming their cowardice at being underassertive in the first place.

There is a Christian form of assertiveness that is not rooted in anger or selfishness. This assertiveness is the way of honesty and Christian love. It tells the truth, but always out of consideration for the rights of others. You know where you stand with such people, and they are free to be themselves, without fear of being manipulated.

How can you know if you are being assertive in a Christian way? If your assertiveness offends the other party, it isn't Christian. Christian assertiveness always heals, never destroys.

INSUFFICIENT SLEEP

I am a strong advocate for improved sleep hygiene for one reason and one reason only: It saved my life from stress destruction. The need for sleep was one of the main discoveries I made when I first started researching the topic of stress. Since then, I have become increasingly convinced that sleep is God's great antidote given to us, not just to counteract the damaging effects of stress, but to enhance our natural tranquilizers as well. This topic is so important that I will discuss it more fully in chapter 14.

GIVING IN TO YOUR TYPE A BEHAVIORS

It has long been known that the so-called Type A personality is prone to developing early cardiovascular disease. The person with a Type A personality has essentially four dominant characteristics: He or she is always in a hurry (never has time for a haircut, overplans each day, finishes your sentences for you), has a deep sense of justice (feels offenses very deeply, expects everyone else to be perfect, is offended by those who don't keep the rules), is quick to become hostile (explosive, quick and overly reactive), and must maintain a sense of control (hates feeling helpless).

Each and every one of these characteristics undermines our natural tranquilizers and destroys our tranquillity. Why? These characteristics all send fight-or-flight signals to the body.

BEHAVIORS THAT INCREASE NATURAL TRANQUILIZERS

Let's examine those behaviors that increase or enhance our natural happy messengers or tranquilizers. Since many of these will be covered more fully in chapters to come, I will only comment on them briefly here.

TAKING TIME TO REST

In the engineering world, engineers who design machines have developed a concept called the "duty cycle," usually expressed as a percentage. If a machine has a duty cycle of, say, 50 percent, it means that it should not be running for

50 percent of the time. If it does, the machine stands the risk of overheating and burning out. When they design a machine, like an electric motor that will operate your washing machine, they decide on what duty cycle they will use. Very few machines are designed to operate 100 percent of the time because such a machine would have to be very robust to do this.

When you look at the human "machine," what you discover is that our bodies are no different than machines. We also have a duty cycle and cannot run continuously without burning out.

What is the human body's duty cycle? I am sure that people differ here, but, in my opinion, our duty cycle is also 50 percent, like most machines. Why do I believe this? The clue comes from the natural cycle of day and night. We are supposed to work during the day and rest at night. What has messed up this cycle is the invention of the electric light. Now our bodies no longer have a sense of daily rhythm—unless we give it to them.

As I mentioned, I grew up in Africa and know many places that do not have electric light. Candles or oil can be expensive. So, with the onset of darkness comes rest, initially, and later, sleep. I would suggest to you that this is a healthier pattern of life than the lifestyle we have created by extending the lighted hours, often with light as bright as the sun.

What is the effect of this increased daylight? Increased stress and depleted tranquilizers. What is the solution? We must build back into our lives some of the rest time that has been taken away from us. Don't misread me. I'm only saying that *some* of the rest time needs to be reclaimed, especially if we are suffering from anxiety or stress problems. I will discuss this further in chapter 9.

MEDITATION

When researching the material for this book, I was quite surprised to discover how effective meditation was in facilitating recovery from a severe anxiety problem like panic attacks. (I explain my reasons for this surprise in chapter 17.) I am convinced that the reason meditation rates so highly in recovery is because it is a powerful restorer of natural tranquilizers. This makes perfect sense to me. If you set aside the spiritual dimensions for a moment, meditation is a powerful form of relaxation. And we know that relaxation is a powerful antianxiety mechanism. Now if you restore to meditation a truly valid spiritual dimension, the total package must be extremely powerful.

Meditation, therefore, cannot be overlooked as an important tranquilizer enhancer. Why, therefore, are many segments of the Christian church so afraid or resistant to the idea of meditation?

The answer lies in the dominant hold that transcendental meditation (TM) has had over our culture on this topic. When most people think about meditation, they don't recall how Christian mystics of old used meditation as a spiritual discipline but think about how transcendental meditators chant mantras and do hocus-pocus. So they shy away from it.

In chapter 17, I will try to rescue meditation from these distortions. TM may be quasi-religious and hocus-pocus, but meditation is not the exclusive domain of pagans. It can be truly Christian and extremely beneficial, both physically and spiritually. So, let us reclaim meditation for Christ and His kingdom.

SEEKING OUT AND ENJOYING HUMOR

Increasingly, we are seeing research that emphasizes the value of humor and laughter in restoring, for instance, the immune system. People who suffer from some very complicated immune deficiency disorders have found laughter (the biblical word is *joy*) to have powerful therapeutic effects.

I want to suggest that laughter, humor, and joy are not just medicines for the body, but also for the mind. I am absolutely convinced that they are natural tranquilizer enhancers. I haven't seen any research to back up this idea yet, but just give it time. In chapter 15, I explore this concept further.

BREAKING OUT OF THE TYPE A RUT

Several times I have mentioned Type A personality patterns. Well, I am here to say that you will need to learn how to break out of some of these patterns if you are going to increase your natural tranquilizers. *All* the patterns of Type A personality work against tranquillity. On your own, you can start to change your Type A habits. Here's how:

Learn to relax. Beyond the formal relaxation exercises I describe in chapter 9, there are other ways to relax as well, and you can practice them at home. When you're ready, pick a quiet place, sit or lie comfortably, and close your eyes.

Several techniques can now be helpful. First, you can listen to soothing instrumental music and let yourself float with the melody. Imagine yourself in a soothing environment, and allow the music to relax your muscles. Second, practice deep muscle relaxation by alternately tensing, then relaxing the muscles of your hands, biceps, face, shoulders, chest, stomach, legs, and feet. Focus on the feeling of relaxation that follows the muscle tensing. Finally, use meditation techniques, such as repeating the phrase "God gives me my peace" with each exhalation. Keep it up for ten minutes. Feel your tension release with each breath.

Once you learn to relax by one of these methods, use them in moments when you feel stress. Take a break from the activity causing your stress, retire to a private spot, and relax. Let your mind drift from the pressure of daily activities. Remember how you felt when you relaxed at home and relive those feelings. *Retrain your reactions.* Once you learn to relax quickly, use imagery to break the emotional reactions triggered by pressures you often encounter. First relax, and then imagine yourself facing a situation that normally makes you tense, such as the pressure that builds up when you face a deadline. As you imagine the situation, retain the awareness of relaxation. Repeat this until you can go through the entire scene without feeling any tension.

Take control of your environment. Type A people often fail to manage their environment properly. Telephones, interruptions, and demands break in, and stress builds. Where possible, take active steps to manage your environment. For example, schedule your appointments realistically; allow enough time on your calendar so that you are not always rushing from one meeting to another. Set your priorities each morning, and stick to that order. Do not overplan your day; schedule enough activity so as to feel you are accomplishing something but not so much as to make you feel you can't finish. Learn how to manage demands from others. Set boundaries. Let them know how much time and effort you're willing to give them; let them know, too, when you cannot accept their requests. Ask the person who wants you to take on another task to help you evaluate the urgency of the request and determine where it fits among your priority items.

Slow down. When you act rushed, you will feel pressure. Take it easy. Practice eating with slower movements and putting down your fork between bites. Slow your steps when you walk. Slow your speech when you talk. As you listen to others, repeat briefly what you hear them say. This will help you understand them better and also reduce your impatience—a very common Type A behavior.

FOODS OR DRINKS THAT REDUCE NATURAL TRANQUILIZERS

Foods can reduce our natural tranquilizers in several ways. The food may directly impact our happy messengers, or it may create internal stress that triggers a fight-or-flight response.

Not a lot of attention has been given to the issue of diet and nutrition and how it affects anxiety, especially how it increases or decreases your natural tranquilizers. But what you put into your mouth has more than just a passing effect on anxiety, including panic anxiety, because it has a direct effect on your body's internal physiology and biochemistry.

While some foods and substances facilitate calmness and a steady mood, others cause increased susceptibility to anxiety. Anyone suffering from an anxiety problem will have to pay careful attention to their food and substance intake.

Most people pay little attention to what they eat and drink. They assume that because "everyone" is eating or drinking something, it must be safe. Some substances, not just drugs, are even addictive. Do you know how often coffee or colas, for instance, are addictive? We excuse these addictions because they are so socially popular. But their popularity doesn't make them innocuous.

More importantly, do you know how these substances lower your tolerance for anxiety? Hopefully, this section will clarify which foods you need to avoid and which ones you can load up on.

SUBSTANCES THAT AGGRAVATE ANXIETY

The most aggravating substances for anxiety are *stimulants.* These substances aggravate anxiety primarily through their effects on the body's arousal and alerting systems, including the stimulation of more adrenaline than needed for a given situation. The heart speeds up, blood pressure skyrockets, and anxiety symptoms appear because our happy messengers are affected.

Of all the stimulants that can aggravate anxiety and trigger panic attacks, caffeine is at the top of the list. Caffeine is the first substance you must drop after becoming panic or anxiety prone. I know I am the bearer of bad news here for many of you, but don't get mad at me. Caffeine alone can trigger panic attacks.

Caffeine, found mostly in coffee, tea, colas, chocolate, cocoa, and several over-the-counter drugs, directly stimulates several systems in your body. It produces the same arousal response (increased adrenaline) as when you are under high stress, which is why it magnifies the stress effects you are experiencing. But that is not all. It also diminishes the calming messengers in your brain, making your sympathetic nervous system more active and responsive.

In the short run, provided the arousal is not prolonged, the effects of caffeine are pleasant and stimulating—which is why people turn to it. But most don't stop there. They gradually increase their caffeine intake until it has control over them. The result is what we see in most people with frequent caffeine intake: a vicious cycle of chronic tension, irritability, and sleeplessness.

If you suffer *any* anxiety aggravation, stop all your caffeine intake *completely* and *quickly*. Merely reducing your caffeine intake won't do it. Sooner or later you will slowly climb back to where you were before.

If you must have some caffeine, then keep your caffeine consumption below the equivalent of one cup of coffee or two colas a day. Sure it is a sacrifice, but the payoff is improved sleep, tranquillity, and, believe it or not, a longer and healthier life.

How can you stop your caffeine intake? You have two choices: cold turkey versus chicken soup. In the cold-turkey method, you stop suddenly and suffer through the withdrawal symptoms, such as headaches and tiredness. In the chicken soup method, you sip yourself slowly into caffeine freedom.

ELIMINATE FOODS THAT CAUSE BAD REACTIONS

If a certain food makes you wheeze or gives you a stuffy nose, diarrhea, or red itchy bumps on your skin, you should obviously avoid that food. Any allergic reaction of this type is a stress on your body that contributes to your *overstress* and by implication, diminishes your natural tranquilizers.

There is another type of food reaction you should avoid. *Any food that you crave or binge* is a brain active food and attacks the happy messengers. You are craving or binging on this food precisely because it is directly affecting your brain's neurotransmitters in a harmful way. Most of the time, these are foods or substances that contain the pick-me-ups, sugar and caffeine. But sometimes the craved substance in the food is corn, milk, or yeast protein.

Many people have sensitivity reactions to corn, milk, or yeast-containing products. The protein in these substances directly affects your brain messenger function.

If, by this point in the book, you are still not feeling well or suspect food may be aggravating your condition, try a corn-free, milk-free and/or yeast-free diet. (Consult a dietician or your doctor for a source of recipes.)

FOODS OR DRINKS THAT INCREASE NATURAL TRANQUILIZERS

Not all foods destroy our natural tranquilizers; some enhance them. These can include natural health supplements or drinks that can increase our brain's production of natural tranquilizers. Obviously, the list here doesn't include candy bars, caffeine, alcohol, nicotine, or any other addictive substances. So begin by eliminating, or at least reducing, these substances.

Since each of us differs widely on what foods trigger allergies or internal stress, you may want to consult a professional dietician. He or she will help you be accountable for what you eat. My guidelines here, therefore, will be general rather than specific. In addition to the comments I have already provided, here are some guidelines to aid you in creating a healthy, balanced, and tranquillity-building diet:

MOVE YOUR DIET IN THE DIRECTION OF VEGETARIANISM. I am not a vegetarian, but I have drastically reduced my intake of all meats. I know many vegetarians, and they appear to be calmer and more tranquil than the rest of us. Meats have many problems, not the least of which is the fat content and the hormones used to grow meat.

INCREASE YOUR INTAKE OF VEGETABLES AND FRUITS. In my cultural background, vegetables play an important role in every meal. Americans substitute a leafy salad, which is not bad, but then they drench it in salad dressing.

EAT FOODS THAT PROVIDE YOUR ENTIRE MINERAL AND VITAMIN NEEDS NATURALLY. An interesting phenomenon of modern times is that we cook away natural vitamins and then supplement them with artificial pills. Of course, supplementing your mineral and vitamin needs may be necessary, but try to prepare food that gives it to you naturally first, then take supplements. Food labels these days usually display vitamin and mineral content.

DON'T EAT SPICY FOOD IF YOUR DIGESTIVE SYSTEM REBELS. I love spicy food. Curries are my favorite. Fortunately, I handle them well, provided they aren't too spicy. What level of "spicy" can you take? Moderation is the way to go.

INCREASE YOUR INTAKE OF DIETARY FIBER. Grains, beans, and *raw* vegetables are good sources of dietary fiber. It took me awhile to get used to the idea that you can eat cabbage raw (in salads, etc.), but I have finally come to enjoy it this way. Cooking seems now to do damage to the cabbage.

DRINK LOTS OF WATER. Six eight-ounce glasses per day of *purified* water is recommended. These days, only a few of us have not yet developed the habit of carrying a bottle of water with us everywhere.

KEEP YOUR CALORIE INTAKE BELOW THAT RECOMMENDED FOR YOUR IDEAL WEIGHT. Counting calories has never been my thing. I have figured out that if I eat about 75 percent of what is put on my plate, I'm doing okay and not gaining weight. So, always leave something behind, unless you are weighing what you are putting on your plate.

BALANCE YOUR DIET FROM ALL THE MAJOR FOOD GROUPS. Fruits and vegetables (four to five servings per day), whole grains (three to four servings per day—including breakfast cereals), protein (poultry, seafood, and eggs or vegetarian equivalents—one to two servings per day), dairy products (low fat—one to two servings per day). Consult a dietary handbook for more detailed advice.

RELAXING HERBS

I have never been a strong advocate for herbal remedies, usually because, even if they are effective, they are not as potent and fast-acting as prescription medications. St. John's wort is an example. I have no doubt that it is a mild antidepressant and that someone with a mild depression will find it helpful. However, you need to take large doses, and it takes quite awhile before you see any therapeutic effects. This delayed response is hardly helpful for someone suffering from acute depression or panic attacks.

As supplements, herbs and natural remedies can be very helpful. However, you should *never* take an herbal supplement with prescription medications because there may be a catastrophic complication from mixing them.

Several natural remedies can have a relaxing effect and thus help to increase your natural tranquilizers. Valerian root is probably the best known, which is not surprising since its active ingredient is similar to Valium. Other relaxing herbs include chamomile, hops (my grandmother used to make a brewed drink out of hops), skullcap, and passionflower. The names may vary in desirability, but these herbs can be used in combination. Some can be boiled to make a tea; others are available in capsules.

If, however, an herbal remedy is not having the desired effect, then seek more conventional forms of treatment without delay. It always saddens me to encounter a patient who has been struggling with a severe panic disorder, desperately trying to cure his or her problem the natural way and getting nowhere. Some have wasted years on such a quest, when quicker relief is readily available.

MEDICATION AS A FOOD SUPPLEMENT

This last point raises a very important issue, so allow me to end this chapter by drawing attention to the fact that in the final analysis, some of the medications you must take for the treatment of an anxiety problem are nothing more than "food supplements." That they are only available by prescription is for your protection. This does not place a stigma on them.

These "food supplement" medications can provide improved sleep, yet they are not sleeping pills. They can stimulate you out of lethargy, but they are not stimulants. They can relieve pain, yet they increase your enjoyment of life. They are a family of nonaddictive, prescription medications that work by rebalancing your brain's chemical messengers, especially the happy messengers.

They do not cause rebound (you don't have a quick upswing followed by a big crash), nor do they develop tolerance (you don't have to take more and more to achieve the desired effect). They can be used to boost your happy messengers while they are in the process of lowering your stress load. And, if you have inherited a very low stress tolerance, *you may safely stay on these medications for a very long time.*

I suggest that you view these medications, including the antidepressant medications used in the treatment of anxiety, the way you view insulin for diabetes or a vitamin supplement for a deficiency.

So if you are still suffering from overstress, you just may be an individual whose genetic inheritance does not allow you to make enough happy messengers to handle your daily stress load. You may indeed benefit from taking these brain chemical rebalancers as a long-term replacement medication. It is food for your brain, so be thankful that God has made it available to us in these modern times.

CHAPTER 8

CHANGING YOUR THINKING HABITS

—⊛⊛⊛—

Be ye transformed by the renewing of your mind.

ROMANS 12:2

If you seriously want to overcome your anxiety problem, you need to approach it from every possible angle. I have carefully reviewed the literature on the effectiveness of various types of treatment and, while anxiety sufferers differ in their response to different treatments, one consistently effective strategy seems to work across the board. Several researchers have highlighted its importance and effectiveness. In fact, the evidence for its effectiveness is so strong that I would stick my neck out and say categorically that if you don't include this strategy in your treatment plan, you will not make much headway.

What strategy am I talking about? *Changing your thinking habits.*

As an example of the research that supports this strategy's effectiveness, let me briefly tell you about a program that is specifically focused on the treatment of anxiety disorders. Known as the Anxiety Disorder Treatment Needs Research Project, the researchers studied 518 anxiety sufferers and found that 29 percent had panic attacks, 23 percent had panic anxiety disorder, and the rest had a variety of anxiety problems. Eighty-two percent had been on anxiety medication with and without therapy, and only 3 percent had received no treatment.

WHAT ARE THE MOST EFFECTIVE TREATMENTS FOR ANXIETY DISORDERS?

A study conducted in Australia has uniquely compared the effectiveness for various treatments among those who found relief.[1] This table shows that the most effective way to ensure that you "cure" your anxiety is to take responsibility for your own recovery by changing your thinking, lowering your stress, and learning relaxation techniques.

Treatment Option	Percent of Those Who Were Successfully Treated Who Considered the Treatment Effective
Self-awareness, working with thinking	95%
Support groups	83%
Meditation	75%
Cognitive-behavioral therapy	78%
Self-help books	75%
Relaxation	72%
Psychotherapy (not cognitive-behavioral)	59%
Graded exposure to anxiety situations	52%
Hypnotherapy	25%
Prescribed medication	16%

(Please note:)

1. Many of these treatments were combined during treatment. Also, 36 percent of those participating considered that none of the treatments they tried were effective.

2. Other studies comparing the relative effectiveness of various therapies have found that cognitive-behavioral interventions report 80 percent panic freedom, while medication based treatments achieve 50 percent to 60 percent panic freedom. The combined treatment is the most effective.

What is interesting is that of all the attempted *professional treatments,* those that were considered to be the most effective in relieving anxiety symptoms in the long run were meditation and cognitive-behavioral therapy. The most effective *self-help strategies* were "working with my thinking" and "increasing my self-awareness." These were effective in both preventing and stopping anxiety attacks.

These findings agree entirely with my own experience in working with anxiety problems. Meditation is also extremely helpful, and I will address this technique in chapter 17. In this chapter, I want to focus on how you should work on your thinking patterns. Though my focus will be mainly on panic anxiety, the techniques I will describe can be applied to all forms of anxiety.

WHY IS LEARNING TO CONTROL YOUR THINKING IMPORTANT?

Every anxiety sufferer must learn new ways of thinking and develop methods for changing their former thinking patterns.

The reasons are obvious. Anxiety always takes our thoughts captive. And our thoughts can create a state of anxiety very easily. The more anxious our thinking, the more prone we become to anxiety attacks.

In the case of panic attacks, the state of depleted natural tranquilizers is primarily created by high stress. Your patterns of thinking both contribute to this high stress as well as set up the "trigger" for a specific attack. As we've discussed, if you interpret a given situation as "dangerous," your brain will respond with a fight-or-flight response that precipitates an episode of panic.

Since the attack is so extremely frightening, you train or condition your mind to think and respond with anxiety. A fear of the anxiety perpetuates the anxiety that causes your attacks. Yes, this is a vicious cycle, and the only way to break it is to interpose some "break" in the circle of thinking. The best break we know is to recondition your thinking patterns.

If you don't do this, you will be dependent on artificial tranquilizers the rest of your life. In fact, 32 percent of the subjects in the study I mentioned earlier report that they have developed a long-term dependence on tranquilizers. The mean time for taking these drugs was forty-three months. Only those who had taken control of their thinking patterns had achieved relative freedom from medication dependence.

STRATEGIES FOR CONTROLLING YOUR THINKING

While the best and most efficient way to change the essential problems in your thinking patterns is to seek therapy, the following may be helpful in guiding your therapy or providing exercises you can practice on your own. Obviously, there are probably other aspects of your thinking that need your attention as well, so I would refer you to my book *Habits of the Mind* for additional help (see Appendix B).

The three techniques I will describe for you here are slowing down your thinking, challenging your mistaken beliefs, and speaking the truth to yourself.

Remember, just as an athlete or musician cannot be at his or her peak without determined practice, so an anxiety sufferer cannot be free of anxiety without determined practice.

SLOWING DOWN YOUR THINKING

Our purpose here is to slow down your thinking processes so you can "capture" the thoughts that are rushing through your mind. To change a thought, you first have to capture it.

Most of us, especially when we are anxious, are flooded with thoughts we are not even aware of. Unfortunately our minds still respond to these thoughts even though we are oblivious to them at a conscious level. In fact, it's not so much that these thoughts are "unconscious" as it is that they flash by the window of our awareness so fast that they come and go before we have time to realize them. Slowing down our thinking is one way to help us capture what we are thinking.

CHALLENGING YOUR MISTAKEN BELIEFS

Mistaken beliefs are at the root of a lot of anxiety. These deep-seated beliefs about ourselves and the world around us are typically so ingrained into us that we seldom recognize them for what they are—*false.* They are deceitful and misinformed, inaccurate and malicious. They prevent us from becoming truly free to achieve our full potential. They also sabotage our tranquillity and create painful anxieties.

Why do these beliefs elude us yet have such a hold over us? Mostly because they are formed in the early years of our lives when we do not have the critical ability to challenge them. So this means we have to learn how to challenge them as adults.

But before we can challenge these mistaken beliefs, we need to be able to recognize them. This is a lot harder than it appears because many of them are quite subtle.

Let's take an example. Suppose I think: *I am nothing unless I succeed*. This is a mistaken belief. It is embedded in a culture that prizes success above everything else. One buys into it uncritically with painful results. Why is it a mistaken belief? For one, it doesn't define success very well. If I am only able to climb halfway up the corporate ladder before I retire, have I been successful? Do I have to get to the top before I can declare success? But only one person gets to the top, so the majority of us will never succeed if this is the formula.

I can't begin to tell you how often this is an issue in therapy for someone troubled with anxiety. Our society demands that we be successful but leaves us dangling when it comes to defining what or how much of anything we achieve constitutes success. So we are left to sort it out ourselves.

The other reason why *I am nothing unless I succeed* is a mistaken belief is that it is more an emotional statement than a factual one. It taps into a much deeper insecurity and fear of imperfection. Result? No amount of success by anyone's standard can fix this insecurity. I know. I have frequently asked someone I consider to be enormously successful whether his success has cured his deep-seated insecurity. The answer is always the same: It hasn't.

This means that the problem with anxiety is very deep, and impotent, mistaken beliefs only make the struggle tougher. This is why we have to identify and challenge our mistaken beliefs.

How can you change your thinking habits without engaging in a lifetime of therapy? One way is to get yourself a little notebook to record your beliefs whenever you catch them. Put the date at the top of a page. Throughout the day try to capture and record thoughts that imply some belief that may be mistaken. Then write down your challenge to that mistaken belief. But remember, no two of us are the same so we have to find our own unique set of beliefs. Here are some examples of my common mistaken beliefs and my challenges to them:

- I am the victim of the way others have treated me. Nonsense. I can take control of my life now and change the outcome.

- I must never take a risk because I always fail. Preposterous. I may have failed before, but always is always a lie. I must try again; this time I may succeed.

- If I worry enough about something, it will go away. My favorite variation is: If I don't worry about this problem all the time it is bound to happen. Ridiculous. There is no evidence in the entire universe that worrying about something prevents or changes anything. Jesus said this a long time ago.

- People should always love and respect me. Who says? People respond to me in the way I treat them. If I want the respect of others, I must first show them respect.

- I don't feel I deserve to be happy or successful. This is asinine. I deserve to be as happy or successful as anyone is.

- People wouldn't like me if they knew who I was deep down. This is foolish, to say the least. The fact is that there is a nasty side to all of us (the Bible calls it "sin"). The truth is that transparent people are more likable than closed people, so why not try being more transparent?

- I'm just the way I am; I can't change. Idiotic. Everyone can change. It may not always be easy, but the gospel is all about people changing. So give up this stupid idea and start doing some changing.

These are just a few examples. Once you start challenging your own mistaken ideas, you will find it gets easier and easier—that is, if you start by challenging the mistaken belief that you can't change your mistaken beliefs.

Here are four questions you can ask yourself about any belief to discern whether it is mistaken:

1. What is the evidence that this belief is true?

2. Is this belief always true, or are there exceptions?

3. Was this belief forced upon me at a time when I couldn't think for myself?

4. Does this belief promote my welfare, or does it work against me?

Speaking the Truth to Yourself

My purpose here is to help you establish a set of well-rehearsed self-statements you can draw on when you need to counter an anxiety-producing thought. These need to be rehearsed frequently so that they spring to mind when you need them. There are several situations in which you will need such statements, so I will suggest a few for each. You should add some of your own so as to feel that it is more personal. I have left you some space to do this.

Practice saying each of the following until you have memorized them. Then use them repeatedly when the occasion requires it.

SITUATION: Anxiety seems to be coming on

1. *I don't need to fight my feelings. They only last a short time, then they go away.*
2. *I am going to focus my thoughts away from my anxiety feelings.*
3. *So I feel some anxiety right now. So what. Everyone feels anxiety some time or other.*
4. *I am going to be all right in a short while, so I will think about something else and continue what I am doing.*
5. *Anxiety is as old as my body. I don't have to allow it to control me; I can control it.*
6.
7.

SITUATION: Having a panic attack

1. *No one has ever died from a panic attack, so try to relax.*
2. *Panic never lasts very long. The peak will pass in a few minutes, then I will take control.*
3. *Panic is just uncomfortable, not dangerous.*
4. *I've survived a panic attack before, so I will survive again this time.*
5. *Right now I am having feelings I don't like. I am not to blame for them, and I know how to treat them so that they will all go away forever.*
6.
7.

SITUATION: Going into a stressful situation

1. *I've been in stressful situations before and survived. I will survive this one as well.*

2. *This may seem like an impossible situation right now, but I must avoid feeling helpless and move forward with courage.*

3. *I have more control over the stress in my life than I give myself credit for, so I will face it head-on. Look out trouble, here I come.*

4. *This, too, shall pass. Troubles don't last if you outlast them.*

5. *When this is all over, I'll be glad I stood up to it and won the battle.*

6.

7.

SITUATION: When you are feeling overwhelmed by your feelings

1. *The feelings I am having right now don't make sense and I really don't want them, but for now I will just live with them.*

2. *I can be anxious but still focus on the task at hand.*

3. *If I think about it correctly, I can turn these feelings of being overwhelmed into my allies. They can help me find the solution I am looking for.*

4. *I have more control over my feelings than I used to think. I can choose to overlook them and focus on other things.*

5. *Feelings are only phantoms—they exist only if I allow them to.*

6.

7.

CHAPTER 9

REST AND
RELAXATION

———∞∞∞———

Come ye yourselves apart into a desert place, and rest a while.
MARK 6:31

In this chapter, I want to cover two related but somewhat different issues—rest and relaxation. Resting is not the same as relaxing, at least not in the minds of most psychotherapists. When you sleep, you are resting, but you may not be relaxing. Your sleep may be fitful and full of tension. Effective relaxation requires that you not fall asleep. It is something you must do while you remain awake, else the benefits do not follow.

In this sense, then, therapists have a somewhat restricted meaning for the term *relaxation.* They see it as an intentional activity that produces a profound "switching off" of all our arousal systems. Deep relaxation refers to a distinct physiological state that is the exact opposite of the way your body reacts under arousal and stress or under a panic attack.

This is the meaning that I will attribute to the word *relaxation* here. But before I can discuss relaxation and its importance for building natural tranquilizers in your brain to fight off your anxiety or panic proneness, I need to discuss its close cousin, *rest.* Relaxation and rest must go hand in hand, else they work against each other. Sleep is a very special form of rest, not relaxation.

GOD'S PLAN FOR REST

Taking time to rest is not an option in today's world; it is a necessity. Yet more people struggle here than in almost any other area of their lives. It is perilous not to take time to rest. Our souls suffer from too much hurriedness. When we rush, we miss out on life. When we live in the fast lane, we neglect so much that is important. Life cannot be appreciated when it rushes past the window of our awareness like a blur.

One of the most powerful arguments in favor of pushing for a greater emphasis on rest comes from the Bible. As we all know, the Bible tells us that after creating the world, God rested on the seventh day. So from the outset, the Bible presents us with the idea that rest is important, and furthermore, that a specific time has to be set aside for rest. Even God rested.

Rest, therefore, is seen in the Bible not as a sign of weakness or laziness, but as a divine activity, a sign of His wisdom and holiness. If resting is important to God, I don't think we can minimize its importance for us as humans. We neglect rest, therefore, to our peril.

A day of rest became mandatory in the laws of the Old Testament. It was called the "Sabbath." An Israelite who violated the Sabbath law paid for this sin with his or her life. Today, death is still the penalty for not resting—only now it is a gradual death because the failure to rest aggravates the destructive influence of stress. We do not allow time for our bodies to recover from the effects of chronic stress, one of these effects being the creation of biologically based anxiety disorders.

This raises another critical question: Were we really designed for today's fast-paced lifestyle? When God designed us, did He have in mind that one day we would be pushing the limits of the human frame as we do today? Yes and no. God knew what we were capable of, but His design for our bodies set certain limits. It is because we need to stay within these limits that rest is so important in God's plans.

I happen to believe (and a lot of scientific evidence is accumulating to support this belief) that we were designed for camel travel, not supersonic jet behavior, as I mentioned in the preface. Except for the last fifty years, which is *very* small in the overall length of human existence, humans have been able to live within the limits set for the human body. Today, however, we are exceeding these limits, not just barely, but by a huge margin. The penalty is an epidemic of stress disease and anxiety disorders, especially panic anxiety.

The only way we can survive in the pace of modern living is by developing effective habits of rest and relaxation. In a nutshell, we have to rediscover the importance of Sabbath-keeping. I don't mean keeping a day of rest in a legalistic way, but implementing the principle of Sabbath-keeping. It is our only hope.

TO REST OR NOT TO REST—THAT IS THE QUESTION

My apologies to Shakespeare, but it seems that our modern dilemma is not whether to live or die, but whether we should rest or work. Resting seems out of fashion. You get branded as lazy, idle, slothful, and even sluggish. Even in my own childhood, if my father caught me just lying about, enjoying the warm sun, he would say, "Haven't you got something to do?" I had to be careful what I said else he would think up something for me to do. Our work ethic demands that we always be busy doing something. Doing nothing has a bad rap.

And here the dilemma gets a little more complicated. How many of us could survive in our jobs if we did not keep working without a break or speeding things up a bit? Who gets promoted? The easygoing, laid-back, don't-take-things-too-seriously sort of person or the triple–Type A person who never stops? You know the answer as well as I do.

So we are caught, then, between the body's need for rest and society's need to keep us busy. What can one do except join the rat race?

The answer is to respect the Sabbath principle and build into one's hectic life the much-needed time for rest. If you want to live a rich and fulfilling life that retains a measure of tranquillity with an abundant supply of natural tranquilizers, a well-honed immune system, and a healthy mind, you have to build time for rest into your life priorities.

WHERE HAS ALL THE TIME FOR REST GONE?

We are so determined to succeed that most of us try to pack each moment of the day with activity. Some of this activity is necessary if we are going to eat, raise healthy and well-fed kids, and save for a comfortable retirement.

But we go beyond this. We also fill our days with so much adventure and excitement that most of us never find time to rest. Resting is not a high priority, so we never set aside time for it. Nothing in our society reinforces the need for rest, so it simply doesn't happen. We are so determined to get to our destination (success, fame, recognition, wealth) that we never take time to reflect on the journey of life, enjoy the scenery, or be grateful that we are on a journey at all.

Sure, when we are delayed at the airport and fail to bring along some work or when the kids are playing a soccer tournament and we have to sit there making believe we are really into the game, we may take a few minutes to rest. In reality, this is forced rest, and being forced to rest doesn't quite do the trick. You are impatiently waiting for time to pass by so that you can get back to that project you are working on. You are frustrated, so your adrenaline doesn't switch off. You are impatient with how long you are being forced to be idle, so your muscle tension goes up, not down. Don't kid yourself. You are not resting.

Real resting takes time. Extended time. Unfrustrated time. Idle time. It also demands that you have nothing waiting in the wings. You have to disconnect, disengage, let go, and forget what you were doing before and what waits for you after. You have to completely separate yourself from your regular routine.

WHAT ARE THE BENEFITS OF TAKING TIME TO REST?

Taking time to rest has implications that benefit our minds and our bodies. Resting also affects our relationships and spirituality.

As an example of how resting affects relationships, let us take a look at the Benefields' case. I had seen both Mr. and Mrs. Benefield separately over several years for personal problems. But one day, they asked to see me together. Their marriage of twelve years was deteriorating. They were really worried about their relationship, especially as it was affecting their children.

Until recently they seemed to get along pretty well. Now they were constantly bickering. The smallest thing would send them ballistic. Their sex life was nonexistent. Both worked at high-pressure jobs that left them stressed-out and tightly wound most of the time.

Believing that part of the problem was they were both living overextended lives, I asked them how often they had an opportunity to be together and really learn to enjoy each other. They sat silently for a moment. They looked at each other, then the wife turned back to me and said: "I don't think we ever spend any time with each other. We just don't seem to be able to find the time."

So I asked them how they spent their "free" time. They confessed they had little free time, but what they did have they used to "relax." I pressed them to tell me what they did to relax. Hubby plunked for golf. I could see the adrenaline scurrying through his eyeballs, rushing to get his brain all pumped up even as we sat there in my office. Suddenly he was alert. "I am most relaxed," he said excitedly, "when I'm on the golf course."

Knowing how busy he was and how short his attention span is when he thinks about golf, I went for the jugular. "When do you get time to play?"

He squirmed for a moment. "Oh, I try to get to the short course we have nearby in the early mornings. I manage to play two to three times a week. It really does make me feel quite relaxed." In this vein he tried several times to reassure me that he "really was taking time to relax." It turns out that he also sneaks off on Saturdays over his wife's protests. It is one of their major tension points: She doesn't see enough of him.

I turned to the wife: "What about you?"

"Oh, I try to take as many courses as I can at the local community college's adult center. They put on all sorts of interesting stuff, like painting classes and pottery." Then she hastily added, "It's all very relaxing. I get a lot of rest through it." It turns out she also does a lot of volunteering at their church, which was a countersource of tension for her husband because she never prepares meals on time and is late for everything. His frustration level is as high as hers.

I tried to explain that they could not expect their relationship to grow and thrive if they never spent time together. They needed relationship "rests," where all they do is attend to each other. Every couple needs to find time to be alone as a couple, just enjoying each other. One way to do this is to build in time for a special type of rest, that which gives priority to rebuilding and strengthening relationships. Failure to observe this type of Sabbath can destroy a marriage as surely as any failure to observe your marital vows.

REDEFINING REST

The Benefields' case illustrates an important point that causes confusion over the meaning of *rest*.

Most people believe that if they merely "do something different" from their normal routine, they are resting or relaxing. I have friends who believe that jogging or working out at the gym is resting. Some even think that just running errands is restful.

But substituting one activity for another, such as becoming passionate about golf or taking all the classes you can, as the Benefields' were doing, is neither resting nor relaxing. These alternative activities are just as demanding on your adrenaline as your regular routine, if not more so.

Take vacations, for example. They were originally designed for rest. Surprised? The travel industry has turned that around and redefined what vacations are all about. In effect, they sell the message: "Vacations are not for rest; they are for exciting adventures. Take off on our exotic escapade to uncharted territories and explore new vistas that will knock your socks off." And I, more than anyone, can be tempted to use up my vacation getting an adrenaline "fix."

I know this principle from personal experience. Recently, I took two weeks of vacation and agreed to take my middle daughter, Sharon, and her two sons, ages thirteen and fifteen, on a backpacking trip to Europe, visiting places I knew well.

As a vacation, the trip was sensational. We planned it as an "overview" trip for my grandsons so as to stimulate their appetites for foreign travel, so we were constantly on the move. The boys chose what they wanted to see, and it certainly was stimulating—also exhausting and demanding, traveling and sleeping on trains and hiking wherever we could.

The pageantry of London was awesome for them. They fell in love with Oxford as I had years ago. The Cotswolds and Blenheim Palace gave them a new appreciation of old England. Then they rushed on the Chunnel high-speed train to Paris, the Louvre and Eiffel Tower, then on to hiking in Switzerland, their first view of a real *Leontopodium alpinum* (the delicate, small white flower known as "edelweiss" to you), a trip around Lake Thun, then on to the Black Forest area, and finally back to London for some shopping at Hamley's toy store and Harrod's.

Restful? No way. Even though my grandsons couldn't keep pace with me, I was exhausted every night. The trip was designed not to be restful, but interesting and exhilarating. I came home and went back to work to rest.

Some vacations are not designed for rest. But here we have a problem. The need for Sabbath rest cannot be delayed indefinitely. The need accumulates and must be cashed in at some time during a busy year. Waiting a whole year to get some rest, therefore, doesn't fix the deficit of accumulated anxiety and stress. That has to be fixed on a regular basis. An annual vacation is just a bonus.

So, let me make a very important point absolutely clear—time for rest must be taken on a daily basis and should never be delayed longer than a week. That is the principle of Sabbath-keeping.

Take a moment and get your Bible. Open it to Exodus 23:12. If you have the New International Version, you will read the following command from God to Moses: "Six days do your work, but on the seventh day do not work, so that your ox and your donkey may rest and the slave born in your household, and the alien as well, *may be refreshed*" (emphasis mine). I find these instructions to Moses very compelling. I cannot ignore them.

Many Protestants play down the meaning of resting every seventh day, the traditional concept of the Sabbath, arguing that the New Testament does not require it. Strictly speaking, it doesn't, not from a legal point of view anyway. But this doesn't mean that the Sabbath principle is no longer important. Does it mean that oxen, donkeys, aliens, slaves (or servants as we would interpret the phrase to mean today), and we don't need to rest? Of course it doesn't. If anything, *we need rest more today than ever before in history*.

And then, did you notice what God says in verse 13? "Be careful to do everything I have said to you." That's a habit shaker isn't it? God is pretty serious here—serious enough to emphasize it a second time. Why do we pay so little attention to the principle of Sabbath rest?

Some Christians believe in a literal keeping of the Sabbath, exactly as it was prescribed in the Old Testament. I respect them for that belief, and I leave it to theologians to work out what is right. I know all about the arguments against keeping a literal Sabbath: Christ brought an end to the Old Covenant and Sabbath-keeping. Keeping the Sabbath would deny the finished work of Christ. We shouldn't mix works and grace in the affair of salvation. Christ alone is enough to satisfy God. Christ our Sabbath rest has come. Any genuine observance of the Sabbath would have to include all the ceremonial laws of the Old Testament.

But the *literal observance of the Sabbath* is not what I am advocating here. It is the principle of a sabbath (lowercase *s*) that I think we need to observe. It is more, not less, than observing one day of rest a week. Every hour needs its minutes of rest, or at least a proper lunch break. Every day needs its hours of rest (a good night's sleep, for example). And every week needs its day of rest (for worship), and so on.

SEVEN WAYS YOU CAN MAINTAIN THE PRINCIPLE OF A SABBATH REST

1. Pay careful attention to developing an awareness of your limits. We all have limits. Not one of us is superhuman. God didn't create us that way. Like all creatures, we not only have our limits, but we have to learn to stay, work, and live within them.

2. Never work until you have reached your limits. Many get into the habit of working until getting a signal to stop, such as exhaustion, fatigue, headache, or dizziness. They just keep going until they are about to drop. Once you start to experience a stress-like symptom, you have gone too far. Learn to stop before you get to the edge of your limits.

3. The moment you realize that you are approaching your limits, stop. I mean stop right there and then. Do not wait until your eyestrain, pain, or headache kicks in. Your goal should be to never create a stress symptom, but to stop well before the edge.

4. Maintain regular breaks during your workday. You will find that if you stop periodically and relax so as to lower your adrenaline, you will in fact be able to keep going longer. It's like running a marathon race. If you keep going full speed, you will drop before you get to the end of the race. If you pace yourself, allowing times of less energy drain, your system has an opportunity to rejuvenate itself during the race.

5. If you exceed your limits and find yourself in stress or pain, back off and allow time for recovery. Once you trigger a pain or other stress response, your body not only needs to rejuvenate itself from the adrenaline overdraft you've created, but it also has to heal the damage you have done.

6. Take a good sabbath rest at the end of every day. The most important discovery I made regarding my own stress abuses is that I neglected to rest every day. I thought I could just keep going and make up for my depletion every week, month, or even year.

Not a good idea. In fact, it's crazy. We need daily renewal. This means you must allow enough time for relaxing, resting, and sleeping each day.

7. Take a good sabbath rest at weekends. As discussed earlier, I am not advocating a literal Sabbath as per the Old Testament, though this may not be a bad idea. The principle I support is "taking a break." Those of us in Christian work are perhaps the biggest culprits. We are deluded into thinking that just because we are doing God's work, we are excused from all the restrictions of being in human bodies. We are not. Rest is just as important in Christian work as it is in daily work.

TAKE TIME FOR RESTING NOW

The need for rest cannot be postponed until an annual vacation because no amount of annual vacation can undo the damage you have already done. Rest, like interest on your investments, should be taken as it is deserved. Only then can a vacation be an escape from the routines of life and an adventure that can open up new vistas of exciting discoveries. If you do not take time for rest regularly throughout the year, you are better off spending your vacation in an infirmary, undoing the accumulated wear and tear on your body and mind.

Sure, we need exciting outlets. We need to have hobbies, recreational breaks, and times for pleasure. But we also need to take time out for pure, non-contaminated rest. Rest is not the time to catch up on unfinished chores, run missing errands, go to the mall, or even take in a movie. These are *activities,* and activities are not rest producing. What characterizes rest is that it is *not* an activity. It is pure, luxurious leisure, a time to rediscover yourself, catch up on your feelings, determine new priorities, recreate a sense of balance, and, most importantly of all, restore your soul. And yes, on the way, you can also reconnect with God. One of the jeopardies of living life in the fast lane is that God will not allow us to set the pace. He prefers country by-paths, not shortcuts. We lose our sense of connectedness when we move faster than God, which results in a feeling of distance between God and us.

Also, resting is not the same as relaxing. We need to learn how to rest as well as relax. We will explore the importance of relaxation next.

RELAXATION AS THE ANTIDOTE FOR
STRESS AND ANXIETY

Everyone attempting to overcome an anxiety problem, such as panic, generalized worry, or phobic anxiety, must first master a very special skill. It is the ability to create, whenever you so choose, a state of complete relaxation. Easy? Not really. Relaxation takes quite a bit of practice before you feel like you have mastery over it.

There is no tool more crucial to recovery from anxiety than the ability to produce a relaxation response. Every other skill you will need to master depends on this foundational skill for its success. If you can't relax, you will not cure your disturbing anxiety. It is as simple as that.

Now let's get straight about what true relaxation is. I hear it all the time. "Oh, I know how to relax. I get on the tennis court and beat the heck out of my buddies." Or, "Relaxation? Sure, I know how to relax. I settle down in front of the old tube and I'm lost in relaxation." Really?

The relaxation response that you must learn to cure anxiety and prevent stress disease is not equivalent to chasing balls on the tennis court, golf course, football field, or any other field. (Ever notice that most sports have to do with chasing balls?) Certainly, unwinding in front of the television is not an appropriate relaxation response either. Take a deep, hot bath by candlelight at the end of the day, and you are headed in the right direction. Or take a nap or a stroll in the park on a Sunday afternoon, and you are beginning to get the idea. But even these can easily become activities if you introduce any level of competitiveness or speed. Unhurriedness is essential, so are no expectations for the outcome, a leisurely spirit and freedom from any demands. Better still, non-activities are the most helpful.

Recreation is not relaxation—not in the sense that clinicians who are experienced in the treatment of stress or anxiety disorders think about relaxation. The relaxation response needed to counteract stress and anxiety is unique in that it involves turning off both your mind and your muscles. It is sometimes referred to as "deep muscle relaxation" because you are able to achieve a dramatic turnoff of muscles firing. The result is you feel that your limbs are not even connected to your body.

It is also a unique state of total "switch-off" of all the activating and energizing systems in your brain and your adrenal system in the body. In fact, your cardiac system, respiratory system, muscle system, and all your systems slow down to a mild tick. Relaxation is more than just sitting down in a comfortable chair. It is a reversing of the gears, not just slowing them down. For most people, it is a completely foreign experience. Naturally, therefore, it takes time and determination to learn.

Herbert Benson first described this state as "the relaxation response." It is a response we are all capable of achieving. However, the further down the stress road you have traveled, the more difficult it is for you to get back. When you do achieve relaxation, however, the rewards are well worth the effort.

THE BENEFITS OF THE RELAXATION RESPONSE

Relaxation as a treatment modality has been around for thousands of years. Sometimes it was cloaked in religion and used to cure disease. But until fairly recently, it was neglected by medicine. Now it is recognized as a powerful resource for treating minds and bodies that have been overstretched by stress. Relaxation is good for everything, and there are no exceptions.

What does relaxation do? For starters, it lowers your stress hormones, including adrenaline and the sad messengers, like cortisol. It also elevates your immune system, raises your tolerance for pain, increases your natural tranquilizers, allows damaged tissue to repair itself, and helps your body to rejuvenate itself. And I have barely begun. You must learn to relax and do it often.

THE RELAXATION RESPONSE

What happens during this very special relaxation response? Your adrenaline drops dramatically, as well as the major culprit in anxiety, cortisol. This is why relaxation so profoundly reverses your anxiety proneness. Other changes directly connected with this drop in adrenaline are:

- Decreased heart rate

- Drop in blood pressure (very effective in treating stress-induced high blood pressure)

- Decreased muscle tension throughout the body (lowers all muscle pain, including muscle contraction headaches)

- Lowered general metabolic rate (reduces "wear and tear" on your body, even slowing down the aging process)
- Increase in your creative abilities.

Notice, nearly all the benefits listed above are due to something being lowered, except the last. When we are in a state of profound relaxation, our brain power is unleashed in a phenomenal way. This is all explained in *Adrenaline and Stress* so I refer my readers to that book for further information about this effect (see Appendix B).

After more than thirty years of teaching patients the art of relaxation, I can honestly say that relaxation is good for everything. I have been involved in the "biofeedback" movement since its inception and was one of the founding members of the California Biofeedback Society. Don't confuse biofeedback with "biorhythm," which is based on the totally useless and misleading idea that the rhythm of our moods is predetermined and follows a pattern that you can determine. Biofeedback, on the other hand, is a scientifically based procedure that uses special instruments that measure muscle tension, skin temperature, heart rate, etc., to provide biological feedback (hence the name) to guide you in achieving the relaxation response. It is used to reduce stress and anxiety symptoms, relieve headaches, increase energy, improve concentration and productivity, reduce insomnia and fatigue, and on and on. I know of no condition, physical or emotional, that is not rejuvenated by the relaxation response. If you have difficulty in teaching yourself this response, you may want to seek out a professional biofeedback trainer.

Is there a downside to relaxation? Only the journey you must take to get there. For most of us who live highly demanding, overextended lives, it is like taking a journey from one mountain peak to another. What lies in between? A valley, of course. For many, this deep relaxation can be a miserable valley.

Why? When we have been at a high level of adrenaline arousal for a period of time, our bodies become "adapted" to this state of high arousal. We actually become comfortable with it, despite its negative payoff. It's like working in a very bright room. Our eyes adapt to the brightness, and after a while we become used to it. This is how our wonderful bodies are designed—we can get used to almost everything.

But when we leave the bright room and move into a dark corridor, the darkness seems perilous until our eyes adapt again. Our eyes are not used to anything but a bright light. The same is true when we move from high to low arousal. A period of adaptation must take place. This adaptation is like the withdrawal experiences of recovering addicts, except here the addiction is to adrenaline.

How, then, do high-stressed people first experience the relaxation response? Miserably. At first, their bodies rebel. They fidget. They squirm. They twitch restlessly. Muscles jerk from the lowered chemicals that keep them energized. They wriggle and try endlessly to find a comfortable position.

I have had patients literally shout at me during the early stages of biofeedback relaxation training: "You must be crazy! There is no way this is relaxation because I feel too uncomfortable." They fight to get back to their higher comfort level.

I calmly encourage them to trust me and continue. Finally, and it varies from person to person how long it takes, they begin to unwind and the withdrawal symptoms disappear. The end result is beautiful to behold: tranquillity, peace, contentment, and serenity.

Can you achieve such depth of relaxation without the assistance of biofeedback instruments to monitor your tension? In the early days I believed not, but I have seen many people learn relaxation effectively on their own. I now believe you can.

HOW TO RELAX

In my book *Adrenaline and Stress,* I provide an exercise for teaching yourself how to relax. Many have found it difficult to do it by themselves, so I am offering a more complete set of exercises on audiotape for a modest charge. (Details on how you can get this tape are provided in Appendix A.)

The tape provides detailed instructions on how to progressively relax all your muscles, but it also provides exercises for relaxing your mind. These include "thought stopping" and "sensory stimulation" exercises that can teach you how to reconnect with your senses. For instance, it surprises even me how often I lose track of my sense of touch when I am caught up in a hectic schedule. By restoring my sense of touch, I open up a very effective sense of pleasure that helps to lower my arousal level. Try these exercises for yourself and see how effective they are.

In the short space I have here, I will provide a general overview of the progressive muscle relaxation exercise so that those of you who are not interested in the tape may have a technique available to you.

Progressive muscle relaxation is a systematic technique for achieving a state of deep relaxation. The technique is based on the principle that tensing a muscle for a few seconds helps to fatigue it enough to facilitate its relaxation. Once mastered, the technique can be used to put yourself to sleep, counteract an impending panic attack, or interrupt your stress buildup during a hectic schedule. I have taught it to lawyers, physicians, teachers, and a host of others who use it preventatively once or twice a day, whenever they get the opportunity, to lower their adrenaline. It is far better to prevent stress and anxiety symptoms than try to relieve them once they are on the attack.

WHEN TO RELAX

Relaxation should be an hourly, daily, and weekly event.

Hourly, you should be checking up on your tensions and saying to yourself, *Relax.* I would suggest placing a small, colored piece of paper or some other kind of mark on your mirror, watch dial, steering wheel, pen, or glasses to remind you to do this often. Perform one or more of the relaxation exercises described later on in this chapter as often as possible until you form a habit. Then practice it regularly.

Daily, you should spend at least thirty minutes in deep relaxation. This is such a small part of the day that everyone can afford to do it—and none of us can afford not to. The best time is when you come home from work or when your early evening duties are completed. Parents of small children may find that the best time is right after the children are put to bed. That's when you're likely to need it the most.

Weekly, you should plan for a longer period of relaxation. Sundays or Sabbaths are ideal. On these days, cut back on your work or regular activities. Take time to put your feet up, have a nap, or *just be lazy*. Much church activity is, unfortunately, geared to make us even busier on Sundays, and I believe this can be a pitfall. If you are not slowing down significantly on your day of rest, you are going against God's intent, as well as courting stress damage.

Many of us have been raised to feel guilty about being idle for even a few minutes. But for the sake of your health—spiritual, emotional, mental, and physical—you must stop your compulsive activity and, if necessary, force yourself into inactivity.

BASIC INGREDIENTS IN ALL RELAXATION

There is nothing mysterious or mystical about relaxation. It is a natural response of the body that can be triggered by all of us. In and of itself, relaxation does not have spiritual significance, but as we shall see, it can be combined with prayer and meditation to become a powerful spiritual exercise. It is something that should become easier as you practice it. Whichever body system you are trying to relax, the following are the basic steps to relaxation:

SIT OR LIE IN A COMFORTABLE POSITION. Pain or pressure will keep you in an aroused state, so try to minimize discomfort. Loosen tight clothing and remove your glasses. Try to provide support for all the undersides of your body.

ENSURE YOU WON'T BE INTERRUPTED. Lock the door; hang out a sign; unplug the phone; tell your spouse, kids, dogs, and neighbors not to disturb you—or better yet, go where they can't find you.

SET ASIDE A PREDETERMINED AMOUNT OF TIME FOR THE EXERCISE. Thirty to forty-five minutes is ideal. Set an alarm so you won't have to keep checking the time.

DON'T FALL ASLEEP. Sleeping is not what relaxation is all about. If you need sleep, go ahead and sleep, but don't confuse sleep with relaxing. Relaxation is a conscious experience, not a trance or sleeplike state. Falling asleep when relaxing is a sign that you probably need more sleep.

REMAIN INACTIVE. Don't fidget, move, get up, or scratch. At first, you'll want to do all these because you will be experiencing withdrawal symptoms from the effect of lowered adrenaline, just as when you stop taking a powerful drug. Just put up with the discomfort, and it will pass away. (If you must scratch, return as quickly as possible to the relaxed position.)

AVOID THINKING TROUBLESOME THOUGHTS. Set aside your worries. Cast all your worries and cares aside. Try to detach yourself from your worrisome world for a while and remain free of the demands that press on you.

131

SPECIFIC RELAXATION TECHNIQUE

I will now describe a more specific relaxation exercise for your muscles. Make yourself comfortable. Close your eyes and shut out the world. Don't cross your arms or legs. Remove your shoes and glasses. Clear your mind of worries or resentments. Claim peace and tranquillity for yourself. Now do the following exercise:

While lying flat on your back, raise your hands above your head and rest them, but don't grasp anything. Take a deep breath. Hold your breath for a few seconds. Relax and breathe out.

Now, stretch your hands up as far as they will go. Stretch them farther. Hold them there. Now push your feet down as far as they will go. Farther. Hold your arms and feet stretched out as far apart from each other as possible. Count slowly to ten: 1 . . . 2 . . . 3 . . . 4 . . . 5 . . . 6 . . . 7 . . . 8 . . . 9 . . . 10.

Relax and let your hands and feet return to their original position. Again, repeat the exercise and count: 1 . . . 2 . . . 3 . . . 4 . . . 5 . . . 6 . . . 7 . . . 8 . . . 9 . . . 10.

Repeat the stretching exercise once more.

Breathe in and out slowly and rhythmically for a few minutes. Try to breathe from your abdomen, not your chest. Concentrate on what you are doing. When you breathe in, push your stomach out and down, so that your lower abdomen expands. When you breathe out, pull your stomach in slightly to help your lungs give up their air.

Now remain immobile, resting and relaxing for another twenty or thirty minutes. (Remember to set a timer before you start.)

When your relaxation time is over, get up slowly. Move slowly. Sit up for a short while. Move slowly and peacefully. Then go back to your normal duties, trying to maintain a more restful posture.

When you have mastered the above exercise, try doing it while sitting. Later you'll be able to do it while driving or even working.

TRY RELAXING THROUGHOUT YOUR BUSY DAY

It is important that you take every opportunity you can to consciously relax. When you find yourself caught up in a conflict with someone, go aside and relax if possible. When you feel a panic sensation coming over you, try relaxing. If you are worried, tense, or anticipating some troublesome encounter, use relaxation to calm your body, and your mind will soon follow.

Don't expect to become good at relaxing without practicing it, however. Like so many other skills we learn, relaxation takes *time* and *practice*. Don't be disappointed if you don't succeed at first, but try and try again. Your very life may depend on it.

When you are relaxing, pay particular attention to the following:

Relax the muscles of your jaw, brow, and forehead. These muscles need special attention. They tend to show your anxiety and confusion very easily. Consciously relax your brow. Drop your lower jaw. Clenching your teeth is never necessary. Whenever you have a problem to solve, remember to smooth your brow and drop your jaw.

Avoid clenching your fists. Also avoid holding on to the arm of a chair or your steering wheel. Sometimes tension creates in us a need to "hold on to something," as if we fear being thrown off our world. Consciously relax your hands, especially when holding a pen, driving your car, or watching TV.

Relax your stomach muscles. If you pay attention, you will notice that you often tense your stomach as if to prepare for a blow. Too often, we live on the defensive, constantly prepared for someone to attack us. The brain receives these protective signals from the stomach and prepares the body for counterattack. But the attack almost never comes, so why not just relax? Don't always pull your stomach in. Forget about your posture and your figure occasionally and just relax.

Watch how you breathe. Our breathing shows our stress. There are two methods of breathing—chest (or shallow) breathing and abdominal (or deep) breathing. Shallow, chest-level breathing is typical of anxious people. It centers around a point high in your chest and the breathing is shallow and rapid. Abdominal breathing is deeper and slower.

One way to test if your breathing is abdominal is to lie flat on your back and place a hand on your stomach just below the ribs. As you breathe, notice whether your hand moves up from your body or down. Moving up is abdominal breathing. Your lungs push the stomach down, and this raises your hand. Shallow breathing pulls your stomach in, and your hand drops down toward your back.

Try not to breathe just with your chest muscles. This is nervous breathing, meant only for emergencies. It takes place high in the chest, expanding the rib cage, and it feels shallow. Use your stomach when you breathe.

Try this exercise for improved breathing: You can develop abdominal breathing by practicing pushing your stomach up as you take in a long breath. (See sidebar for a breathing exercise.)

Lie on your back and place your left hand on your stomach just below the sternum (breastbone). As you breathe in, make sure you do so by pushing up the stomach. You should see your hand rise when you do this; if it doesn't, try pushing it up. As you breathe out, the hand must fall. This is abdominal breathing. It is relaxing, peaceful—the breathing style of calm people. When you breathe from your belly, you can't remain tense, so always try to breathe this way.

A BREATHING EXERCISE

The following exercise can help you calm yourself when you are anxious. It also helps to prevent the onset of hyperventilation. You can do it lying down or sitting up. You can even do it inconspicuously with others around you.

1. Sit or lie down on a comfortable surface. Make sure you will not be disturbed.

2. For the first five minutes, lie still and just observe your breathing pattern without trying to change it. How fast are you breathing? Is your breathing shallow or abdominal?

3. Then, when you are comfortable with the first exercise, try to slow down the inhaling of air, making it last as long as you possibly can. Count: a thousand and one, a thousand and two, . . . and see how long you can drag it out. Make sure your stomach is rising as you breathe in. Then start exhaling as slowly as possible, counting again and slowly dropping your stomach.

4. Repeat this exercise over and over again, trying to make both inhaling and exhaling last as long as possible.

5. After ten minutes or so, continue this pattern of breathing without trying to control it or counting. As you inhale and exhale, observe the process. Concentrate on the air filling your lungs and imagine it transferring to your blood and circulating around your body.

6. After five more minutes, you can get up and return to your regular duties. Be careful when you get up, however. You may be so relaxed that you may miss a step and easily fall over.

Relaxation gives you a wonderful opportunity to develop your spiritual disciplines. These are wonderful opportunities for meditation, prayer, Scripture memorization, or simply pondering the marvelous ways of God. You can listen to tape-recorded scriptures or audiobooks while practicing your relaxation. Much of what we do as Christians is by its very nature peaceful and tranquillity building. Capitalize on that and claim it for yourself.

CHAPTER 10

DEALING WITH
OVERSTRESS

———— ∽∾∾ ————

We are troubled on every side, yet not distressed;
we are perplexed, but not in despair.

2 CORINTHIANS 4:8

S tress! Some hate it; others love it. If you love it, it is more than certain
that you will die from it. Stress is both exciting and painful. It exhilarates
us and gives us energy to achieve, but at the same time, it causes an accelerated wear and tear in our bodies. In a nutshell, stress is accelerated dying.
And the problem with stress is that if it doesn't take you to an early grave, it
will make your living painful and uncomfortable through the anxiety it will
create.

After writing *Adrenaline and Stress,* I thought that I had said everything
there was to say on stress and how to manage it. And its principles are still a
good foundation for controlling stress. But since I wrote that book, several
important new bits of information about stress have come to light. I am going
to lay them out here as concisely as I can.

First, a personal testimony. When I started doing the research that led to
writing *Adrenaline and Stress* fifteen years ago, I really wrote the book for
myself. In fact, most of the books I have written have been for myself. (This one
is no exception.) I needed its message more than anyone because my own stress

levels were through the roof. My blood pressure was too high, I experienced frequent headaches, and my sleeping habits were atrocious. I was headed for some serious trouble.

What can I say about my stress message now? It has saved my life—literally. I am more convinced of the importance of paying attention to our adrenal system and the threat of becoming addicted to its thrills now than I ever was. Is it also important here? Absolutely. To cure your anxiety problem, especially anxiety that causes panic, you cannot ignore your stress. You must become its master, not its slave.

So in addition to the stress management principles I set out in *Adrenaline and Stress,* here are some very important additional strategies that can help you build your resistance against anxiety.

OUR MODERN-DAY PLAGUE

I recently went to see the animated movie *Prince of Egypt* with my grandchildren. This epic portrayal of the life of Moses graphically and frighteningly depicts the stories of the plagues that God sent the Egyptians. My grandchildren cringed, and I was reminded that throughout history, humankind has had periodic episodes of plaguelike illnesses that have decimated the population. The bubonic plague ravaged Europe in the Middle Ages. Syphilis killed one in four Europeans when it first surfaced in Europe in the 1500s. One in two Hawaiians was killed by measles in the 1700s. Meanwhile, Native Americans were dying from smallpox and other diseases imported by the early explorers.

Are we plagued today? Medical science has advanced tremendously, so it is unlikely that we will ever have any disease as serious as our ancestors had to face. But there is one insidious plague that haunts us today, and medical science has done little to prevent it. It is the plague of stress and its consequent diseases. We know how to treat some of the symptoms of stress disease, but it seems that there is little interest in preventing it.

How serious is this disease? Today, one in ten persons falls victim to *over-stress.* Those who are becoming chemically dependent on some of the palliatives we use for stress symptoms are walking a fatal path. Others "drop out" at an early age to join the ranks of society's "marginal survivors."

The cost to our society is immense—overstress costs our society at least sixty billion dollars a year. Our society loses through lost productivity, medical care for the complications of overstress, job accidents, and traffic fatalities (half of which are related to driving while using alcohol or drugs).

TELLTALE SIGNS OF TOO MUCH STRESS

How can you tell if you have too much stress in your life? Here is a baker's dozen of important symptoms. Look at these telltale signs and give yourself the following scores:

0 if you never experience this symptom
1 if you sometimes experience it (say, once a month)
2 if you experience it between once a month and once a week
3 if you experience it often (more than once a week)

1. Do you experience headaches of any sort?
2. Does your heart pound, feel irregular, or skip beats?
3. Do you feel a lot of muscle tension or stiffness in your joints?
4. Do you ever feel dizzy or lightheaded?
5. Do you get sick often (colds, flu, or throat problems)?
6. Does indigestion, nausea, or other stomach discomfort bother you, or do you suffer from stomach ulcers?
7. Do you have difficulty sleeping, falling asleep, or waking up too early?
8. Do you typically have to wake up to an alarm still feeling tired?
9. Does your mind become very active and race a lot?
10. Do you grind your teeth or does your jaw ache?
11. Do you become very excited when you engage in challenging activities?
12. Do you get angry quickly or feel a deep sense of injustice whenever things go wrong?
13. Do you suffer from high blood pressure or elevated cholesterol?

How did you fare? Obviously, the higher your score the greater your stress.

- If you scored between 0 and 8, you probably have little or no stress. Seek help only if the one or two points of discomfort bother you and especially if you answered yes to question 13.
- A score of 9 to 15 indicates a fair amount of stress. If any of the symptoms has been around a long time you may need help in getting rid of it.
- A score of 16 to 30 indicates a high level of stress. You could benefit from professional help.
- If you score is more than 30, your stress level is extremely high. You should seek professional help right away.

WHY IS STRESS A PROBLEM?

Stress is a problem for several reasons:

IT IS EMOTIONALLY AND PHYSICALLY TREACHEROUS. Emotionally, stress can cause anxiety and depression problems, and, physically, it can kill you. And if it doesn't kill you, it will cause so much pain and discomfort that you will sometimes wish you were dead.

WE ARE ONLY "JARS OF CLAY." This means that we are, by design, fragile and vulnerable. This is what the apostle Paul discovered. In 2 Corinthians 4:7, he explicitly makes the point that, as humans, we live in fragile bodies: "jars of clay" (NIV). His point is that *we have our limits*, and when we violate these limits stress will begin to do its damage. We are not superhuman. We need to take care of our frail and human bodies just as someone in times of old, before they learned how to glaze and bake clay pots as hard as steel, had to tenderly care for their earthenware vessels.

OUR CULTURE DOES NOT TRAIN US TO MANAGE STRESS. If anything, it capitalizes on our stress. Do you want a promotion in your job? Then you have to work harder and longer than your nearest rival. Competition is the name of the game, and, if you don't play the game, you lose. Unfortunately, most of the stress we experience is the result of this competition in some form or other. Do we need to feel competitive in order to succeed? I believe not. I think I can perform at my best without having to psych myself into feeling I am in a race to win over someone else.

STRESS ITSELF IS NOT SINFUL

Many devout believers are bothered by feelings that if they are under high stress, they must be sinning. Let me take a moment to correct this erroneous idea. Stress, in and of itself, is not sin. True, a lot of stress can be avoided, but some of it is very much beyond our control. Take tragic bereavement, for example. The sudden and unexpected death of a child or spouse is about as tragic as life gets. The stress that follows such a tragedy is quite natural. The same applies if you lose your job due to the downsizing of your company. You can't help what is happening to you. Your spiritual responsibility is to utilize the resources that God has given you to help you cope with and minimize the effects of this stress. Don't make it worse by condemning yourself as sinful.

Certainly stress can have sinful consequences. Often, when Christian leaders fall, it is because they have been in a period of extreme stress. Stress lowers our ability to cope with life or make clear judgments, so we make stupid mistakes that we regret afterward.

Stress, therefore, is not inherently sinful. But it can certainly set us up for a fall.

WHAT IS STRESS?

Because I encounter so much confusion and misleading information about what causes stress, I first want to make sure you know what stress is.

Many of us succumb to stress because we look for it in the wrong places. For instance, most of us think of stress as coming from the unpleasant things of life. We think of the tension in our lives, the conflicts that are going on around us, or even a catastrophic experience such as the death of someone in our family. While all these unpleasant experiences are stressful, the fact is that the kind of stress that kills us—the stress that is most damaging—does not come from the unpleasant things of life. When things bother and hurt us, we take steps to avoid them, mostly. But stress that comes from the exciting, challenging things of life is often the major source of our destruction. Often, the exciting stress that comes with doing things that keep us wired is so pleasant that we do not take steps to remove it.

And if there's one thing we know about stress it is this—*whether the stress comes from the good things or the bad things of life, its damaging effects are always the same.*

So, what is stress? Let me suggest a few examples:

STRESS IS BEING STRETCHED BEYOND YOUR LIMITS. Whenever you are confronted with challenges that you don't seem to be able to cope with or demands that you don't have the skills to deal with, your system goes into emergency mode. Your body starts to pump adrenaline, and the effect of this adrenaline surge is what we call stress.

STRESS IS OVEREXTENDING YOURSELF WITHOUT ADEQUATE TIME FOR RECOVERY. If you have a series of crises in your life where one thing upon another is thrust upon you, your stress level will increase very dramatically.

STRESS IS BELIEVING YOU CAN DO MORE THAN YOUR HUMAN FRAME CAN TAKE. Remember my earlier engineering analogy using the term "duty cycle"? It applies here. Electric motors have a duty cycle, if you recall, that indicates what percentage of time the motor is designed to run. If you use it for longer than its duty cycle, it will burn out. That's a fact of engineering. No engine or motor is designed to run all the time without a break—without some sort of rest. Remember that the human body is no different. In fact, the human body has a much lower duty cycle than most machines.

Right now I can almost hear what you're thinking: *But not all stress is bad. I need to have some stress in my life; otherwise I'm not going to feel very good about myself.* Am I right? Let's take a moment to look at the notions of "good" stress and "bad" stress.

It would be unfair of me to suggest that all stress from challenges, changes, excitement, or fervor for your work or play is bad and should be avoided. No, not all these things are entirely bad. However, these exciting things in your life are also the source of a lot of stress. If you maintain a high level of excitement for a prolonged period of time, the stress will kill you no matter whether it is "good" or "bad."

So, what is the difference between "good" stress and "bad" stress? What we should be asking is whether there is really such a thing as good stress. One of the great myths is the idea that stress is really a positive thing and that you should channel it in the right direction. But this view is not scientifically valid. Years ago, a pair of researchers by the names Holmes and Rahe examined the whole issue of good stress versus bad stress. They came to the conclusion that *any stress,* if it is prolonged, is bad for the body.

Perhaps the best way I can explain what stress is really about is to draw several analogies:

"HILLS AND VALLEYS": First, think about stress in terms of a series of hills and valleys. Every mountain of high arousal, whether from the good things or the bad things of your life, should be followed by a valley of recovery. Each day should end with a return to a low state of arousal so that your body can recuperate. Each challenge of the day should end with a calming of your body and of your mind. And each week of work should end with rest. If you can do this, you will be healthy in mind, body, and spirit. In fact, your stress will be good for you. But if you don't follow the "hills" of stress with the "valleys" of rest, your body will not have time to rejuvenate; thus, you will develop a slow pattern of burnout.

"HIGH-POWERED SPORTS CAR": Another analogy is to think of stress as a high-powered sports car in the fast lane. Sports cars can travel very fast on a short journey. They are not designed for long-distance travel. The gasoline they use is high octane, and the engine is tuned almost to the edge of destruction. So the sports car's engine is capable of a short burst of high speed. Big deal. But can it go the distance? No, it can't. So if you try to live a high-octane life, don't be surprised if your "engine" disintegrates after the first lap. We are just not designed for that sort of high-powered, fast-paced lifestyle.

"CAMEL TRAVEL": As I mentioned earlier, we were not designed for high-speed travel; we were designed for camel travel. We were designed to finish the race, not win it. This means that we need to build lots of time for rest and recovery into our busy lives.

"CLOCKS AND HURRIEDNESS": Hurry sickness, which causes us to feel we are racing against time, is a killer of innocent people—people who don't know that the disease does its damage right before their eyes. Our culture is a hurried culture. Unlike many other nonwestern cultures, we think of time as "the enemy." So we're always trying to beat the clock as if time were against us. Also, we practically worship time. We place big clocks on tall steeples where we can all stare at them. Then we attach large bells that clang out the hours to remind us how little we are accomplishing.

Often, it is very helpful to remind yourself that there was an era when the reminder of the passage of time was helpful in slowing us down. My grandfather used to say, "There's lots of time" as the big clock in the hall chimed ten in the morning. "Let's take a break and go fishing down at the river." These days, my digital wristwatch beeps to remind me that the hour is up, so I have to say to a patient, "Time is gone; I need to hurry on to my next client." And my stomach doesn't feel quite the same as it did when my grandfather's clock did the chiming.

ADRENAL EXHAUSTION

Hans Selye, the grandfather of all stress research, was the first to describe how prolonged stress caused the adrenal glands to be in such a chronic state of exhaustion that they are not doing their job properly. I have referred to this effect at several times throughout this book.

This condition of underfunctioning doesn't happen overnight but progresses through a series of stages. In the *first stage* of fighting stress, the adrenal glands tend to overproduce. They produce high amounts (hyperfunction) of adrenaline, noradrenaline, and cortisol. As the stress keeps going, the glands begin to expand their production and can begin to feel overtaxed.

The *second stage* now begins as the glands begin to temporarily underfunction. You will find that the adrenal glands "crash" because they are depleted. This leaves you feeling fatigued a lot of the time, especially when you let down at weekends or in the evenings.

If you are healthy, the *third stage* now sets in. Your glands compensate for coming up short and begin to rebuild themselves, adapting to the higher demand by actually enlarging so as to compensate for the higher demand for their services.

If the high level of stress continues, a *fourth stage* sets in. The glands will again eventually exhaust themselves and remain in a chronic state of under-functioning. At this stage, they can oscillate between overproducing adrenaline, causing panic or mood swings like depression, then crashing and underproducing adrenaline the rest of the time. With insufficient stress-fighting hormones, you will tend to have difficulty handling any stressful situation. You will feel as if you are falling apart. At this point, your stress tolerance is exhausted. You are on your own without the God-given help your adrenal system was designed to provide.[1]

How can you know if adrenal exhaustion has set in? Here are some telltale signs:

- A sense of chronic low stress tolerance
- Frequent feelings of fatigue
- Repeated bouts of depression, especially when you stop work or try to relax
- Worsening allergies or asthma
- Cravings for substances that provide stimulation
- Addiction to caffeine

How do you recover from a chronic state of adrenal exhaustion? By consistently working at lowering adrenal arousal to allow your system to "reset" itself. Your body needs time to heal and to adapt to a lower level of functioning. Here are the general guidelines:

- Simplify your lifestyle and reduce stress to the absolute minimum. Take up a hobby. Get lots of fresh air and sunshine.
- Increase your sleep to a minimum of between eight and a half to nine hours a night. (I'll have more to say about this in chapter 14.)
- Eliminate all stimulants, especially caffeine, as well as nicotine, alcohol, and recreational drugs. These play havoc with your body's chemistry.
- Eliminate all foods that may disturb your digestion or cause allergies.
- Supplement your diet with vitamins such as B-complex, C, and E.
- Take yourself less seriously and treat life more respectfully.

HIDDEN STRESSORS

Not all our stressors are easy to recognize. Some sources of our stress are "hidden," meaning that they are doing their damage behind our backs where we can't see them.

How can stress be so damaging yet elude our awareness? Because we are born with the amazing human trait of *adaptability.* Our bodies have remarkable ability to adjust to a wide variety of conditions-from—heat to cold, high to low altitudes, hard physical work to sedentary inactivity. As I mentioned earlier, if we walk into a dark room from bright sunlight, we cannot see anything at first. But as our eyes get accustomed to the darkness, we begin to see more clearly. This is adaptability, and it operates in every system of the body, including the stress system. While most times, adaptability is a good thing and helps us to adjust to changing life circumstances, there is a negative side. Our bodies can run the risk of becoming so adjusted to a circumstance that we lose any awareness of its presence.

For example, let's look at blood pressure. In a moment of crisis, your blood pressure will go up. You may be angry and need to deal with some situation that is threatening to you. But if that anger is not resolved quickly, the blood pressure continues to climb, and your body slowly adjusts to the high level of blood pressure. After a while you don't even notice it; in fact, many of us cannot tell whether our blood pressure is high or low. That is because our body has adapted to the high level of blood pressure, and we can no longer feel it.

Let me put it simply: When you experience a lot of stress for a long time, your body adapts to this prolonged stress by keeping you in a protracted fight-or-flight state. That is what the stress response is all about. Stress is an *emergency* response designed to help you fight or flee. However, when you live an emergency lifestyle, your adrenal system is no longer helpful. It becomes the enemy because it will slowly destroy you.

So, any of the following things can cause you stress without your knowledge:

- driving on busy freeways
- noise from your teenager's stereo system
- living near noisy freeways or train lines

- loneliness
- complaining neighbors
- bad lighting at work or home
- bad time management
- always being late for appointments
- too many deadlines
- dogs that bark in the night

All of these can be the source of continuous stress. Because you adapt to their presence, you no longer can recognize them as stress.

BELIEFS THAT CAN CAUSE STRESS

One very important source of stress that we must not overlook is how our beliefs can, by themselves, set us up for more stress.

A particular brand of thought can cause as well as aggravate stress. What sort of thoughts are stress-producing? Usually these are thoughts that send alarming or distressing messages to your body. They are directives that scream out "Emergency!" even when there is no emergency. In order to decrease your stress level, you need to send yourself calming or reassuring messages and carefully attend to the beliefs that lie behind all your self-messages.

What beliefs tend to feed inappropriate alarming or emergency self-messages? Following is a list of the more important stress-inducing beliefs that you should begin to change. Under each category, I will suggest some important questions you should ask yourself. The answers you give should suggest where you should begin to change your thinking.

PEOPLE-PLEASING MESSAGES

- Does your self-esteem depend on everyone else's opinion of you?
- Are you better at taking care of the needs of others than you are of taking care of your own needs?
- Do you avoid confrontation or conflict because you fear displeasing someone else?

- Do you often keep your opinions to yourself because you think others are smarter than you are?

- Do you suppress your negative feelings to avoid displeasing others?

- Do you go overboard to please your boss because you feel you have to please him or her at all costs?

CONTROL MESSAGES

- Are you uncomfortable when you don't feel in control of a situation?

- Do you believe that a lack of control is a sign of weakness or failure?

- Do you find it difficult to delegate responsibility to others?

- Do you tend to do things yourself because you believe others may not do it as well?

IMPRESSION MESSAGES

- Do you frequently pay too much attention to what sort of impression you make on others?

- Are you very self-conscious when you are in a crowd?

- Do you try to "manage" the impression you make on others so that they will feel better about you?

- Do you tend to feel shame when you make a mistake?

- Do you find it difficult to forgive yourself when you fail at something?

SELF-CONFIDENCE

- Do you have a strong sense of self-competence, like you can handle most things in life?

- Do you compare your performance with that of others a lot?

- Are you confident in making decisions or judgments about life matters?

- Are you a person of good, common sense?

- Do you accept compliments honestly, recognizing that they are true?

PERFECTIONISM

- Do you feel a strong pressure to perform better than others do?
- Do you punish yourself with criticism and self-rejection when you fail?
- Do you often feel uncomfortable because you haven't finished a project?

Any of the tendencies I have just mentioned could be originating in long-standing irrational beliefs and causing you to be sending high stress-building messages to yourself. Take a little time to evaluate your responses and change the beliefs that underlie them. If you get your thought life back on track, you will significantly reduce your stress and anxiety.

OVERUSING YOUR ADRENAL SYSTEM

In the final analysis, as I have mentioned several times already—and I intend to repeat myself often on this point because it is so crucial—overstress is the result of churning out too much of the emergency stress hormones from the adrenal glands. In a nutshell, you are under stress whenever you pump too much adrenaline. Your body is being mobilized for a fight-or-flight response when there is probably no threat, and this increased flow of adrenaline causes many stress symptoms, especially panic anxiety.

What are the effects of all this adrenal flooding? Let me summarize them for you:

First, and the most serious, is an increase in the production of blood cholesterol. Your cholesterol level is not just tied to diet; it is also tied to stress. And whenever your adrenaline is high, your liver produces more cholesterol.

Second, there is a narrowing of the blood vessels that control the blood supply to the heart muscle. This can have serious consequences, of course, if you have a heart attack.

Third, there is a decrease in your body's ability to remove cholesterol. The body needs the cholesterol, so it hangs on to it.

Fourth, there is an increase in your blood's tendency to clot. This occurs because this high level of adrenaline is designed for emergency when you are likely to cut or injure yourself and could bleed to death. You are created in a way that whenever your adrenaline is high, your blood's capacity to clot goes up. However, when your blood vessels in your heart have been narrowed by all that bad cholesterol, the high adrenaline arousal causing the blood to clot may be the final thing that causes you to have a heart attack.

But let's keep this all in perspective. Short bursts of high levels of adrenaline are not damaging nor dangerous. After all, adrenaline is what makes us feel life's excitement. We all have moments of challenge when our arousal revs us up and leaves us idling at a high speed. But if your life is balanced, then that high rev will settle down slowly to a slow tick, and your system will gradually return to normal.

What does this all mean? It means that we have to learn to live on less adrenaline. We have to learn to live at a lower level of excitement and build into our lives the necessary time for our bodies to recover. And, of course, since anger, frustration, irritation, and aggravation can all be adrenaline triggers, we need to learn the skills necessary to bring these emotions under control. The accelerated pace of our modern lifestyle robs us of our natural recovery times. The night is shortened; we don't get as much sleep as we need; and, especially for pastors, weekends can also be extremely stressful. So many pastors don't take time to achieve an adequate level of rest, and they pay for it in increased stress symptoms.

STRESS BUSTING YOUR LIFE

Obviously, prevention is always better than cure. So what are some of the ways you can prevent stress buildup in your life?

To manage your stress effectively, you should do the following:

SET BOUNDARIES IN YOUR LIFE. Your body needs to "be told" when there is an emergency and when there isn't. Therefore, be clear in your mind whether you are working or relaxing. Be intentional about setting boundaries for your feelings of responsibility for others; don't assume responsibility for things for which you are not responsible.

RESOLVE CONFLICTS QUICKLY. No emotions are more stressful or stress producing than anger and resentment. Whenever you are in a conflict, your body goes into accelerated fight-or-flight mode. It feels threatened, but it doesn't know what to do. It is up to you to tell your body what it should do. The most obvious thing to do, therefore, is go and solve your problems right away. If you allow a conflict to stay with you into the night, it is going to disturb your sleep. You're not going to sleep well, and this is going to make you less effective when you try to resolve that conflict the next day. Festering conflicts are one of the major sources of stress disease.

TAKE CARE OF UNPLEASANT TASKS FIRST AND GET THEM OUT OF THE WAY. Some of us are procrastinators. I know that I am. But procrastination doesn't keep you in low-stress mode; it increases your level of stress. So wherever possible, try to do things on time, especially unpleasant things. These tasks need to be taken care of right away. The sooner you get them off your body's agenda, the sooner your body will go back into a low-stress mode again.

"INOCULATE" YOURSELF AGAINST STRESS. Just as being inoculated with a mild dose of a disease causes your body to build a resistance against it, so also dealing effectively with small amounts of stress can help to build your body's resistance against stress. People who are at greatest risk for stress are those who never experience any stress at all. Suddenly they are thrust into a whirlpool of crises, and they do not have any skills for dealing with that. On the other hand, don't take things too seriously. Try to understand where others are coming from and don't take matters too personally. Learn to forgive other people very, very quickly because you will benefit from giving that forgiveness.

BE FIRM ABOUT SETTING UP YOUR "RECOVERY TIMES." You must build recovery time into your life after every period of stress. Failure to do this means that your body never catches up; it never heals itself and gets back to its original state. It is extremely important, therefore, that you take a Sabbath rest. You need rest times; you need a day off; you need periodic vacations; and, especially, you need to build into your life some personal retreat time.

KEEP YOUR ADRENALINE AROUSAL TO A MINIMUM. The problem with adrenaline is that it is so energizing, so exciting, we seek it even to the point of becoming addicted to it. Many people like the thrill of challenge or the thrill of change simply because it gets their adrenaline going and makes them feel good. This is dangerous. Too much adrenaline will kill you in the long run because this is the high-octane gasoline or petrol of your body. As I mentioned earlier, high-octane engines don't last very long. They are designed for short bursts of high speed and then they must be replaced. Remember, our bodies are designed more for camel travel in the sense that they must go the distance, not just finish the high-speed race. So learn to enjoy a little bit of boredom in your life every now and again. Take time for leisure and recreation because these, in the long run, will help to prevent stress from killing you.

MAINTAIN OPEN AND HEALTHY RELATIONSHIPS. We need one another, but we also need to live in harmony with each other. This is important to us spiritually and emotionally, but it also important to us physically. People who live in conflicted environments—for example, in families that are always fighting or in churches that have lots of conflict—are always under a lot more stress. Make sure that you have people around you who love you and care for you, the kind of friends that you can rely on in moments of crisis.

GIVE YOURSELF A BREAK BY LEARNING TO SAY NO. One of the greatest sources of stress in many of our lives (I know it is in mine) is the inability to say no. Result? We become busier and busier, and we have little time for renewal—spiritually, emotionally, and physically. Under such stressful conditions, our happy messengers fly the coop. We are left holding stress at arm's length, but fighting stress is as stressful as being stressed. If you really struggle with the word *no,* then perhaps you need some basic training in Christian assertiveness, that form of assertiveness that lovingly declines being trampled on or overwhelmed by activities that other people think up for you. Remember this: Your *no* gives meaning to your *yes.* If you say yes to everything, you are essentially saying yes to nothing because the stress will eat you up and spit you out as a hollow shell.

POSTPONE MAKING MAJOR DECISIONS DURING STRESS. Remember, *change is stressful.* If you are already under stress, don't make it worse by welcoming more stress. If it can wait, let it wait. So relax and postpone any big moves or changes for a while. Some examples of things that can wait are remodeling your house or apartment, moving to a new house or apartment, elective surgery, looking for another job, or making major financial investments or purchases that will put you under more stress. There are many things we do impulsively that can wait for more considered reflection. Impulsiveness always raises our stress levels.

TAP INTO YOUR SPIRITUAL RESOURCES FOR STRESS BUSTING. I have more to say about this point in the last chapter of this book, because it is so foundational that I want to make sure it is given the attention it deserves.

If you have tried all these suggestions and are still very anxious, depressed, or stressed-out, then it is time you got some professional assistance. This is *not* a sign that you are weak, simply that you are human. It's really not all that bad to accept your humanness. It sure beats trying to play Superman or Superwoman. Or should that be Super-stupid-human-who-tries-to-do-everything? I must confess that description fits me better than most. How about you?

CHAPTER 11

A SEVEN-WEEK PLAN FOR BREAKING THE WORRY HABIT

———— ∞∞∞ ————

Look at the birds of the air;
they do not sow or reap or store away in barns,
and yet your heavenly Father feeds them.

MATTHEW 6:26 (NIV)

D o you ever wonder why some people are perpetually happy, while others are perpetually miserable? It's not such a mystery. The answer has been clearly demonstrated in the previous chapters: It is mostly in the brain's chemistry.

But let us not take this idea too far. Up to a point, brain chemistry has a lot of say about how we feel. But what upsets our brain chemistry? Is the imbalance all "biological" so we have little control over it? Or can the imbalance be due to what is going on in our heads? As I have tried to show throughout this book, some forms of anxiety start as disturbed brain chemistry and find their way into our minds, while others start in the mind and work their way through to upsetting our chemistry. Worry anxiety is the latter.

Someone has so rightly said, "Worry is like a rocking chair. It will give you something to do, but won't get you anywhere." It is the one form of anxiety that Scripture clearly warns us to avoid. By and large, worry is useless, unnecessary, bothersome, unfruitful, uncalled for, and vexing. I say "by and large" because worry is essentially a *warning signal*. It tells us that danger lurks in hidden places. And if we could only keep it within reasonable limits and use it to point us to ways of avoiding the danger, worry would be of help to us. But it goes overboard. It warns us of dangers that don't exist. It exaggerates petty pitfalls and drives us crazy by bedeviling our tranquillity.

Herein lies the struggle in learning how to deal with worry anxiety: How can we preserve its good function (to warn us of impending danger and to force us to take action) while reducing or even eliminating the useless worry? We can only eliminate worry by eliminating all anxiety. If you do this, you will end up as a sociopath—a dangerous person with no conscience. So, we must seek to achieve a proper balance. We want to preserve worry that is constructive but eliminate worry that is futile.

EVERYBODY WORRIES

For those of you who worry excessively, let me reassure you on one important point: *Everybody worries.* It's all a matter of degree. We were designed to worry. It is a part of anxiety that we cannot survive without.

Suppose, in looking at a mirror when getting out of the shower, I discover that I have a small, dark, ugly growth on my back that I hadn't noticed before. Growing up in South Africa, I had a lot of exposure to strong sunlight and I know that this puts me at risk for deadly skin cancer. But I don't want to be bothered about it right then. I have a speaking trip coming up that can't be delayed. So I put the growth out of my mind and tell myself I will have it seen to after I get back from my trip.

During breakfast on the plane the next morning, I catch myself obsessing about the growth on my back. I realize that it has been worrying me all the time. Is it cancerous? Skin cancer grows very fast, so if I don't catch it early it can metastasize and I'll be in real trouble. My mind is racing. I try to set my thoughts aside, but they won't stop. I push my breakfast tray aside because I can't eat. I scold myself. Why didn't I have my doctor take a look at the growth right away? I was stupid to ignore it.

Tell me, what is going on in this scenario? My mind is only doing its job. It is warning me that there is danger in my neglect. It is trying to force me to take action. Thank God for such worry anxiety because it could save my life.

Let us now suppose that after a miserable few days I return home and go to see my doctor. He assures me that it is just a normal age-related growth, removes it, and sends me on my way. But I don't believe that it is normal. I fear that it will come back. I have nightmares about it and wake up in the early hours of the morning worrying about the growth. So many questions. What if the doctor is wrong? What if he missed something? I can't get back to sleep. The next day I call to ask him whether he is sure it isn't cancerous. He assures me it isn't. Half an hour later, I am worrying again.

Obviously, what I am doing now is useless and unnecessary. Such worry disturbs my tranquillity. It doesn't help me but makes me miserable. And if I worry frequently like this, I will get into trouble emotionally. Worry can be a cruel tyrant when it gets out of control. For some people, it even feels like an addiction—they just cannot stop doing it.

While some have applied the concept of addiction to worry, I don't think it is comparable. True, useless worry seems to have an addictive quality about it in that you can't stop doing it, but it doesn't bring any pleasure. Yielding to an addiction arouses great relief, euphoria, and pleasure. Worry is misery all the way, before, during, and after. So, I prefer to refer to it as a "habit." As a bad habit, useless worry knows no equal.

There is much to worry about today. The economy, the AIDS crisis, the epidemic of broken marriages and teenage pregnancies, job security, promotion prospects, and turmoil in the world. Jesus was right. "In this world you will have trouble." (John 16:33 NIV). Some of us seem to get more than our share of it. But the truth is that useless worry drains away our energy for living and reduces our efficiency and effectiveness. We tend to worry most over things we have least control over. Ninety-five percent of the things we worry about never come to pass, and the remaining 5 percent will happen whether we worry about it or not.

The famous author-physician A. J. Cronin sorted out worry this way:

- Things that never happen—40 percent
- Things in the past that can't be changed by all the worry in the world—30 percent
- Health-related worries—12 percent
- Petty, miscellaneous worries—19 percent
- Real, legitimate worries—8 percent

I must say that Dr. Cronin's estimate that only 8 percent of worry is over real, legitimate matters fits my experience. And it has always been so, which is why Jesus poses this question to make the same point: "Who of you by worrying can add a single hour to his life?" (Matthew 6:27 NIV)

THE SIN OF WORRY

In calling worry a "sin," I do so more to make a point than to be judgmental. Worry anxiety, as Scripture clearly shows, is bad for us and therefore runs contrary to God's good plan. It involves relying on self rather than on God, and it gets in the way of faith. As such, worry is sin. When we worry, we need God's healing and forgiveness, just as we do when we lie or commit adultery.

In addition, worry is an intriguing problem from a clinical point of view. We all have an inherent tendency to anticipate or prepare for future events by thinking about them in advance. We use thoughts and images to help us either understand or solve our problems. But worry is more than just thinking about things; it seems to take on a life of its own. It becomes an "enemy within," distracting us from our work with its relentless flow of bothersome thoughts. While it may fool us into thinking that it is directed at solving problems, it never delivers the goods. We never get closure on anything we worry about.

One research group at Pennsylvania State University defined *worry* as "a chain of negative and relatively uncontrollable thoughts and images." Another person described worry as "interest paid in advance on a debt you may never owe," a description that probably captures it best of all. Most worry focuses on the future (what will happen tomorrow, next week, or next year), but a lot of it also focuses on the past.

Most worry follows a circular path; it starts nowhere and ends up back where it started. "I've got to meet that deadline. . . . Deadlines are important. . . . My boss puts a lot of emphasis in meeting deadlines. . . . If I don't meet the deadline, I won't get a raise. . . . My promotion will be dead too. . . . Maybe I'll even get fired. . . . What will happen to me? . . . This is the only job I know. . . . How do I make the house payments? . . . What will my kids do? . . . If I don't stop thinking like this, I won't get this assignment finished on time. . . . I've got to meet that deadline."

About 15 percent of the population can be classified as *chronic worriers*. That's about one person out of seven. But what is a chronic worrier?

Researchers tend to think that if you worry for fewer than one and a half hours a day, you do not have a worry problem. Isn't that amazing? But then, you see, a lot of worry goes on unconsciously; it is not until you catch yourself putting shaving cream on your toothbrush that you realize you've been worrying.

What are some of the consequences of worry? Misery, certainly, but there are many other consequences as well: headaches, lack of sleep, loss of appetite, overeating, lower tolerance of frustration, irritability, and bad disposition. There is even some suggestion that worry creates high blood pressure, heart disease, and ulcers. While there is no hard evidence yet, worry is even suspected to be an aggravating factor in cancer.

BREAKING THE WORRY HABIT

Many of you reading this are, by now, impatiently thinking: *Yes, I agree that worry is a waste of energy, but how can I stop worrying?* I have devoted the rest of this chapter to establishing a seven-week plan for breaking the worry habit. My strategy will proceed along the following lines. Having made the point that we cannot, nor should we even try to eliminate all worry, we need to first sift through our worries and figure out which of them are necessary and which are not. This isn't as easy as it sounds. Follow the strategies outlined very carefully, and then you will begin to eliminate the useless worries while setting up a strategy for dealing with the necessary ones.

Here are some directions, then, about how to work through this seven-week program:

- Each week's exercises must carry through subsequent weeks. In other words, keep doing the previous week's exercises as you practice the new week's exercises. All the exercises must be seen as a whole.

- If you find any of the exercises to be difficult or to take longer than anticipated, then let them flow into the next week and delay moving to the following exercise. There is no hurry, so don't become anxious about your progress if you need more time.

- At all times follow the famous Alcoholics Anonymous adage: "One day at a time." Very few alcoholics can imagine being sober for the rest of their lives. But they can imagine being sober "one day at a time." Days roll into months and months into years. Many alcoholics have remained sober for the rest of their lives just one day at a time. Breaking the worry habit is a one-day-at-a-time project. Be content with being worry-free just one day at a time.

A SEVEN-WEEK PLAN FOR BREAKING THE WORRY HABIT

WEEK 1

PURPOSE: *To discover and systematically record all the things that worry you.* Get a spiral notebook that you can easily fit into your pocket or purse. It must be of such a size that you can keep it with you at all times. Starting, say, on Monday, every time you catch yourself worrying write it down. Capture the day, time, place, how long it bothered you, circumstances leading up to the worry, and what, if anything, you did about it. For example, let's say you just got to the office and caught yourself worrying about whether you turned off the stove. Write down the day, time, what worried you, etc. It's best if you write it down at the time, but this may not always be convenient. In that case, write it down when you get an opportunity. Equally important, record what, if anything, you did about it. Did you go back home later? Did you just spend the rest of the day worrying? Did you call a neighbor and ask her to check the stove for you?

At the end of the week, take your notebook and review your worries. Ask yourself two questions:

1. How many of my worries turned into reality? Was I fired? Did the house burn down? Did the plane crash? The idea here is to prove to yourself how useless your worries are.

2. What themes can I detect in my worries? Are all my worries over work? Family matters? The past? The future? Money? Dying? Illness?

Look for themes and see which are more common. This will help you decide which aspect of your life gives you cause for more worry than others. From now on, work only on those worries that have to do with this theme. You can repeat the rest of this plan for the other worry areas of your life once you have conquered the most common one you have found here. Now we are ready to move to the second week's activity.

WEEK 2

PURPOSE: *To separate out "concerns" from "worries."*
Perhaps the most confusing aspect of worry anxiety for most of us is that we do not or cannot distinguish it from a healthy (but related) emotion that can best be labeled "concern." It is very helpful to separate worry from concern. The one is unhealthy, the other is not.

Simply put, the word *worry* should be reserved for that kind of fruitless mental activity which keeps thoughts revolving endlessly but takes no action to solve the problem—either because no action is possible or because we refuse to take action. Such fretting is pointless; it goes nowhere. When we worry, we cause an emergency reaction throughout our body, and as a result we become exhausted, disorganized, and disoriented—without moving one inch toward solving our problem.

Concern, on the other hand, refers to that kind of mental activity that focuses on a problem with a view toward taking action to resolve the problem. Concern springs naturally from love and caring and is directed toward an end.

Let us suppose, for example, that a loved one is about to undergo surgery. I know the feeling well because just a few years ago my wife, Kathleen, had major surgery. I recall sitting in the waiting room with my stomach in knots and my hands sweating. Was that feeling worry or concern? I must admit that there was an element of worry when I allowed my imagination to get away from me. But a lot of my feeling was nothing more than concern. Because I love my wife, I wanted her to feel comfortable, the surgery to go smoothly, and the outcome to be satisfactory. This concern helped me to focus my prayers and to pray for the surgeon and for my wife.

For the second week, therefore, I would like you to concentrate on the worry theme you selected in the first week's exercise, and this time record only those worries that fit this theme. Again, record all the details as you did in the first week. At the end of the week, sit down again with your notebook and review each worry carefully. This time ask yourself the following questions:

1. Was the worry really a worry, or was it a "concern"? The point here is to clearly differentiate a worry (useless, meaningless, and

nonproductive) from a concern (a genuine, caring, or considerate thought). In red ink, mark each one of your worry bouts accordingly. Count the number that fall into each category because later we will want to see if you are increasing your concerns over your worries.

2. Consider each worry and ask yourself: *How can I turn this worry into a concern?* In other words, what self-talk could you use to reframe the worry into a concern? Let's suppose you worried about whether a job you completed was going to be acceptable to your boss, who is a perfectionist. Worrying about it, now that you have handed it over to her, isn't going to make it more perfect. So you could say to yourself: *I have done my best. I am not perfect, so perfection is beyond my, or anyone's, reach. If my boss wants me to do the job again, I will at least know where to go from here. I will stay concerned but will let my worry go free.* At this point you have effectively converted your worry into concern. Is there a difference? There certainly is. Your mind and body gets a totally different message when you worry uselessly than when you acknowledge that you are concerned. The former triggers a fight-or-flight response; the latter has a calming effect.

WEEK 3

PURPOSE: *To apply the difference between worry and concern in your everyday activities.*

In the previous week, you recorded your worries and at the end of the week categorized them into "concerns" and "worries." Afterward, you saw how you could transform even your worries into concerns by reforming them through self-talk. Every worry can be turned into a healthier concern merely by changing your attitude toward it or seeing it in a more positive light. Are you worried about that surgery next week? Then convert your useless worry into a concern by saying toward yourself: *I will pray that the surgeon will do his best, that God will keep me safe, and that I will have a speedy recovery. The rest is up to God, and my worry isn't going to make anything better. I remain concerned but will not worry about it.*

Now this week I want you to continue recording each worry, but this time try to reframe it into a concern *at the moment it happens*. This is a bit more challenging, which is why you needed last week's exercise to give you some practice. Do three things:

1. Record the worry. This rule always applies because the very act of writing down your worry will help you to identify which are the most common, and it also helps us to see your worry for what it really is—useless.

2. Examine your worry and try to find a way to convert it into a concern—*at that moment.* You are now implementing your first real-life intervention, challenging your worries as they occur, and converting them into something more positive. Record the reframing. If the worry is so useless as not to lend itself to being converted into a concern, then you have your message and know what to do: Dump it.

3. At the end of the week, review your success at changing worry into concern. You will not have succeeded every time, so if necessary keep the exercise going the following week. In fact, you should continue to do the reframing from here on all the time until it becomes a habit you do without thinking about it.

WEEK 4

PURPOSE: *To catch automatic thoughts that creep up on you.*
Automatic thoughts are involuntary thoughts that creep up on you. Usually they cause anxiety because you were not expecting them. Many worriers find automatic thoughts to be the bane of their lives. Often these thoughts start a chain of worrying, so our exercise here is to try and head them off before they get a foothold. The best way to do this, interestingly, is to bring them into your awareness *before* they creep up on you. In other words, if you choose to examine them, they do not produce as much anxiety as when they catch you by surprise.

The following exercise will help you capture and bring into the open your automatic thoughts:

1. Set aside twenty minutes for contemplation at the end of each day. Get a small notebook specifically for this exercise, and during these

periods of contemplation write down *every* worry, anxiety, concern, bothersome thought, event, or person that comes into your mind. Your notebook is confidential, so write down everything, no matter how petty it seems. Try to survey your day and recapture every troublesome thought.

2. Review your list of bothersome ideas. Ask yourself, *Which of these can I take care of right now? Is there anything I can change?* Then take that action immediately and cross that concern off your list.

3. Take a moment to pray about the rest of your list—those concerns you cannot take care of there and then. Commit to God any concern you cannot change. Then close your notebook and go about your business, trusting that God is in control and you cannot control every aspect of your life.

4. If any concern continues to bother you, make a note of it once more in your notebook. In next week's exercise, I will teach you how to select and substitute a pleasant thought for the bothersome one.

I cannot stress strongly enough the value of writing down, as fully as possible, all thoughts and ideas that bother you. Writing them down helps to get them out of your memory, where they will otherwise be kept alive by the memory-refreshing mechanisms of your brain. Your notebook, therefore, serves as an external memory. It can be taken with you everywhere.

Variation: A variation of this exercise is to use your notebook whenever you are bothered by a thought. As soon as it comes into your mind, write it down. It doesn't matter how often you write down the same thought—just keep doing it. This helps the brain to "give up" unwanted material as it knows that the information is being stored somewhere else.

WEEK 5

PURPOSE: *To learn how to initiate pleasant thoughts to displace unpleasant ones.*

1. Take a card and write down five or six activities you know will give you pleasure. These can be events from your past (memories of

happy childhood outings) or present (your last visit to the beach or to see a friend), or they may be activities you anticipate with pleasure in your near future (such as an upcoming vacation).

2. Next to each pleasant activity or event, write down two or three specific ideas or aspects of the event that interest or captivate you. For instance, if you are planning a vacation, you may wish to write down "plan clothes to take" or "examine travel brochure for places to visit" as specific ideas.

3. Keep this card with you at all times. Every hour or two, take out your card, select a pleasant activity or event, and deliberately begin to think about one of the specific ideas you have written down. Take a moment to enjoy the feelings that it generates. Savor the pleasant feelings that follow. Try to think about it for four or five minutes. Then return the card to its place of safekeeping and go about your business.

Variation: Instead of places or events, make a list of personal qualities you would like to encourage in yourself. Would you like to be more loving? More caring? Ponder these. Or you may prefer to keep a favorite poem or portion of Scripture with you. Review these. Think about them deliberately and consciously and try to enjoy the thoughts as much as you can.

WEEK 6

PURPOSE: *To explore your self-talk and turn it around.*
Are you aware of the conversations you have with yourself and how often they are responsible for your worry tendencies? Try writing down every conversation you have with yourself over your spouse, kids, boss, employees, pastor, or friends. You might be surprised at the sorts of things you say to yourself. It isn't until we see these thoughts written out that their irrationality becomes obvious. Think about the following characteristics of self-talk:

- Self-talk tends to be emotionally charged. It comes from hurts (real or supposed) and is fed by other feelings.
- Self-talk is fed by a vivid imagination. It seldom keeps in touch with reality. It exaggerates and oversensitizes us.

- Self-talk overgeneralizes. It takes one little event and tries to prove that everything is the same.

- Self-talk is irrational and illogical most of the time. It feeds off doubts and uncertainties and is seldom satisfied with reality.

- Self-talk usually leads to a "catastrophizing" of everything. It always ends with statements like *I am jinxed, I am terrible,* or *Nobody cares for me.*

- Self-talk is usually self-pitying and selfish. You are the center of the conversation and the victim of all offense, and you want to wallow in your mire.

Improving your self-talk is the object of this week's exercise. Healthy and successful people can recognize and stop their negative self-talk. They can analyze its content and argument, set aside the ridiculous and imagined, test reality and take whatever action needs to be taken, or inject healthier and more realistic ideas into the self-conversation. This keeps them from being influenced by worrisome thoughts.

Here is an exercise to help you monitor your self-talk:

1. Set an alarm or use some device to signal you at least once every hour. You can use class breaks, coffee breaks, or any other natural breaks in your day to signal the time for the exercise.

2. At the moment you are signaled, stop what you are doing and review very carefully the conversation you have been having with yourself during the previous five minutes. Write it down in your notebook. Try to recall as many ideas or self-statements as possible. Pay particular attention to the conversation you are having with yourself at the moment the signal occurs.

3. Take your list of self-talk sentences and review each one. Ask yourself the following questions about each of them: Is it true? How do I know it is true? Is it reality? Am I overreacting? What's the real issue here? Where will this thought take me?

4. Deliberately counter your negative self-talk with positive, realistic, reassuring sentences. For example, say to yourself, *It is unfortunate*

that this has happened to me, but it is not the end. Or, *Who says I must be this way? I am being irrational and illogical, and, therefore, I will not pay attention to what I am thinking.*

5. Find someone (a friend or spouse) to share your thoughts with. Irrational self-talk is best challenged in open conversation with another person. In addition, share it with God. After all, this is what prayer is for.

Variation: You can monitor your self-talk at any time. Once you know how to do it when cued by set times, try catching your self-conversations at random times during the day. Monitor your self-talk while you are having a conversation with a friend or while standing in line at the supermarket. Generally increase your awareness of what you say to yourself. This will help you to catch the stream of your thought.

WEEK 7

PURPOSE: *To intentionally prolong your worry.*
Even chronic worriers are known to have periods when they don't worry. This phenomenon—times of worry followed by periods of no worry—has led to some interesting and useful discoveries. Research has shown that short periods of worrying (say, for less than ten minutes) or very long periods (greater than thirty minutes) tend to cut down on the tendency to worry. It is the "middle" range of worrying, between ten and thirty minutes, that produces the worst consequences. This effect is called "incubation" and is thought to explain why worry tends to "feed on itself."

We don't worry all the time, even if we are chronic worriers. If we did, we would probably extinguish the worry. Nor do we tend to worry for just a brief period and then set it aside; this would also extinguish the worry. Instead, we worry enough to entrench our anxious feelings, and then we leave our worry alone for a while so it can incubate. Later, we return to our problem to find that it is ready and waiting for more worry. This pattern entrenches the worry and makes it very resistant to extinction.

It's very much like painting a barn door. Put on one thin coat of paint and leave it, and the paint will wear off quickly. Put on a very thick single coat, and the paint will drop off as quickly because it doesn't dry properly and therefore doesn't adhere well. But put on just the right amount of paint, give it time to set, add a second layer and let it dry, then add another and another, and you build up a strong, impermeable, almost indestructible covering.

Now, this process may be good for painting barn doors, but it is not good for protecting the psyche from anxiety. When worry is entertained in just the right amount and repeated at just the right interval, it will build up to become an entrenched habit that is resistant to almost any therapy, and, I might say, to the Holy Spirit as well. That is why, I'm convinced, that Scripture pegs worry anxiety as sinful. We need to work hard at eradicating it.

For our last exercise, therefore, I want to show you how to use this incubation principle to your advantage and extinguish your worry habit. The procedure is as follows: Whenever you catch yourself worrying about something (and you should be pretty adept at this by now), go aside where you can be alone and keep that worry in your mind. Now focus on it. Think about it. Keep thinking about it. Don't let it slip from your mind. If it does, pull it back. Just keep it going as hard as you can for as long as you can, but make sure it is no longer than ten minutes. In other words, you should *deliberately* choose to think about your worry, but limit it to less than ten minutes.

What happens here? First, by *choosing* to worry about something you interrupt the dynamics of worry. Worry is a problem precisely because we fear it and try to avoid it. So if you choose to worry, it has lost the game to begin with. Second, by forcing yourself to think about the troublesome thought, something else happens: Your mind gets tired of it and gives it up. It wants novelty so turns to thinking about something else.

This procedure, if practiced consistently, can be powerful in extinguishing worry and the anxiety it causes. At all times, however, be in a spirit of prayer. God is interested in your problem and will help you to overcome it.

WINNING OVER WORRY

Winning over worry takes work and patience. You didn't succumb to worry overnight, and it is not going to vanish that quickly either.

Whatever else you do, avoid people who tell you, "Don't worry." It's easy to say. I've even seen it on T-shirts and bumper stickers, as if it's the greatest psychological or spiritual discovery ever made. But it's not really helpful just to tell people not to worry. That's like telling a person who is overweight, "Just don't eat so much." It's true, but it's not really helpful. To overcome worry anxiety, you need to understand *why* you worry, come to see how useless it is, and learn how to turn your worry into action.

I have presented you with a seven-week plan for breaking the worry habit. Let me close this chapter with a few final thoughts.

Remember, first of all, that there is enormous help available to us in combating worry in our Christian faith. My own faith in Christ has helped me survive many times when I thought worry would do me in. God understands how we are made, and whatever practical help I have offered here from a psychological point of view must be taken with a *massive dose of spiritual renewal.* I am convinced that the first line of defense against worry must be an understanding that God gives us power to live meaningful lives and sustains us through every experience we face and every challenge we must cope with. God can deal with *every* situation that gives us cause for worry—of this I am certain.

Second, remember that *not all your anxiety is useless, only the worrying sort.* Sometimes anxiety is a call to action, to get you out of your helplessness and take control of your life. We are designed to experience a form of existential anxiety that will drive us crazy if we are not achieving our full potential or moving forward with our lives. So try to understand what your anxiety is calling you to do before you rush to take a tranquilizer and demolish it.

Third, do you remember what Joseph in the Old Testament said to those who plotted his death? "You meant evil against me, but God meant it for good" (Gen. 50:20 NASB). Begin each day trusting that this is as true for you as it was for the young Joseph, and the need to worry your way out of your predicaments will diminish.

Still there are times when worry is overpowering and no amount of praying or believing seems to enable us to withstand it. Remember that God understands this also, so take heart as you try your best to deal with it in the ways I have suggested.

CHAPTER 12

THE ANXIETY-DEPRESSION CONNECTION

Why art thou cast down, O my soul?
and why art thou disquieted in me? hope thou in God:
for I shall yet praise him for the help of his countenance.

PSALM 42:5

I f only anxiety would stick to itself and not team up with other problems, it would be a lot easier to cope with. But it doesn't. Anxiety always has fellow travelers. Some just go along for the ride, but others insist on getting into the act as well. So anyone struggling to overcome an anxiety problem must also learn how to deal with these freeloaders as well, especially depression. They sponge off the anxiety and make life more complicated than we would like it to be.

WHICH COMES FIRST?

There was no doubt in my mind that Mercy was depressed when her husband first brought her to see me. All the symptoms of depression were there: the tired look in her eyes, the lack of eye contact, the resistance to treatment, the lethargy, even the way she slouched in the chair. Depression was written all over her face. And when she began to talk about how life wasn't worth living and she wished she were dead, I knew this case was going to be a challenge.

Not that her treatment isn't helpful. In fact, her type of depression has a very good prognosis and treatment is usually very effective. But it is quite a struggle to gain cooperation, especially in the early stages. One slip on my part and Mercy could have easily gotten up and walked out. It has happened—not often, fortunately—but enough to keep me on my toes.

It wasn't until our third session together, however, that Mercy's husband mentioned, in passing, her panic attacks. I had not specifically asked about them because her depression was so profound as to mask every other possible diagnosis. So I immediately began to explore Mercy's so-called panic attacks.

"How do you know they were panic attacks?" I asked the husband. Mercy had started having them shortly after they got married. The very first time scared them so much they took her to the emergency room. After a thorough checkup, the doctors concluded that she was having panic attacks and sent her home to follow up with her family physician. She never did. Shortly afterward, the panic subsided and they forgot about it until the depression hit. At almost the same time, the panic feelings began to return.

I heaved a sigh of relief. The clinical picture was now all falling into place. I knew exactly what we were up against, and fortunately there are now effective treatments for even the most complicated-looking emotional problems.

But the question that arises here is this: If anxiety and depression can coexist, even in their most severe forms, which comes first? I regret to say that we don't know. Sometimes someone will begin with panic attacks and later depression will emerge. The depression could be a reaction to the loss of control felt by most panic sufferers. But at other times, panic emerges in someone who is already struggling with depression. They can even come on simultaneously.

While there may very well be a common denominator leading up to both these problems, such as stress or a common genetic factor, the important point for me to emphasize here is that the two are treated as separate problems, merely coexisting. Effective treatment includes a combination of both psychotherapy and pharmacotherapy. Fortunately, the newer anti-depressants like the selective serotonin reuptake inhibitors (SSRIs) offer a broad efficacy for treating multiple disorders with fewer side effects and risks. I will have more to say about this treatment and how you should cooperate with it.

HOW COMMON IS IT FOR ANXIETY AND DEPRESSION TO COEXIST?

It is very common for anxiety and depression to coexist. I would even go so far as to suggest that you seldom see depression without some anxiety, or anxiety without some depression. They are two sides of the same coin. It just depends which side lands faceup.

From a clinical perspective, the more important question is whether the "other" problem needs to be treated. In other words, if your main problem seems to be depression and the anxiety is not very severe, does the anxiety need to be treated? Or, if the anxiety is the dominant problem, do you need to be concerned about the depression? The answer is that it all depends on whether the secondary problem is severe enough to be debilitating. If it isn't, then it probably will get better as the main problem is treated. It may be nothing more than a symptom of the main problem.

But what do the experts think? Anxiety coexists with depression for a majority of patients seen in routine medical practice, according to John Zajaecka, M.D., assistant professor of psychiatry at Rush-Presbyterian-St. Luke's Medical Center, Chicago. Speaking at the ninth annual U.S. Psychiatric and Mental Health Congress recently in San Diego, Dr. Zajaecka noted from a literature review that up to 60 percent of depressed patients have a full comorbid anxiety syndrome, arising at any point in the course of a depressive illness. Typically, the anxiety can include generalized anxiety disorder, panic anxiety disorder, obsessive-compulsive disorder, social phobia, posttraumatic stress disorder, or mixed anxiety-depression.[1]

For other depressed patients, anxiety may develop as less than a full syndrome, yet it may still impede full recovery from an affective episode. It may also persist as a residual phenomenon after depressive symptoms improve during treatment.

THREE COMPLICATING PROBLEMS

To put the coexistence of anxiety with depression in a larger perspective, let me also explain that *three complicating problems* can all increase the symptoms of either anxiety or depression: hypoglycemia, premenstrual syndrome, and alcoholism. Depression, therefore, is not alone in muddying the waters here. These three very common problems can really make anxiety and/or depression a much more difficult problem to deal with. They need to be treated at the same time as the depression or anxiety.

HYPOGLYCEMIA

As touched on earlier, the term *hypoglycemia* simply means "low blood sugar." It is the experience of uncomfortable physical symptoms during times when there is a lower than normal level of glucose in the bloodstream. The condition is found in people with diabetes mellitus, but it may also occur in people who have not yet developed clinical diabetes. They have "functional" or "reactive" hypoglycemia.

The important point to remember is that when the symptoms of hypoglycemia are severe, they appear to be identical to most of the symptoms seen in a panic attack. In fact, the body may well be reacting with panic to its state of internal emergency signaled by the low blood sugar. Symptoms include trembling, lightheadedness, perspiration, anxiety, rapid heartbeat, and weakness, all seen also in panic attacks.

The similarity between the symptoms of panic and hypoglycemia is not coincidental. Guess what? The common link is adrenaline. Whenever the blood sugar level gets low, the adrenal gland sends out adrenaline to help release extra sugar from its storage in the liver and dump it rapidly into the bloodstream.[2] But as we already know, adrenaline is also the fight-or-flight hormone that fights emergencies by raising blood pressure, increasing heart rate, triggering perspiration, and tensing muscles. So the two responses resemble each other very closely, a fact that can complicate diagnosis.

So the first thing I did with Mercy, the panic case I mentioned earlier, was to send her to her family physician with a request that she have a thorough physical examination. This doesn't always catch functional or reactive hypoglycemia, but physicians can usually alert you to the possibility that you may have a problem here just from the symptoms. One must always first rule out obvious physical disease before starting any form of treatment for panic, except perhaps to provide some symptom relief. I can't tell you how often someone has come to see me after years of psychotherapy and a few basic tests reveal that the problem is physical, not psychological. The potential for misdiagnosis is enormous.

You can help your doctor by observing and evaluating your panic attacks. Consider the following questions:

- Do you wake up with panic attacks? If so, this could be because your blood sugar levels are lowest in the morning.

- Can you see regular patterns to your panic attacks? Blood sugar levels are also lowest just before meals or two to three hours after your last meal.

- Does sugar in some form completely remove your panic? If something sweet like candy, juice, or a sweet roll makes you feel better, you may want to be checked out for hypoglycemia.

PREMENSTRUAL SYNDROME

Commonly known as PMS, premenstrual syndrome occurs in women in the days or weeks before menstruation. It is extremely common, with 30 to 95 percent of all healthy women experiencing some form of it, according to several studies. The dominant symptoms are depression, irritability, and anxiety during the period before menstruation.

Because stress can aggravate the menstrual cycle, causing delayed or even skipped periods, it can also intensify PMS symptoms. Panic before, during, or after menstruation on a regular basis points to the stress surrounding menstruation as an aggravating factor. It is not sufficient to treat only the panic. Treatment needs to consider providing some relief for the PMS as well.

The topic of PMS is a vast one and since it is well covered in my book *Secrets of Eve* (written together with my daughter, Dr. Catherine Hart Weber), I will not spend too much time on it here. (See Appendix B.) The treatment of PMS can proceed along several lines, some of which overlap with the treatment of panic. If you suffer from PMS, you must pay special attention to your diet. Especially avoid foods that are high in sugar, salt, or fat. Eating binges are a no-no, and lowering your weight can certainly help. However, *never* go on a weight-loss program if you are taking an antidepressant without consulting your doctor. A sudden drop in your fat level will free medication normally bound to fat molecules and cause you to be overloaded with the medication. While the SSRIs are quite safe here, the older TCAs could cause a toxic reaction. Beneficial foods are those high in protein and those derived from whole grains, vegetables, seeds, and nuts. Vitamins, especially the B-complexes and A, may need to be taken as a supplement.

On the medication front, the SSRIs like Prozac are proving to be very effective in fighting PMS. Since SSRIs are antidepressants, they are also helpful in treating depression and panic. So one medication can tackle all three problems very effectively. Killing three birds with one stone seems to be a sound idea—figuratively speaking, of course.

ALCOHOL

While I am primarily writing for a Christian audience, I can't assume that my readers are free of any risk from alcohol. The consumption of any amount of alcohol, even if you are not an alcoholic, is a seriously complicating factor in panic anxiety and depression. For one thing, alcohol disturbs the body's metabolism of the standard medications used in treating panic and depression. The same enzymes that are used to get rid of the alcohol are also used to remove the antidepressant medication. If you drink alcohol, you increase these enzymes, and they aggressively go after the antidepressant, effectively removing it and reducing your protection against anxiety and depression.

Furthermore, alcohol is primarily a central nervous system *depressant.* It slows down and "numbs" the brain, including the emotions, which is why so many use it as an escape. It removes inhibitions and tensions, fears, and anxieties. Many depressed people use alcohol as a form of self-medication. The trouble is that you've got to keep taking it to keep up the numbing. If you stop, you are more depressed than before.

As you consume larger amounts of alcohol, your entire nervous system becomes depressed, leading to impaired judgment and coordination. That's why you see the cops giving a suspected drunk driver the "walk the straight line" test. An intoxicated person can't walk straight.

For our purposes here, alcohol has several effects that are important to understand. It can lead to a hypoglycemic reaction because the liver stops manufacturing glycogen, the precursor to glucose. Result? Lower blood sugar. And since some panic prone individuals are more susceptible than others to low blood sugar, a panic attack may soon follow.

Alcohol also diminishes balanced judgment, so anxiety increases when you wake up to the effects of your embarrasing actions or bad decisions. Drinking alcohol to relieve your anxious feelings or to overcome your social discomfort only sets you up for more anxiety later. I believe many people are driven to alcoholism because of a deep-seated and untreated anxiety problem. This has certainly been true for the alcoholic patients I have seen over the years. Alcohol probably does relieve panic and other anxiety feelings temporarily, but in the long run it has serious, negative consequences.

One prominent politician I know started drinking only after he went into politics and found he was beginning to have panic attacks. Before a meeting or dinner party he would become panicky and feel socially very inadequate and uncomfortable. He had never consumed alcohol before, but very early in his career he tried some whiskey and found that it relaxed him and took away his anxiety. He was hooked, and he self-medicated his anxieties this way for a long time until his wife began to confront his increasing dependence on alcohol for his "Dutch courage."

When I recommended to him that he use appropriate medication together with some cognitive and relaxation therapy to help overcome his anxiety (which would be safer than becoming an alcoholic), he really balked. The alcohol was an instant fix. Everything else would take too much time and trouble. So, as far as I know, he still drinks heavily but denies he has a drinking problem. Recently, when I encountered him socially, he was beginning to show all the signs of alcoholic liver damage. But he still believes he is not an alcoholic.

If alcohol has become your crutch, you must remain alert to its seductiveness and be honest about its power over you. Facing up to your anxiety is demanding and time-consuming, but in the long run it provides a more permanent cure.

TREATMENT FOR YOUR DEPRESSION

If you suspect you are depressed or have been diagnosed with concurrent depression, how should it be treated?

Each case of coexisting depression and anxiety falls into one of the following scenarios: Your anxiety may be the dominant problem and the depression may be a side effect of the anxiety; your depression may be the dominant problem and the anxiety a side effect of the depression; or you may have two independent, coexisting problems.

Let me discuss each of these in turn and help you understand what you should expect from your treatment.

ANXIETY IS THE DOMINANT PROBLEM

In all likelihood, if your problem is primarily anxiety, the treatment of your anxiety will relieve the depression. Often, the treatment of panic anxiety disorder or other anxiety conditions requires the use of an antidepressant. This is fortuitous because you will be able to help both conditions at the same time.

However, if the anxiety problem is dominant, you will need more than an antidepressant to deal with your problem, if only in the early stage. While some antidepressants are very effective in treating anxiety, they are slower to take effect because they approach the problem through a different route. If you are experiencing panic attacks, therefore, you will need more immediate relief to prevent the recurrence of the attacks. As I have already mentioned, the attack itself is so frightening that it creates a fear-of-fear response. You begin to fear having an attack, which raises your anxiety to the point where you actually have an attack. The use of appropriate tranquilizers can minimize these attacks in the early stage of treatment.

Also, psychotherapy is extremely important here. It is very easy to become demoralized by a severe anxiety problem, which can lead to reactive depression. Therapy can help to deal with your negative thinking and maintain an optimistic outlook. This, in turn, lowers your stress level and helps to restore some of your natural tranquilizers or happy messengers.

DEPRESSION IS THE DOMINANT PROBLEM

In this case, the depression must receive priority in your treatment. While a mild tranquilizer may be added to relieve the anxiety symptoms, the anxiety is secondary to the depression and will go away once the depression begins to lift. Often the anxiety is "reactive" in the sense that it is caused by your concern for the depression. You are not sure about what is happening to you or how you will come out of the depth of your despair. It is only natural that you should feel some anxiety over this. The anxiety will soon pass as you see the progress of your treatment.

How can you tell if the depression is your primary problem? There are several clues. First, if you have a history of depression in your own life, as well as in the lives of any close family members, it is very likely that what you are experiencing now is a depression problem. Major depressions are "episodic." They return over and over again, unless you have sought out long-term treatment with maintenance medication that can help to prevent fresh episodes.

Also, the relative seriousness of the symptoms can determine whether depression is the dominant problem. It all depends on which overshadows the other. Are you constantly depressed but only occasionally anxious? Then it is more likely that the depression should be the main focus of treatment.

You Have Two Independent, Coexisting Problems

There is nothing to prevent a person with a serious panic disorder or other anxiety problem from also developing a major depression. The underlying mechanism for each of these is quite different, with different messengers and locations within the brain being affected.

The dosage may have to be adjusted to a high enough level to treat whichever is dominant. In other words, if you only had an anxiety problem, you would require a lower dose of the antidepressant. With concurrent depression, the dose may have to be raised to ensure that it is adequate to treat the depression as well.

Initially, your treating clinician should determine whether the anxiety in your depression is just a symptom of depression or the result of other factors, including other substance abuse disorders, underlying medical illnesses, medication side effects, or environmental stresses.

THE INTERACTION EFFECTS OF CERTAIN MEDICATIONS

During pharmacotherapy for depression, anxiety may be a common side effect of the shorter half-life selective serotonin reuptake inhibitors (SSRIs). Also, if you abruptly discontinue most antidepressants, you can cause withdrawal symptoms, which involve anxiety. Thus, patients who miss even one or two doses of some antidepressants may experience "rebound anxiety" within twenty-four hours. Withdrawal after discontinuation appears less commonly with Serene, Prozac, and Wellbutrin. So check with your doctor before you stop *any* medication.

The treatment of mixed anxiety and depression, where both are very prominent, requires using multiple medications that must often be tailored to individual patients. As a result, there may be more side effects than seen with a single medication. This should not put anyone off with a combined problem like this since combined drug regimens are at times more effective.

Antidepressant agents, in general, afford the best efficacy for depression with anxiety and represent a first-line treatment. The caution is, as always, to "start low and go slow" with medications that may be especially activating, such as SSRIs. Medications with little or no anxiety-producing properties are often best suited for many anxious and depressed patients. SSRIs, for example, are effective for depression as well as obsessive-compulsive disorder, panic anxiety disorder, and social phobia, but they may be activating and lead to withdrawal phenomena if abruptly discontinued.

Tricyclic antidepressants, like SSRIs, are effective for depression with anxiety as well as for specific anxiety syndromes (e.g., imipramine for panic attacks), but they can be activating and carry lethal risks in overdose. Monoamine oxidase inhibitors (MAOIs) are often underutilized yet may be highly effective for treatment-resistant cases. Your doctor will be able to give you up-to-date information on the current strategies for treating coexisting depression and anxiety.

Undiagnosed and untreated anxiety can severely aggravate the course of depression for a majority of patients. Accurate recognition of anxiety and its causes remains a critical first step for the successful treatment of many complicated depressive episodes.

I cannot stress strongly enough how important it is for you to get help promptly and to stick with it. Early intervention, drawing on a wide range of therapeutic options, is essential for the effective treatment of depression with anxiety. The careful selection of single or combination therapies with the fewest side effects is the key element in maximizing treatment response and recovery.

CHAPTER 13

FIGHTING YOUR FEARS

❦

I sought the LORD, and he heard me,
and delivered me from all my fears.

PSALM 34:4

Given the right circumstances, every one of us could develop unreasonable fears and phobias. We are all able to become phobic over one thing or another. The cause of phobias are not in the genes, but in your life experiences. There is no proven drug treatment for specific phobias, but certain medications may help reduce symptoms of anxiety before you face a phobic situation.

This means, therefore, that there are also no medications that can cure phobias. You have to take control of your fears and deal with them yourself.

Take Sally, for instance. She is an extremely competent business executive who grew up in a healthy, functional family. Her parents were Christians—loving, caring, and not possessive. Even Sally admits that her childhood was generally free of any trauma or bad experiences. Yet she has claustrophobia. She is afraid of being in small spaces like elevators and closets. She is not afraid of heights, flying, snakes, muggers, or even dying. But put her in a small room and close the door, and she begins to panic. She is overcome with the most intense anxiety and fear—and it's difficult for her to separate the one from the other.

At first, sitting in my office was a bit of a problem for Sally. It's not a small office, but then it's not a big one either. The real problem was closing the door because, obviously, we didn't want everyone down the corridor to know what we were talking about. The very first session, I left the door a little ajar, and we talked softly so our voices wouldn't carry. The next session, we closed the door for a few minutes every ten minutes or so, and by the third session, she was comfortable with the door closed.

This illustrates perhaps the most important point I want to make about fears and phobias: *They must be confronted,* but not in a way that reinforces them. It is possible to overcome almost every phobia. It just takes time and effort. Real-life exposure to whatever situation you might fear is the most effective way to overcome that fear.

How did Sally's phobia develop? As best we could determine, her claustrophobia was the result of a single incident in kindergarten when she locked herself in a toilet and couldn't unlock the door. She panicked, started screaming, and finally fainted before they could get a handyman to take the door off by undoing the hinges. If she had gotten some help right away, the damage could have been minimized. But the whole incident was hushed up, and Sally, thereafter, would never close a toilet door again. You can imagine what problems this posed for her as a young child.

Interestingly, you don't have to know the origin of a phobia in order to cure it. I have long since given up wasting time on exploring early possible causes. At best, you can only come up with plausible explanations. Treatment can continue without knowing the cause anyway.

HOW PEOPLE EXPERIENCE PHOBIAS

Many people experience specific phobias—intense, irrational fears of certain things or situations—such as dogs, closed-in places, heights, escalators, tunnels, highway driving, water, flying, and injuries involving blood. Phobias aren't just extreme fear; they are irrational fear. You may be able to ski the world's tallest mountains with ease but panic going above the tenth floor of an office building. Adults with phobias realize their fears are irrational, but often facing, or even thinking about facing, the feared object or situation brings on a panic attack or severe anxiety.

Specific phobias strike more than one in ten people. No one knows just what causes them, though they seem to run in families and are a little more prevalent in women. Phobias usually first appear in adolescence or adulthood. They start suddenly and tend to be more persistent than childhood phobias; only about 20 percent of adult phobias vanish on their own. When children have specific phobias—for example, a fear of animals—those fears usually disappear over time, although they may continue into adulthood.

No one knows why phobias hang on in some people and disappear in others. If the object of the fear is easy to avoid, people with phobias may not feel the need to seek treatment. Sometimes, though, they may make important career or personal decisions to avoid a phobic situation.

FEARS VERSUS PHOBIAS

While all phobias have their origin in fears gone wrong, the ability to feel fear is designed into us from the start. You are capable of becoming afraid; therefore, fear is perfectly normal, even necessary. Phobias, however, are needless. I don't know any expert who would argue that some phobias are healthy and necessary. The main difference between the common fear and the less common simple phobia is one of degree. The common fear can be faced, though with discomfort, but causes little or no interference with everyday life.

By contrast, a phobia is defined at least in part by the disability associated with it. Thus a fear of heights might cause dizziness and anxiety, but you still are able to take a trip up to the top of the Empire State Building. When you look over the edge of the balcony you will be startled, and your *fear* would drive you back. A height *phobic,* however, would avoid at almost any cost going into a tall building or would never venture higher than the first few floors.

A fear causes little interference with the ordinary course of life, but a phobia causes considerable interference. If you were phobic, you would go to great pains to avoid the feared object, even to the point of depriving yourself from some basic life pleasures.

Most important of all, a phobia is more than avoidance of a feared situation. The perception of the feared event sets off a chain of physiological and behavioral sequences that have significant effects. You stand frozen like a statue, motionless and breathless, or you crouch down instinctively as if to escape. Your heart beats so quickly and violently that it feels like the palpitations will knock your heart out of your chest. A phobic attack is the ultimate fight-or-flight response.

CAUSES OF PHOBIAS

Phobias, like Sally's claustrophobia, are attributed to two causes: *trauma* and *conditioning*. They can be created by a very frightening or traumatic experience that you are unable to resolve at the time, or they can be "conditioned" into you.

I knew a woman (not a client, but let's call her Nancy) who grew up in a home where there was a morbid fear of disease. From her earliest years, her mother, a one-time nurse, continually described all sorts of horrible diseases to Nancy and threatened that Nancy would catch these diseases if she wasn't careful. From her earliest years, Nancy was told to wash her hands, always wipe things clean before touching them, pay attention to her pains, avoid friends who were sick, and preferably always stay at home. Constantly, she was reminded that germs were everywhere and that death-threatening illness was just around the corner. At the slightest hint of a fever, imagined or real, she was rushed to the doctor.

As you can imagine, Nancy became morbidly fearful of disease. The slightest cold caused her to think she had a deep-seated cancer. But it went further. She became phobic of doctors and hospitals. Nancy feared illness and everything associated with it. Illness meant certain death. But in her irrational thinking, she could avoid illness if she *didn't* go to the doctor. To Nancy, it was *discovering* that she had a serious illness that had to be avoided. Just going to the doctor or having a medical test done would send her into the most intense panic reaction.

So some phobias don't need a specific bad experience like a severe illness to create them. They can be learned by repeated exposure to distortions and lies. The good news is that they can also be unlearned.

CORE FEARS

Behind all phobias is a set of core fears. Unless we are afraid from the beginning, we can never really develop a phobia. If, for example, you are claustrophobic, you have a fear that you might suffocate or be imprisoned in an enclosed area.

While knowing what your actual fear is won't take away the phobia, it can go a long way toward motivating you to work at resolving it.

Knowing, for instance, that the reason you have a flying phobia is because you risk dying in a plane crash doesn't cure your phobia. A phobia is much more irrational because it doesn't respond and go away logically. It is based much more on a set of feelings than beliefs.

COMMON FEARS AND PHOBIAS
(and their technical names)

Heights	Acrophobia
Open spaces	Agoraphobia
Cats	Ailurophobia
Thunder	Asterophobia
Lightning	Ceraunophobia
Enclosed spaces	Claustrophobia
Dogs	Cynophobia
Horses	Equinophobia
Dirt and germs	Mysophobia
Darkness	Nyctophobia
Snakes	Ophidiophobia
Running water	Potamophobia
Fire	Pyrophobia
Animals	Zoophobia

KINDS OF PHOBIAS

There are many kinds of phobias or fears. You can be afraid of certain things, places, or situations, such as specific animals, flying in a plane, or getting an injection. These are known as *simple phobias*. You may have a fear of being in a social situation, such as a party or a meeting. This is a *social phobia*. Regardless of the type, a phobia is always an irrational fear.

Phobias can start at any time in life and are rather persistent. Some fears that occur in childhood, such as a fear of the dark, are often developmental and dissipate with age. However, those that begin in later years rarely disappear without professional help.

Most phobias arise from the following basic fears:

THE FEAR OF DEATH OR SEVERE PAIN. The instinct to live is so strong that any threat of dying is overpoweringly frightening. The prospect of suffering from severe pain is intolerable for all of us, especially if we have seen loved ones go through terrible pain and suffering.

THE FEAR OF LOSING CONTROL. We all need to feel a sense of control over our lives and naturally resist surrendering that control to others. We need to feel in control of the present and the future, and we become extremely anxious when someone we don't trust gains the power to affect our future. Severe illness can also create a feeling of being out of control as can a sudden death of a loved one.

THE FEAR OF BEING RESTRAINED OR CONFINED. Both emotionally and physically, the fear of being trapped provokes an instinct to escape. This is as true for being trapped in a broken elevator as it is for being trapped in a bad life situation. For a brief period of my life, I felt trapped in a bad work situation and was quite alarmed by the feelings of panic that I felt.

THE FEAR OF BEING RIDICULED, EMBARRASSED, OR SHAMED. To be "unmasked" or to have the truth about our deepest self exposed to ridicule is a basic fear in all of us. We need acceptance not rejection, understanding not judgment because our personal value is determined or destroyed by it.

THE FEAR OF BEING ABANDONED. The human baby is about the most helpless of all living creatures. Starting in childhood, therefore, we have a need for security and are threatened by any prospect of abandonment. This fear can also create a special problem called "separation anxiety," which is not only seen in children going off to school for the first time, but also in adults who were abandoned by their parents in childhood and later become anxious when separated from their families.

THE FEAR OF SOMETHING STRANGE OR UNKNOWN. Humans don't handle change very well. Mostly we are creatures of habit and need routine and orderliness. (Try telling your teenager that.) The unfamiliar provokes anxiety. Young children go through a period of "stranger anxiety" because strangers are unpredictable. Change is also very stressful and places demands upon us that go beyond the routine. And the change doesn't have to be traumatic to be stressful. Even "good" life changes, such as taking a new job, getting married, or having a milestone birthday, can cause stress.

Experiencing any of these fears, therefore, can cause you to develop a phobia that is in some way connected to that fear. You can trace the roots of almost any phobia to one or more of these basic fears.

But how does a simple fear become transformed into a phobia? Mostly it happens in early childhood. But there is now some evidence that phobias can develop later in life when these fears are severe. Even an adult who is trapped in an elevator for a few hours can become phobic of elevators.

ORIGINS OF FEAR BEFORE CHILDHOOD

A fascinating and important issue to consider here is whether phobias and fears can be formed even at or before birth. In the past twenty years, considerable research has looked into the possibility that some fears are imprinted even earlier than childhood. The emerging field of perinatal psychology (the psychology of the unborn infant) is investigating the effect that traumatic birth has on the child's personality development. It has been found, for example, that fears of confinement later in life have been correlated with a difficult birth during which the newborn infant was particularly slow to pass through the birth canal. Or a fear of death may derive from the experience of having come close to death at the time of birth when the newborn had to be revived from unconsciousness by artificial or mouth-to-mouth resuscitation.

Evidence for fears from birth comes from the fact that some psychotherapy clients have been able to finally resolve some of their phobias when they were able to relive their original birth experiences under hypnosis.

I don't have any experience of such cases, so I cannot evaluate the validity of these claims. I have no doubt, however, that some form of phobic imprinting can take place at a very early age. I just don't trust so-called "recovered memories" that much. I'm a skeptic at heart because I've seen these so-called memories to be wrong more often than right. There is legitimate evidence, however, that the unborn fetus can be imprinted with fear prior to birth. That is all we really need to know to realize that one cannot always discover the cause of a phobia. A phobia sufferer needs to accept the presence of the phobia and not waste too much time on figuring out what caused it. Instead, he or she should work at removing it.

APPROACHES TO RECOVERY

How can you deal with your fears and phobias? Twenty-five years or more of research on psychotherapy has repeatedly and unequivocally demonstrated that approaches that "desensitize" the fear or phobia are the most effective.

One of the reasons I am skeptical about therapeutic approaches that are purely insight-oriented is that the best we can come up with when you explore early life experiences for the origins of phobias, or any other emotional problem, is a "plausible" explanation, which may not be the right explanation. Memory distorts over time, so it's not possible to get at the absolute truth. What you get is usually a distortion (at best) or a fabrication of your mind (at worst) of the supposed childhood experience that caused your phobia. I recall one patient who suffered from a fear of swimming and claimed that she had fallen into a pool of water as a child and was rescued by an aunt. She is adamant that she was the one who fell into the water because she can vividly recall the feelings of fear and the experience of swallowing the water as she went under. Yet the patient's mother explained to me that it was the patient's cousin who fell into the pool, not the patient.

Of course, it doesn't really matter who fell in. Just observing a near drowning can easily put the fear of life in you. But the problem is that we can never really actually discover the absolute truth about early events in our lives. As I've said, we have to settle for plausible explanations. Frankly, if the explanation is plausible to sufferers and helps to free them of their fears, it doesn't matter if it isn't the absolute truth. As a psychologist, I am prepared to settle for "plausible" explanations if they can be helpful. I never walk away from a therapeutic encounter believing that what we have uncovered is the real story. It just doesn't matter, so long as it brings freedom. The real truth may never be known.

SELF-HELP FOR YOUR PHOBIAS

While I strongly recommend that you seek professional help for a phobia, there is a lot you can do for yourself, especially if you only have a single, uncomplicated phobia. The danger in trying to treat yourself is that you may, in fact, end up reinforcing the phobia rather than curing it. So if the help I offer here doesn't bring immediate improvement, I recommend that you see a therapist experienced in the treatment of phobias. I say this for two reasons—not all therapists are trained to treat phobias, and not all therapists use the right approach for this rather specialized problem.

A fear of flying is a very common phobia that lends itself to self-help treatment. Listen to one sufferer's story about how problematic it can be:

> I'm scared to death of flying, and I never do it anymore. It's an awful feeling when that airplane door closes, and I feel trapped. My heart pounds, and I sweat bullets. If somebody starts talking to me, I get very stiff and preoccupied. When the airplane starts to ascend, it just reinforces that feeling that I can't get out. I picture myself losing control, freaking out, climbing the walls, but, of course, I never do. I'm not afraid of crashing or hitting turbulence. It's just that feeling of being trapped. . . . Whenever I've thought about changing jobs, I've had to think, *Would I be under pressure to fly?*

So, whether you do it for yourself or work with a psychotherapist, there are two steps to your cure. Even if you intend to see a professional therapist, the following explanation of the treatment process will help you familiarize yourself with what to expect. A psychotherapist must follow this sequence. The first step is called "imagery desensitization," and the second, "real-life desensitization." The only way you can overcome a phobia is simply to face it square-on. That may seem daunting, but it is the way you do it that makes it possible.

Desensitization is the process of *unlearning* the connection between your anxiety and the particular situation that is causing it. You break its power over you. One of the ways a phobia continues to have a hold over you is that you avoid doing what you fear. Part of this process is also learning to reassociate good feelings with the object or place you fear. You do this by associating feelings of calmness, tranquillity, and relaxation with the object.

IMAGERY DESENSITIZATION

You cannot break the power of the true phobia simply by forcing yourself to confront the phobic situation. If you can, it probably isn't a true phobia to begin with, but merely a bad fear. Any attempt to jump into the water, pick up a snake, lock yourself into a closed cupboard, or otherwise confront your phobia will almost certainly trigger the fight-or-flight response and reinforce your phobia. So you have to approach the phobia *very gradually,* so slowly that it doesn't even know you are creeping up on it. The slower you do it the better. And the best place to begin is *in your imagination.* Once your imagination no longer triggers a massive psychophysiological response to the phobia, you are halfway home to a full recovery. Naturally, you shouldn't try to deal with more than one phobia at a time. Conquering the first will go a long way in helping you with any others, so start on one that is not as threatening just to learn the technique.

You need to prepare yourself in two ways:

1. Learn to attain a deep state of relaxation. (Since I covered this in chapter 9, you know why it is so important. If necessary, order the relaxation tape listed in Appendix A.)

2. Set out a gradually increasing series of steps (called a "hierarchy") that will take you closer and closer to the thing you fear.

Developing an imaginary hierarchy for, say, a snake phobia is quite simple. All you have to do is imagine that the snake is in a heavy glass case a mile away. Your hierarchy begins by simply moving closer and closer, ever so slowly, to the case. The same is true for a phobia for flying. Place the airport a few miles away in your imagination; moving closer is the hierarchy.

Now imagine what would be the worst scenario. For the snake, the case would be right in front of you where you can touch it, or for flying it could be sitting in a seat on the plane. Now write out a series of steps that will move you from the one end of your hierarchy to the other. You need about ten or more steps. For a flying phobia, the following could be an example:

1. Imagining the airport two miles away and watching the planes take off and land.

2. Moving to one mile away and watching.

3. Standing just outside the airport and watching.

4. Walking into the terminal and watching.

5. Going up to the ticket counter and buying a ticket to a favorite place.

6. Walking to the departure gate and watching the activity.

7. Entering the plane and sitting down in a comfortable seat with the freedom to leave if you so choose.

8. Watching flight attendants close the doors but not departing.

9. Hearing the engines start but not departing.

10. Experiencing the thrill of takeoff.

11. Flying high.

12. Arriving at your destination.

The actual hierarchy should be tailored to your specific fear.

Now you are ready to carry out your own imagery desensitization. Just preparing the hierarchy may have made you anxious, so find a comfortable reclining chair or lie down on a bed. Do your deep muscle relaxation for ten or fifteen minutes, and when you feel completely relaxed, imagine the first step of your hierarchy. Try to visualize it, and keep imagining it until any anxiety you feel goes away. Say some calming affirmations if you have any anxiety. Reassure yourself that you are a safe distance away.

If the anxiety doesn't subside after a few minutes, stop imagining but continue relaxing until your anxiety is under control. Then restart the imagery while relaxing. You need to spend at least thirty minutes doing this, taking it very slowly.

Repeat this exercise for as many times as it takes for you to no longer feel *any* anxiety. Sooner or later, you will be able to complete the imagery without a single bout of anxiety. Then, and only then, continue to the next level of your hierarchy.

It may take some time, but finally you will have completed the complete hierarchy without any anxiety. True, this scenario is only in your imagination, but you will have begun to train your body to relax in the imagined presence of your phobic object. You are halfway home.

REAL-LIFE DESENSITIZATION

This is the more difficult step, so you may want to recruit a patient family member or close friend to assist you. The idea is to take your phobic hierarchy that you have stepped through in your imagination and try it out, in the same increments and *very slowly,* in real life.

The procedure is as follows:

1. Before you start, spend ten or fifteen minutes in deep relaxation. Whenever your anxiety goes up a bit, return to your relaxation exercise. This relaxation counters your fight-or-flight response.

2. With your supportive friend, take the first step in the hierarchy. For instance, in the flying phobia example, you will drive to within two miles of the airport and sit and watch planes going and coming for, say, thirty or forty minutes, relaxing. If your anxiety goes up, counter it with relaxing affirmations. Then go home. Never try to jump over the steps you trained yourself within your imagination. Repeat this first step until you have no anxious feelings.

3. Next time, if you are sure that there is no anxiety, go to the next step in your hierarchy. Stay here and repeat it until there is no anxiety even if it means several trips. Persistence is the name of the game.

4. Then move to the next step, all the way up your hierarchy, except that buying a ticket and actually flying may have to wait until you have a reason to fly. Time for a trip to Hawaii perhaps?

5. Go through each cycle as often as necessary. If one step creates a lot of anxiety, retreat to the previous one. Be patient with yourself; some days you may do better than others.

This approach to treating phobias is very effective. If you can't succeed on your own, then invoke the help of a professional therapist. You owe it to yourself, and to God, to get over your phobias.

WHAT TREATMENTS ARE AVAILABLE
FOR SOCIAL PHOBIAS?

Social phobias are in a class by themselves because they often have to do with personality factors rather than early life traumas. One sufferer described the difficulties created by social phobia: "I couldn't go on dates or to parties. For a while, I couldn't even go to class. My sophomore year of college I had to come home for a semester."

Another social phobic explained: "My fear would happen in any social situation. I would be anxious before I even left the house, and it would escalate as I got closer to class, a party, or whatever. I would feel sick to my stomach; it almost felt like I had the flu. My heart would pound, my palms would get sweaty, and I would get this feeling of being removed from myself and from everybody else."

As you can see, social phobias can be quite troubling and debilitating. People with a social phobia are aware that their feelings are irrational, but they still can't control this fear except by dint of sheer will power. Still, they experience a great deal of dread before facing the feared situation, and they may go out of their way to avoid it. Even if they manage to confront what they fear, they usually feel very anxious beforehand and are intensely uncomfortable throughout. Afterward, the unpleasant feelings may linger, as they worry about how they may have been judged or what others may have thought or observed about them.

About 80 percent of people who suffer from social phobia find relief from their symptoms when treated with cognitive-behavioral therapy, medication, or a combination of the two. Therapy may involve learning to view social events differently, being exposed to a seemingly threatening social situation in such a way that it becomes easier to face, and learning anxiety-reducing techniques, social skills, and relaxation techniques.

Some social phobias also respond to the desensitization technique I described in the previous section, but it is different in that it is much more controlled by irrational thinking than early trauma. It can be effectively treated with medications, including MAOIs, SSRIs, and high-potency benzos. People with a specific form of social phobia called "performance phobia" (like having to sing a solo or make a speech) have been helped by medications called beta blockers (Inderal) that help to dampen the adrenaline rush when they are trying to perform.

So there are some ways to help you take control and deal with phobias yourself. Let's look at more things now that you can do for yourself.

CHAPTER 14

SLEEP
AND TRANQUILLITY

———&———

I laid me down and slept; I awaked;
for the LORD sustained me.

PSALM 3:5

There is no greater God-given gift that can help us maintain a tranquil, nonanxious existence than sleep. Sleep is one of the most powerful healing mechanisms given to us, and the inability to sleep creates a high state of distress. Without adequate sleep, your brain and body become dysfunctional. Deprived of total sleep, you will become crazy and ultimately die. Fortunately, nature protects us here so that the more we are sleep-deprived, the greater is the chance that our brains will force sleep upon us. It is the in-between state of not getting enough sleep that is the problem.

But we are looking at a two-way street here. Disturbed sleep is both a *symptom* and a *cause*. It is a *symptom* of too much stress and anxiety and the *cause* of excessive stress and anxiety.

The "happy" brain messenger, serotonin, does many good things for us, including being the key player in helping us get to sleep. It must not only be in abundance, but it must be working properly and in the right places in order for you to sleep well. Serotonin is responsible for ensuring that your body's physiology is *set* for sleeping, and then it controls *how* that phenomenal mechanism called the "body clock" sets off drowsiness and starts you on your journey into slumberland. If serotonin does not do its job properly, you will not be able to get a restful sleep, no matter how hard you try.

INSOMNIA

One of the most dreaded words in the English language is the word *insomnia*. Just the mention of it is enough to cause some people to panic. It represents pain, confusion, frustration, and fear. Nothing is more debilitating than being unable to sleep.

How common is insomnia? About half of all adult Americans cannot fall asleep at night. Forty-nine percent of American adults suffer sleep-related problems such as insomnia, says a recent Gallup survey of more than a thousand adults. Many are reluctant to seek help. "The frantic pace of modern society is leaving more Americans awake when they shouldn't be," says Dr. Allan Pack, medical director of the National Sleep Foundation, which sponsored the Gallup survey. In addition to difficulty in falling asleep, about one-quarter to one-third of the population suffers with some degree of insomnia—difficulty staying asleep or waking too early. Half of these rate their problems as "serious."

In a society driven by high energy and expectations, little virtue is seen in insisting on a good night's rest. And for millions, healthful sleep is just a dream.

So sleep problems are pretty common. But what is the main cause for these sleep difficulties? Most sleep experts say it is stress and work problems. Causes for three out of four cases of insomnia can be pinned down. They include medical or psychiatric illnesses, the use of medications, environmental disturbances, biological rhythm disorders triggered by poor shift work schedules, and problems intrinsic to sleep, such as sleep apnea.

Insomnia that lasts more than six months seldom goes away by itself, and about one in six American adults suffers from chronic insomnia. Many experts believe that insomnia is undertreated in the doctor's office today, despite the fact that about eight out of ten people with chronic insomnia can benefit from a combination of drug-free treatments that aim to alter erroneous beliefs about sleep or provide instruction in healthy sleep habits. Sufferers may need to try a number of techniques to find the ones that work best for them.

WHY DO WE SLEEP?

The simple answer is because we are tired. But that is really too simple. We sleep because something needs to be restored. Sleep is essential for rejuvenating all our systems, physical and psychological. I would even add that sleep is important to our spiritual well-being.

Delving into the brain has given scientists the best insight into why we sleep and what happens during sleep. Shortly after the discovery that the brain produced electrical activity that could be recorded on the scalp, researchers discovered that sleep was composed of two types: REM, or rapid eye movement sleep (dream sleep), and non-REM sleep (non-dream sleep). Each caused a distinctive pattern of electrical activity in the brain. The area of the brain most clearly connected with sleep has been found to be the frontal area of the cerebral cortex. Just put your hand up to your forehead and you'll be grasping this area. This very busy part of your brain is responsible for speech, short-term memory, and flexible thinking.

Our bodies may relax during the day if we are not doing heavy manual labor but not our brains. They continue to work all the time. And the frontal area of the cerebral cortex is most in need of relaxation and rejuvenation at the end of a busy day. Sleep, therefore, is not only needed for physical rest and rejuvenation, but also for mental rest and rejuvenation. The problem, as we will see shortly, is that most of us don't do enough physical activity to balance the rest needed for the body against the rest needed for the brain.

IS SLEEP REALLY ALL THAT IMPORTANT?

Since so many people, including Christians, are convinced these days that we don't need all the sleep we are getting and that "sleeping your life away" is a form of "sloth" (a good old-fashioned English word meaning you are idle and lazy), they feel guilty if they get too much sleep. (It always fascinates me how easily we find things to feel guilty about.) So, how important is sleep? Believe me, it is a lot more important than 95 percent of the population thinks it is.

One line of research that emphasizes the importance of sleep is the study of sleep deprivation. You may find the following account helpful in convincing yourself of the importance of sleep.

Dr. Allan Rechtschaffen, from the Sleep Research Laboratory at the University of Chicago, studied sleep-deprived rats to see what happened to them physiologically. What he found is that when deprived of sleep for long enough, the rats died. And it didn't take that long; it only took between two and three weeks to kill the rats in this way. If the animals were deprived only of REM sleep, the stage of sleep in which we dream—and rats dream too, by the way—they died after seven weeks.

During these experiments, the physiological changes that the rats underwent were monitored, including body temperature. At the beginning of the experiment, their temperature went up as they tried to seek warmth. Later, even though their metabolic rate increased, their temperature started falling. However, their heart rate, muscle tone, and electrical brain activity remained virtually constant until the day before death. The exact cause of death remains a mystery. All we know is that if we don't sleep, we can't go on living.

Other studies of the effect of sleep deprivation on humans have shown that if you prevent dream sleep, in less than a week subjects develop schizophrenia-like symptoms. Since schizophrenia is linked to problems in the frontal lobe, there may well be a connection here. The frontal lobes are the ones most active through the day and in most need of rest during sleep. Dream sleep is what they need, so if you deprive them of dream sleep you could be mimicking the effects of what causes schizophrenia. Fortunately, the effect is temporary and passes away after a return to normal dream sleep.

THE EFFECTS OF INADEQUATE SLEEP

A lack of sleep affects all aspects of life, as several studies have shown. Underslept people are tired most of the time, sluggish in their thinking, and tend to be more irrational and irritable. A third of those with sleep problems admit to having fallen asleep while driving, while 4 percent have had an accident because of fatigue. And each year sleep disorders add almost sixteen billion dollars to national healthcare costs, contributing to problems such as anxiety and heart disease, say the experts. That does not include accidents and lost productivity at work.

About one-third of adults report they normally sleep less than six and a half hours on weeknights and make up for lost sleep on weekends. Alertness falls after even a single night of only six hours of sleep. After several nights with only five to six hours of sleep, people become significantly sleepy. Their reaction time, judgment, and creativity suffer, and they make more mistakes on a variety of performance tests.

This finding is worrisome because lack of sleep has been linked with a higher likelihood of errors on the job. Several major catastrophes, including the grounding of the Exxon *Valdez* and the explosion of the space shuttle *Challenger,* have been blamed, at least in part, on insufficient sleep in those involved. In a group of train drivers, 70 percent reported dozing off while driving the train. The National Transportation Safety Board found that fatigue was a factor in 57 percent of trucking fatalities.

Insufficient sleep affects every aspect of our life. Before you get on a bus, you may want to ask if the driver has had a good night's sleep. I certainly wouldn't want a surgeon operating on me or an airline pilot flying for me who hasn't had a good night in slumberland.

For my purposes here, though, the most important effect of insufficient sleep is its effect on the happy messengers, GABA, natural benzos, and serotonin. They are all impacted by insufficient sleep, and, when affected, cause us to feel more anxiety, which in turn makes it difficult for us to sleep. It is an incapacitating cycle that must be corrected if you are going to cure yourself of serious and debilitating anxiety.

Most people suffer quietly instead of getting the medical attention they need. They try home remedies that often do not work, such as reading to make themselves drowsy (attempted by 64 percent of those with sleeping problems), taking a warm bath before bed (47 percent), and relaxation techniques (41 percent).

WHY DON'T WE GET ENOUGH NATURAL SLEEP?

So why is getting enough sleep a problem? Why don't we all get enough restful and rejuvenating sleep every night? Why do so many have problems naturally getting to sleep? (By "natural" sleep, I mean not the artificial kind out of a bottle.)

The answer lies, once again, in our adrenaline—more specifically, in its close cousin, cortisol. As you will recall from earlier chapters, cortisol goes up whenever adrenaline goes up, and adrenaline goes up when stress goes up. Both are the body's chief stress-fighting hormones. When cortisol secretion is high, the body shifts to a war footing, helping us to fight stress whether it be running away from an attacker, fighting for our rights, coping with trauma, completing a deadline, or battling a severe illness. These events all elevate our stress-fighting hormones.

Our adrenaline and cortisol usually drop substantially in the evening, assuming, of course, that the danger or excitement is over. As you settle down, relax, and prepare to go to sleep, serotonin plays a key role. But since serotonin is usually the first happy messenger to fail under stress, the first sign that you are under too much stress is your inability to obtain an adequate and restful night of sleep.

So there you have it. Serotonin and sleep are connected. If you want to get to sleep as well as stay asleep, you need to be kind to your serotonin. Too much stress increases your cortisol and depletes serotonin, which, in turn, stops you from getting to sleep. It also interferes with how much sleep you get. But the story doesn't end there. Without proper sleep, you won't function well, and your coping skills will diminish. Result? You become even more stressed, which further increases your cortisol. A vicious cycle is established that repeats itself over and over again. This is the story of many people's lives today.

THE BODY CLOCK AND SLEEP CYCLES

In order to take control of your life and restore some sanity to your sleeping habits, you need to understand how your body regulates the sleep cycle. Ignorance of this simple mechanism causes many to abuse it.

Designed into our brains is a very accurate "clock." But it is more than just a clock. It also functions as the conductor of the brain's orchestra keeping all the players on time and in tune. Imagine that. The rhythm of the brain is controlled by one central clock.

The body clock, or more correctly "brain clock," is located deep within the center of the brain in what is known as the pineal gland. And guess what? It is a region of the brain that is a storehouse of the happy messenger serotonin. It has been called the "main spring" of the brain clock. At a certain time each day, serotonin is converted to melatonin. Yes, this is the same compound that is now being sold in many stores as a sleep inducer. Later it is converted back again to serotonin.

What is absolutely fascinating is that the complete cycle of serotonin to melatonin and back again to serotonin takes exactly twenty-five hours, *not* twenty-four hours. Researchers discovered this by placing subjects in a mine deep within the earth where daylight could not have any effect, and they found that the subjects followed a twenty-five-hour daily cycle.

What causes us to follow a twenty-four-hour cycle? Sunlight. Bright light resets the pineal gland every twenty-four hours with the rising of the sun. This way, our brain's clock is kept in time with nature's daily cycle of light and darkness. If the natural cycle were less than twenty-four hours, we would experience chaos. Each of us would be on our own brain clock's time and never get to sleep at the same time of the day. We would all have our own rhythms.

The twenty-four-hour cycle of the brain clock is extremely important. It adjusts your body chemistry for sleeping in the evening (with the onset of darkness) and in the morning for waking (with the onset of sunlight). This is why it is important to darken your home some time *before* you go to bed and to ensure a lot of light when you wake up. Since we don't sleep under the stars anymore and use artificial light for the nighttime, we have lost contact with the natural cycle of light and darkness. Good sleep hygiene, as we will see, requires that we enhance darkness before going to bed and get plenty of light when we arise.

One practical outworking of the need for a natural cycle of light and dark-ness is seen in a special form of depression called "seasonal affective disorder." This form of depression is found in northern countries where there are long periods of cloudiness or darkness. With insufficient light to reset the pineal gland, too much melatonin is produced or not converted back to serotonin. This means there is insufficient serotonin in the brain, which causes depres-sion. Remedy? Quite simple. "Light rooms" are set up in these climates that duplicate sunlight, and affected people spend a part of each day getting a high dose of the right sort of light.

But here my concern is the effect of stress and cortisol on destroying the natural sleep process. It never ceases to amaze me how little information has disseminated on the effects of stress on depriving us of adequate sleep and how this, in turn, makes for more anxiety. I can say with strong conviction that improving your sleep habits can go a long way toward enhancing your natural tranquilizers and interrupting cortisol's destruction of your happy messengers.

HOW MUCH SLEEP DO PEOPLE REALLY NEED?

Are most people sleep deprived? Or do most get enough sleep? I have developed a bit of a reputation around the country, and in several other parts of the world, for advocating more sleep for everyone. I did so more than sixteen years ago on a radio program with Dr. James Dobson, and that program has been rebroadcast many times to changing audiences. And I have never wavered from what I advocated back then. Furthermore, I practice what I preach and have benefited unbelievably from my own advice.

The debate over how much sleep we need has raged for a long time. To contrast how difficult it has been to settle this issue, let me cite two examples from recent sleep journals. Most adults report that they average about seven and a half hours of sleep per night. This is too little, according to Michael Bonnet of the Dayton Veterans Affairs Medical Center and Kettering Medical Center and Donna Arand of the Kettering Medical Center in Dayton, Ohio. But Yvonne Harrison and James Horne of Loughborough University in Leicestershire, England, assert that most people function adequately on seven and a half hours of sleep. Getting more sleep, they say, is like gorging on food or drinking to excess.

I don't care much for the analogy between eating and sleeping. Sleep is not like food: Your body will only sleep for as long as it needs, whereas you can eat way beyond what your body needs. But it is a problem when we cannot get all the experts to agree.

In a 1993 study conducted at the National Institute of Mental Health, people given the opportunity to sleep as long as they could averaged about eight and a half hours of sleep per night. This number is now cited as the amount of sleep most people need. The subjects in this study, who previously averaged a little more than seven hours of sleep a night, said that the extra sleep made them feel more energetic, happier, and less fatigued.

SLEEP AS AN ANTIDOTE FOR STRESS

As you have probably detected, I am trying to make a case for most of us to get more sleep. Sleep simply is the best antidote for stress and, therefore, for anxiety as well. Sleep enhances our natural brain tranquilizers and reverses the effects of the damage we do to ourselves through overstress.

As I mentioned, I have made a particular study of the value of sleep, especially as it relates to the problem of stress. In my very carefully considered opinion, sleep is probably God's most important provision for our rejuvenation from a stressful day. He has designed the need for sleep into our lives so that it happens daily, and perhaps this is because He knew that one day's worth of stress was about as much as we could handle.

The problem is, of course, that our Western culture has taught us not to respect sleep. *Sleep* is a dirty word. "We should all try to sleep as little as possible so that we can do as much as possible for God" is the message of many preachers. Many people feel guilty if they sleep too much, so they force themselves out of bed, violating their body's needs, in order to keep going and alleviate their guilt. This all works to their detriment.

To help you determine a reasonable formula for your own sleep hygiene, let me remind you of something I mentioned earlier in the chapter. There are two basic types of sleep: dream sleep and non-dream sleep. The function of non-dream sleep, that part of your sleep before you actually dream, is to provide physical rest and rejuvenation. This is the time when the muscles and those parts of the body that have been used physically get to heal themselves. If you do a lot of physical work, you probably need a lot of non-dream sleep.

For most of us in ministry or in academia, our work is mainly mental. And this is where dream sleep comes in. Its function is to *rejuvenate the mind*. During dream sleep, the brain consolidates memory, clears out unresolved issues, and helps us forget things that we don't need to remember. Without a lot of forgetting, the brain would run out of memory very soon, and we could be in some serious trouble. It is like the hard drive on your computer. Every now and again you have to do a "cleanup" of your drive as well as defragment it. That is what dream sleep does for your mind.

But there is a Catch-22 here. In order to get enough dream sleep to accommodate those of us who do mainly mental work, we have to earn the time for dreaming with a certain amount of non-dream sleep. The cycle goes something like this: We sleep in ninety-minute blocks and wake up at the end of the block. Most times we just fall asleep again.

Our dreaming only comes near the end of the ninety-minute cycle. So if we don't get enough physical activity to keep us sleeping, we are not going to get the right amount of dream sleep. This is why so many of us experience fuzzy-headedness and headaches when we don't get enough dream sleep.

One further point: One of the reasons why the length we sleep is important is that as the night progresses, we spend increasing amounts of time dreaming. So, during the first ninety-minute cycle we may only dream for, say, three minutes. The next cycle it goes up to six minutes, and so on. By the fifth or sixth cycle (seven and a half to nine hours), we are getting twenty minutes or more of dreaming time.

What this means is that the most amount of dreaming time is only available after about the fifth cycle. If you only sleep for six hours, you will be missing out on several major periods of dreaming and will not be getting enough dream sleep. So, it is not that you need that much sleep for physical rest, unless you do heavy manual labor, but for mental rest. And in our modern lifestyle, most of us need more mental rest than physical rest.

So what conclusions can we draw to guide us in setting up a healthy plan for sleep? First, dream sleep is just as important for our tranquillity as non-dream sleep. Second, in order to feel the need for more sleep we may need to increase our physical tiredness through exercise. Third, we may have to change our lifestyle in order to build in more time for sleep.

EXERCISE IMPROVES BOTH TYPES OF SLEEP

Since I will not be discussing the importance of exercise elsewhere, let me comment on its importance for improved sleep.

Physical activity, of which exercise is only one component, is essential to physical health. Everybody knows that these days. But exercise is also essential to emotional health. A sedentary lifestyle remains a risk factor for many health problems, including high blood pressure, elevated cholesterol, heart disease, obesity, and the like. But it is also important in improving sleep.[1] Studies show that 60 percent of Americans engage in little or no recreational physical activity, but 80 percent of the U.S. population is considered to be not adequately physically active.

What are the benefits of increased physical activity? It will improve your sleep. Causing some muscle fatigue helps to prolong your need for non-dream sleep. Exercise also stimulates endorphins (natural painkillers) and improves blood circulation, digestion, and elimination. We know it reduces depression and anxiety as well. Most importantly, it helps to metabolize excess adrenaline, the presence of which tends to keep you in a state of arousal and vigilance, making it difficult to go to sleep.

Contradicting the common idea that exercise has to be energetic is the more recent finding that exercise doesn't have to be vigorous to be beneficial. The greatest benefits of physical activity can be derived from moderately intense activities outside of formal exercise, like walking or biking. You should always first get a physical examination before starting *any* exercise program, no matter how light. *Also, if you suffer from panic attacks, don't start exercising until your treating clinician says you can. Some forms of panic attack are actually triggered by exercise.* A sign that you are getting better is that you begin to be able to tolerate physical activity.

One interesting test to see if your activity qualifies as adequate to count for exercise is that you should be able to carry on a conversation with some labored breathing, but exertion should never be so intense that you cannot talk. This means that you are exercising to at least 60 percent of your maximum heart rate.

Approach exercise gradually. Keep a record of how much you do so you can see your progress. After a month of exercise you tend to forget just how little you could do at the start. Don't become competitive or push yourself too fast. Keep your Type A personality characteristics out of the picture.

COMMON EXCUSES FOR NOT EXERCISING

A psychotherapist hears them all. You may want to check the list to see where yours is and try to challenge it.

- "When I come home from work, I feel too tired to exercise." Everyone feels this way at the end of a workday. However, most of this tiredness is a symptom of being underexercised. Force yourself to start exercising, and your tiredness will begin to go away after the first week. Soon you will actually look forward to exercising.

- "I really don't have the time to exercise." Of course not. We all fill our day with activities that are important. You have to rearrange your priorities and make time. Your problem is not time, but priority.

- "I don't enjoy exercising." You mean that when you first start exercising it is not pleasurable, and you are right. Your body, when lazy, resists physical activity and tells you that this is about the most miserable thing anyone could be doing to themselves. Don't listen to your body. It is confused. Enjoyment comes when you start to function better.

- "I'm too old to start exercising now." This excuse just has no merit whatsoever, sorry. Provided you've been cleared on your physical and you start slowly, everyone can start at any age. In fact, as you get older, exercise should become a greater priority because the quality of your life will depend on your level of fitness.

If you are not a physically active person, how can you naturally increase your level of physical activity without joining an expensive health club? Here are some suggestions:

- Park farther away from your workplace and force yourself to walk briskly to your office.

- Take the stairs instead of the elevator (if you don't live or work in a skyscraper).

- Walk to lunch instead of driving.

- If you are having a meeting with your boss or a subordinate, suggest you go for a walk. They will benefit as well as you.

- Take breaks through the day and walk briskly around the office.

- At the end of each day, take a long, brisk walk in a nearby park, and make sure you walk to it.

- Find activities that you usually pay someone else to do, and do them yourself (such as mowing the lawn, weeding the garden, washing the windows, cutting wood, etc.).

- If you are confined to a wheelchair, find similar physical outlets that will exercise whatever parts of your body you can.

- Participate in community events that foster physical activity (such as bird walks, heart walks, etc.).

If you are already quite active, you may want to graduate to more strenuous aerobic activity. However, avoid being too competitive. Too much competitiveness can undo all the benefits of a vigorous exercise program by creating more adrenaline than you can burn off.

The best time to exercise is late afternoon or early evening because it helps to burn off some of that surplus adrenaline that has accumulated all day. This is also a good time to do a "mental wash" when you review anxieties that are cluttering your thinking and dump those that are not important.

HOW CAN YOU IMPROVE YOUR SLEEPING HABITS?

The following suggestions for improving your sleeping habits may help you get over your sleep problem, whether it has only been around for a short time, or if you have had a lifetime of difficulty sleeping. If my suggestions here don't work for you, then I strongly suggest you consult with your doctor and be examined by a sleep-disorder specialist. Sleep disorders are now so common that clinics are available within a short distance of anywhere.

Here are some of the ways you can improve your sleep habits:

GO TO BED AND GET UP AT THE SAME TIME EVERY DAY, INCLUDING WEEKENDS. The body has a clock that is set by the arrival of daylight, but, more importantly, by the time we regularly go to bed. If you go to bed at a different time every night then don't be surprised if you don't have good sleeping habits. Your body gets too confused by the erratic times you go to bed.

TRY NOT TO DO ANY WORK THAT GETS YOUR ADRENALINE GOING AFTER A CERTAIN TIME IN THE EVENING. I find my limit is around eight o'clock. After that, I dare not touch a book or go to my computer because this will only get my adrenaline going again, and I will have a long time to wait before I can get to sleep. People who watch television late at night suffer from sleep problems mainly because this stimulates their adrenaline when the body should be allowed to lower its adrenaline in preparation for sleep.

AS EARLY IN THE EVENING AS POSSIBLE, REDUCE THE AMOUNT OF LIGHT IN YOUR HOME. Turn down the lights to provide a darkened environment. Darkness starts the production of the very important brain hormone melatonin. This hormone helps us with the onset of sleep. Too much light prevents your melatonin from kicking in.

AVOID ALL FORMS OF STIMULANTS IN THE EVENING. This not only includes caffeine-based drinks and foods, but also spicy foods or large amounts of food. A glass of water or a light snack may be helpful just before you go to bed.

DO NOT FORCE SLEEP ON YOURSELF. Falling asleep is as natural as falling off a log if you first learn to keep your adrenaline arousal low and establish regular sleeping habits. If you find yourself lying awake and not getting to sleep, then remember that non-dream sleep, which is what you experience when you are just relaxing or slightly dozing in bed, is still important in earning you the right to dream.

MAKE SURE THAT YOU HAVE A QUITE PLACE TO SLEEP. A noisy environment will disturb your sleep or keep you in a light state of sleep. If necessary, invest in earplugs (the soft plastic ones are the best because they mold to your ears).

MAKE SURE THAT YOU EXERCISE REGULARLY. As I explained earlier, you need a certain amount of non-dream sleep in order to earn your dream sleep. If you don't get any physical fatigue, then your body will not want as much non-dream sleep as you will need. The best time to exercise is the last thing in the evening before you go to bed. This helps to burn off surplus adrenaline.

LEARN A RELAXATION TECHNIQUE. I covered the topic of relaxation in chapter 9, so review that chapter for specific techniques. When combined with prayer or any other spiritual discipline, relaxation can help to improve the quality of your sleep.

UNTROUBLE YOUR MIND BEFORE YOU GO TO BED. If things are bothering you, get a notepad and write them down. You need to get everything out of your mind that might keep you awake during the night. The brain is merely doing its thing by keeping you alert to what you need to remember, so you can help it by writing it down into some sort of external memory.

IF YOU WAKE UP DURING THE NIGHT, DON'T GET UP UNLESS YOU ABSOLUTELY MUST. The moment you get up physically, your adrenaline starts to flow again and wakefulness will ensue. It's a good practice to learn how to stay in bed, do a relaxation exercise, and allow your body to go back to sleep naturally.

One last thought on the matter of sleep: I believe we need at least nine hours of sleep a night to rejuvenate our bodies and minds, but this doesn't mean you have to sleep all the nine hours at one time. You can break it up. If you have a bad night, you can catch up by sleeping in the afternoon the next day for the same amount of time that you lost the night before. Also, during weekends you can catch up on your deprived sleep. Wherever possible, however, try to get a full night's sleep each night.

WHAT ABOUT SLEEPING PILLS?

Pharmacologic therapy may be helpful if it is determined that periodic movements in sleep are contributing to insomnia and require treatment. Particular problems like sleep apnea (an obstruction that stops your breathing) and insomnia due to another medical condition need to be ruled out.

Sometimes insomnia is transient (a few days) and just related to grief or temporary stress. The use of a "hypnotic" medication for short-term use may be necessary. Long-term use (more than three weeks) is not a good idea unless your physician has reasons for it. Sometimes a sedating tricyclic antidepressant like Elavil is preferred for long-term treatment. "Restless legs" syndrome is sometimes treated with Klonopin, and periodic limb jerks or movements are treated with Restoril. If there is a lot of anxiety underlying the insomnia, then it can be treated with a tranquilizer until the sleep improves.

The biggest problem with using a sleeping aid is breaking your brain's dependence on it. The longer you use a sleeping aid, the more your brain depends on it and shuts down its own sleep-producing mechanisms. Invariably, then you have to go through a period of withdrawal in order to force your brain to come back on-line and help you get to sleep.

Other general measures, such as educating yourself on sleep hygiene, should always be used as adjuncts to the treatment of a specific cause of insomnia and tried when the cause is not clear or is unspecified. Sleep hygiene measures include regularization of bedtime (generally later rather than earlier); the use of the bedroom primarily for sleeping and sexual activity, not as an office; exercise; avoidance of alcohol and caffeine; reduced evening fluid intake; and, in the case of esophageal reflux (heartburn or pain in the esophagus when you lie down), elevation of the head of the bed.

Short-term, intermittent use of hypnotics and sedative tricyclics may be useful for temporary problems such as bereavement, dislocation, and situational anxiety. There are no studies that demonstrate their long-term effectiveness. Given the changes in drug metabolism associated with increasing age, all medication should be used with caution, especially those with long half-lives. Older people should avoid over-the-counter sleep medication due to their side effects and questionable effectiveness.

WHAT ABOUT MELATONIN AND OTHER "NATURAL" REMEDIES?

Melatonin is a widely publicized sleep aid that is selling briskly at health food stores, even though the hormone has not been proven scientifically safe nor effective. Experts at a recent National Institutes of Health conference described this medical situation as "scary." Many sleep experts feel that people are taking melatonin in a sort of uncontrolled experiment, and they are nervous about the possible long-term effects.

Health food advocates, of course, allege that the experts' negativity is born out of fear that melatonin might undermine a lot of "business" in the professional world. And while I am well aware of such professional "resistance" to new treatments, especially if they don't come through the normal drug company channels, their concerns are nevertheless valid here.

Most of the research on melatonin has been basic laboratory studies.

There have been no organized, definitive clinical studies yet to prove that melatonin supplements help people sleep or that the hormone pills are safe when taken over a long period of time. So if you use melatonin to help you sleep, you do so at your own risk. I know some physicians who swear by it, and some research has suggested that the elderly, for example, can benefit from it.

Because of the uncertainty of what it actually does, you should not experiment with melatonin without some supervision by your doctor. Even if research shows it can help people sleep, the safe dosage is still not known. More seriously, its manufacture (which can be anywhere in the world) is not regulated, and some stores often sell pills that can raise blood levels of melatonin ten times or more above normal, which could have serious side effects. There is no control over the purity of the product, so you have no idea what impurities or toxins might still be in the pill when it comes off the line. Some ruthless manufacturers are more interested in the buck than your well-being. So be careful where you buy it.

Also, high doses of melatonin can cause the body to secrete another hormone, prolactin, well known for depressing the sex drive in males. This effect has not been studied sufficiently yet, so be cautious.

I would like you to have pleasant dreams, not a nightmare of consequences from misguided enthusiasm for something that you think is acceptable just because it is called "natural." Always remember this: *Insomnia is a symptom.* You should always try to find the underlying causes, if only in your lifestyle. You cannot spend the rest of your life just treating that symptom.

Regarding other natural remedies, I need to comment on one in particular. A natural remedy from the South Pacific that has been used for centuries to induce relaxation and sleep is a herb called kava. This herb is now popular in this country for relieving insomnia and anxiety.

While it might be effective, a problem arises when you take kava with other medications. A recent *Dateline NBC* report described the experience of a man who took kava with Xanax and ended up in the hospital in a comatose condition. Fortunately, he recovered, but his case does flag the reality that just because a herb or natural substance is "natural" doesn't mean you can take it with anything. Some natural remedies are, in fact, powerful drugs and should be treated with the same caution as all drugs.

The rule is this: Never mix natural remedies with prescription drugs without checking with your doctor.

CHAPTER 15

ENHANCING YOUR HAPPY MESSENGERS

———— ⚬⚭⚬ ————

Happy is the man [or woman] that findeth wisdom,
and the man [or woman] that getteth understanding.

PROVERBS 3:13

The idea that you can actually enhance your "happy" messengers (as described in chapter 2) is not as ridiculous as it seems. Our minds are designed so that we actually have a degree of control over the production of those brain neurotransmitters that are classified as the happy messengers—serotonin and GABA. We can certainly do a lot to reduce the "sad" messengers, and just getting rid of a few can go a long way toward increasing our general feeling of well-being and tranquillity.

What are some of the key activities we can engage in that can enhance these happy messengers? There are, no doubt, many. In addition to the topics I have already covered, such as dealing with your thinking habits, rest and relaxation, and sleep and tranquillity, here I will discuss several more activities that will contribute substantially to increasing your happiness and tranquillity hormones.

INCREASING YOUR SENSE OF HUMOR
AND LAUGHTER

No one denies the value of humor or the benefit of a hearty bout of laughter. The reason is simple: Humor has a wonderful way of restoring our sanity, and laughter lowers our stress levels. But they do more than this. They actually reshape the chemistry in our brain. In a nutshell, they help to increase our happy messengers. Finding humor in a situation, and more specifically, laughing freely with others, can be a powerful antidote for stress, depression, anxiety, and about everything else. Our sense of humor and the laughter it generates can help us extract meaning from bad life experiences, joy from unhappy tragedies, and tranquillity from even the most tension-filled relationships.

RESEARCH BACKS UP THE VALUE OF HUMOR
AND LAUGHTER

First, what is humor? The word *humor* has many meanings. The root word is *umor,* from the Latin for "fluid." In the Middle Ages, humor was believed to be an energy related to a body fluid or an emotional state. This energy determined your health and disposition. So we say of someone in a bad mood that "he is in a bad humor."

Today we define *humor* as "the quality of being laughable or comical." But the idea of it being fluid is still there. Humor "flows" through our personality and emotions, as well as through our body.

What is laughter? We don't know a lot about it. We don't know what part of the brain controls it or quite what gives rise to the explosive sounds of the voice nor the characteristic movements of the facial features and body. Animals can't laugh like we do. But babies can do it almost from the start and in every culture on earth. We intuitively know that laughter is beneficial psychologically. When we laugh, we feel better, our troubles seem to diminish, our depression lifts, our anxiety vanishes, and a feeling of general well-being comes over us. Happy people also happen to laugh a lot too.

But, biologically speaking, laughter must be very important, or why would we do it? Nothing in the body that is natural causes us harm, so laughter must be beneficial.

What research is there that humor actually brings healing to our body and minds? Quite a bit. There is an Association for Therapeutic Humor, so psychotherapists think it is important, and an institute as well as a journal for *Humor and Health,* so scientists also think it is important. Perhaps at the forefront of this thrust was Norman Cousins, a man who spent the last twelve years of his life at the University of California Medical School exploring the scientific proof of his belief that laughter is healing. He established the Humor Research Task Force, which coordinated worldwide clinical research on humor.

But long before any of us lived, Scripture recorded that "A merry heart doeth good like a medicine" (Prov. 17:22). The word *merry* here means "cheerful," but I believe it also implies a lot of laughter. I can't imagine a merry person who does not occasionally let out a loud chuckle.

THE PHYSIOLOGICAL AND PSYCHOLOGICAL BENEFITS OF LAUGHTER

Just as there are psychological dynamics associated with humor, mirth, and laughter, there are physiological changes as well. Even mere giggling or chuckling will cause an increase in certain bodily activities. We now have laboratory evidence that demonstrates that most of the major physiologic systems of the body are stimulated or activated during mirthful laughter. Laughter is clearly a total body experience—the whole body participates in the experience of mirth.

The laboratory evidence collected to support the involvement of most physiological systems has shown that laughter has an impact on the skeletal muscular system, the central nervous system, the respiratory system, the cardiovascular system, the immune system, and the endocrine system.[1] We have scientific laboratory evidence that *all* of these systems are responsive and active during the response of laughter. Biochemically, humor has been shown to increase immunoglobulin A and decrease stress hormones. It has also been shown to increase our tolerance to pain.

Cognitively, humor helps break rigid thinking, resulting in our ability to perceive the world more "realistically" and without distortions. Our emotional state is greatly influenced by our perception of the events around us. A stressor is not inherently stressful. The intensity of stress we experience is directly related to the way in which we perceive the stressor. As Shakespeare stated, "Nothing is good or bad. It is thinking that makes it so."

Humor also changes our behavior. We know that humor changes how we feel, and how we behave is linked to how we feel. When we feel good, we reach out and connect with others. We are more open to trying new things, taking risks, and being open to possibilities. When we feel bad, we tend to withdraw and close off relationships and opportunities. When experiencing humor, we feel good; therefore, we behave differently. People who are depressed tend to become lethargic and do very little, while happier people are energized and connect with others.

We also know that laughter is a general body exerciser. It appears that people can get much-needed physical exercise through laughter, especially if they are not ambulatory. In working with handicapped people who are bedridden or confined to a wheelchair and who do not have much opportunity to get a great deal of formal exercise, laughter has proven to be very helpful.

HUMOR PROVIDES MANY PSYCHOLOGICAL AND SPIRITUAL BENEFITS

One of the ways laughter and humor (and they go together for me) are beneficial in building up our happy messengers is that they restore our perspective whenever it has shifted off-base. Ashleigh Brilliant (known for his one-liners often found on postcards) says, "Distance doesn't really make you any smaller, but it does make you part of a bigger picture."

Laughter also provides energy and gets us going when we are lethargic. Do you notice how often good preachers and lecturers use jokes, stories, and anecdotes? They use humor for a reason. Humor gets our attention, yes; but more than that, it energizes us. An office bulletin board loaded with cartoons, one-liners, jokes, and pictures perks up employees and invites them to be alert, no doubt increasing productivity as the newly energized employees return to their tasks.

LAUGHTER AND GOD

On a much deeper level, laughter not only teaches us something about ourselves, but it also teaches us about God.

I must confess that I have an intense interest in all things Jewish. Part of my interest comes from growing up with many Jewish friends, but mainly it is because I value so much the Old Testament heritage of my Christian faith. I'm fascinated with the Talmud, Jewish feasts, and Jewish customs. I particularly enjoy Jewish comedians and ponder why so many comedians are Jewish. And this is not just a modern phenomenon. It goes back centuries. The Talmud tells that a famous lecturer named Rav always started with a joke.

In the Jewish calendar, the official day for laughter is the feast of Purim. Everyone dresses up in funny costumes and acts silly. I love it. What is fascinating is that although Purim is a feast of laughter, it is really all about an impending annihilation of the Jewish people. Of course, it's because the threat was turned upside down. Haman was hanged and the Jewish people were rescued. (You can read all about it in the Book of Esther.) And the Jews set up a two-day feast so that their rescue would never be forgotten (see Esther 9:28).

But why a feast of laughter? Rabbis teach that it is because when you think you are in danger and then find you are safe, you naturally respond with an outburst of joy and laughter. Further, when you think you are alone and abandoned in a hostile world and suddenly discover that God is there, you burst out loud in joy.

So Jews believe that laughter is an opportunity to transcend the limitations that blind us to seeing God more clearly.[2] Or, to put my slant on it, if you really believe that God is in control of your life, then why don't you laugh at your stress and dangers a little more? I don't mean you should deny the dangers in your life; instead, you should merely confront them with a laughing spirit. Laughter can snap you out of your fight-or-flight response, overcome your melancholic self-pity, and provide the momentum you need to grab your problems by the throat and dispose of them.

GET MORE LAUGHTER INTO YOUR LIFE

What does laughter have to do with anxiety? There are important implications here for the curing of anxiety problems. Anxiety and laughter cannot coexist in the same body. The one will displace the other. Yes, laughter is an important way to build a greater level of joy into your life, but my focus here is specifically on the benefits of laughter and humor for restoring those depleted brain neurotransmitters that have been ravished by stress. Our happy messengers return more quickly when we send the signal to our body that the emergency is over or has been exaggerated. And the evidence is overwhelming that the simple act of seeing something funny and laughing about it can boost our recovery from many disturbances.

I don't mean to imply that this process is all mechanical. Obviously, deeper issues need to be addressed also. If your *Titanic* is sinking, standing on deck singing happy songs isn't going to boost your brain's happy messengers. You better find a lifeboat and listen to your fight-or-flight messages as well. But most of the life circumstances that we confront are not exactly of *Titanic* proportions. They are everyday, minor hassles and need a good laugh in their face to get them off your back. Try it. It really works.

LEARNING TO LAUGH MORE

How can you increase your laughter quotient? The key is to find reasons to laugh. One way you can do this is to crank up your ability to see humor in ordinary things.

A word of caution first. Sometimes humor can be abused. Here are some examples of how it can be abused:

- Ridiculing others. Laugh with others, never at or about them.

- Excessive laughter. Laughter is fun when it gives itself a break. Silliness is a sign of immaturity.

- Sarcasm or cynicism. Certain types of humor reveal deep-seated emotional problems, as do dirty or ethnic jokes.

- Off-limit humor. Some subjects are serious and off-limits to humor. If you don't know what they are, then you have an even greater problem: You are an insensitive person and out of touch with today's realities. You need to get some help.

How can you increase your funniness factor? Here are some ways:

READ FUNNY BOOKS. Make it a habit to always have a humorous book handy to relieve your stress. I don't mean just joke books. They have their limits because you have the urge to constantly tell funny stories, and that isn't what I'm talking about here. (I avoid people like the plague who are always telling jokes, don't you?) I mean, read humorists . . . like Andy Rooney and the late Erma Bombeck. You don't have to agree with them, just enjoy them. There are also many humorous Christian authors who are worthy of your funny bone. Check them out and do your body and mind a good service.

WATCH FUNNY MOVIES. You'll probably have to turn back the clock a bit to Laurel and Hardy, but whatever tickles your funny bone is okay. There are many "clean," but funny movies available in your local video rental store. Make a habit of watching them regularly. I particularly enjoy British humor, so *Fawlty Towers, Yes, Prime Minister, Mr. Bean*, and a host of others are my favorites.

READ THE NEWSPAPER COMIC SECTION. See if you can make the comic strips funnier. I regularly treat them as a challenge to see if I can modify them a little to be really hilarious. It's my equivalent of doing the crossword puzzle. Nothing humorous there, unfortunately. Cranking up the humor on something funny can be a real laughter stimulator. Not only does it develop your humor IQ, but also you laugh best at your own jokes.

AT THE END OF EACH DAY, REVIEW ANY EMBARRASSING INCIDENTS YOU MAY HAVE EXPERIENCED AND SEE IF YOU CAN TURN THEM INTO HUMOROUS EXPERIENCES. Let's say you got a traffic ticket. How would Mr. Bean handle it? He would probably think he was getting a cash refund for good driving and try to cash the citation at the local bank. Or imagine that as the officer walks away he finds another officer giving him a ticket for parking behind you in a "Handicapped Only" parking space. Even policemen aren't exempt from the law. This helps to transform an unpleasant memory into a happier one.

IN A SERIOUS CONVERSATION YOU MAY BE HAVING, SAY, WITH YOUR WIFE ABOUT THE GARDEN, STOP FOR A MOMENT AND SEE IF YOU CAN FIND A HUMOROUS POINT, WITHOUT OFFENDING HER, OF COURSE. "I'm sure I saw that ant there in the *Antz* movie. Look, he walks just like Woody Allen." Not so funny? Then try to do better. What is important is that you *try* to find something humorous in even the most serious of life matters.

OCCASIONALLY, BUT NOT TOO OFTEN, PLAY THE FOOL. Do something really silly. Dress up in a funny way (such as putting your shirt or pants, skirt, or dress on backward) and surprise your family at dinner. Suggest that you all sit on the floor and eat your dinner, or play "drop the handkerchief" or some other child's game while eating. Just "funny up" little things and create a humorous atmosphere. It can do wonders for family relationships, but more importantly, it will destroy your reserved, uptight, tense, or nervous reputation. It will free you to laugh and relax more.

In summary, what are the reasons you should try to laugh more? Humor and laughter will increase your happy messengers, strengthen your immune system, exercise your cardiovascular system, lower your adrenaline, increase your joy, make people like you more, replenish your creative juices, help you to think more clearly, make you wiser, rebalance the chemistry of your body, lower your blood pressure, reduce your risk for heart disease, release your emotional pain, lower your susceptibility to panic attacks, give you a clearer perspective on life, put a devilish twinkle in your eye, and draw you closer to God.

And it will do it all for no cost. What a deal.

MAINTAINING A POSITIVE LIFE OUTLOOK

On a recent *Loretta LaRoche* comedy show, LaRoche presented her message on how to beat stress with a rubber chicken by doing her entire show with glasses (those plastic ones with the fake nose, moustache, and eyebrows), a Viking helmet, and a costume cape with "TA-DAH" emblazoned on the back. (It stood for "The Association of Delightfully Alive Humans.")

Under all this, of course, lies the same serious message I am sending to you. In this episode, LaRoche recounted the following story (my paraphrase):

> Everyone's always complaining about being so tired and so busy it would be a good idea to sell a "martyr kit." It's made up of two pieces of Velcro and it works as follows: You attach one piece to your forehead and the other to the back of your hand. And when you're feeling overly stressed, smack the back of your hand to your forehead and take up a kind of "woe is me" pose so everyone will know you're suffering. Actually, you can maintain this pose for quite a long time because your arm won't even get tired—the Velcro will hold it up all by itself.

There are times in my life when I feel like buying one of those martyr kits, not just because I'm feeling sorry for myself, but because maintaining a positive outlook on life is hard work.

I mean, really hard work. Take this morning, for instance. I sat down to write this section on the importance of "Maintaining a Positive Life Outlook." I thought I would access the Internet and see what others are saying about this subject at the present time. I loaded my favorite search engine and searched for "positive outlook." Promptly the search turned up quite a few entries. I tried to open the first one and got the message back that the site was closed. So, optimistically, I tried the second. Same message. Something about the site no longer being available. I tried the third and the fourth.

To cut a long story short, I tried every Web site listed by my search engine, and *not one of them would open.* Talk about disappointment. Not a single positive response from any site that had advice to give on maintaining a positive outlook. Where was *my* martyr kit?

So much has been written and said about the value of maintaining a positive outlook. A positive outlook is known to improve recovery from surgery and the immune system's ability to fight off disease as well as aid in cancer recovery, to reduce the fight-or-flight response and hence stress disease, and to ensure success in business or career. I think we intuitively know that the opposite, a negative outlook, kills off everything good in our minds and bodies. It even rains on our spiritual parade and makes us nasties.

Can changing from a negative outlook to a positive outlook actually help to restore our tranquillity and turn our unhappy, anxiety-producing hormones into happy ones? Without a doubt. The important question is: How can we set about reversing our outlook?

In my book *Habits of the Mind,* I discuss the value of a positive mind. In that book, I asked the question: What are the characteristics of a healthy mind? One of the characteristics of healthy people, I argued, is that they are able to accentuate the positive, even when the negative is overbearing. They are able to look into the face of disaster and find a ray of hope that gives them a little foothold on the face of a steep cliff. (Pardon the mixed metaphors.) With just that little foothold, they are able to climb back up to the top of the cliff from where they had lost their footing.

But a positive outlook is more than this. True, it is important that we see crises as challenges to be overcome if we are going to be successful either in work or in our marriage or other relationships. But this is *survival* mode. And important as it may be, another mode is equally important: I call it *tranquillity* mode.

What is the difference? In survival mode, we are using a positive outlook to solve problems, avoid helplessness, and be creative. But what happens when the crisis or challenge is over? Your postadrenaline depression robs you of your positivity, and you submerge yourself in a negative or self-defeating outlook.

What I am suggesting is that many of us, myself included, have a fantastic ability to deal with the major issues of our life. I often boast (in a good way I hope) that I can deal with any crisis, personal or professional. I come alive. My adrenaline serves me remarkably well. I become a creative problem-solver and see the whole crisis as a game to be won. I operated this way when I was an engineer, then as an academician, and also in my clinical work. Show me a client falling apart, needing emergency help, and I come alive. No negative, defeatist attitudes with me.

But then I crash. After each crisis is all over, my positive outlook seems to vanish into thin air, and, with it, my happy messengers.

So the challenge then, in addition to maintaining a positive outlook during challenging times, is to keep your optimism going when your adrenaline crashes. Why? Because it doesn't matter to your brain whether there is a good reason for your negativity or not. All that matters is that adrenaline isn't there at that moment. And the absence of adrenaline means that your brain must suppress its happy messengers in order to cope with the crisis.

It has been my observation, therefore, that generally optimistic people, like me, become negative whenever they are in a downhill run without a challenge to bring out their positive outlook. (If you assess yourself to be generally low on positivity, then *Habits of the Mind* will help you learn how to crawl first before tackling much of what we've been talking about in these pages.) If you lose your positivity during times of low challenge, then the following suggestions may be of help:

DON'T TRUST YOUR FEELINGS DURING YOUR POSTCRISIS TIMES. You *will* be depressed because that is what happens when your adrenal system crashes. Your brain is demanding an opportunity for rejuvenation and restoration, so it turns off your interest in outside activities and removes your energy. This way you won't rush off to do more damage to your overdrawn adrenal system.

TELL YOUR BRAIN THE TRUTH. If, at any point when you are down, you "believe" your negative feelings, you will be sending the wrong message to your brain. Cognitive psychologists call this "attribution" because what you believe about an experience tells your brain how to interpret it. For instance, if you drink a strong cup of coffee and half an hour later have an argument with someone, you will interpret your raised pulse rate and stimulating effects of the caffeine as being the result of your anger. Just believing this, as opposed to accepting that the rapid heartbeat is just the coffee, can make a huge difference in how your brain reacts. Always tell your brain the truth.

SAY A POSITIVE SLOGAN OR MOTIVATING MOTTO TO YOURSELF OVER AND OVER AGAIN. When you are in a funk, your mind isn't working properly. Everything looks negative, and you can't think clearly. The best way to counteract this is by persistently challenging your negative thoughts by replacing them with positive ones, preferably slogans or motivating mottoes, that you can throw at your unresponsive mind to direct attention away from your self-defeating thoughts.

My friend and former student, Rick Warren, currently pastors the large Saddleback Community Church in Orange County, California. I have always admired Rick's approach to ministry and have the privilege of preaching for him occasionally. He has developed a "purpose-driven" approach to ministry, and one of the ways he communicates his message is through slogans, maxims, mottoes, and pithy phrases. Rick believes that many key events in history have hinged on a slogan, such as "Remember the Alamo" or "Give me liberty or give me death." In his best-selling book *The Purpose Driven Church,* Rick writes, "Simple slogans like this, repeatedly shared with conviction, can motivate people to do things they wouldn't normally ever do—even give up their lives on a battlefield."[3] He regularly develops slogans to reinforce his message. "We're saved to serve," "Every member is a minister," and "Win the lost at any cost" are just a few examples.

What has that got to do with building resistance to negativity when our adrenal glands are exhausted? A lot. At times like these, we need a dozen strong slogans or maxims to keep us from sinking into despair or inactivity. If a slogan will encourage men to risk their lives in battle, then surely it can help get us out of a funk.

Where can you find suitable mottoes? You can borrow them from other settings and adapt them for yourself. Want to know some of mine and where I get them? "Troubles never last" (from a slave spiritual). "Slump? I ain't in no slump . . . I just ain't hitting" (from Yogi Berra). "Never stop, never weary, and never give in," "Who said it would be easy?", and "Sleep and gather strength for the morning" (all from speeches by Winston Churchill).

Here are a few more of my often-used maxims or slogans:

- "Just let it go. It's not the end of the world."
- "I don't have to like everyone, just love them."
- "Have the courage to accept my imperfections."
- "I don't have to win, just finish the race."
- "I have a right to make mistakes."
- "I can't expect forgiveness if I don't give it."
- "I can't expect respect if I don't give it."
- "Failures are to grow by."
- "Disappointments are always blessings in disguise."

Many good slogans are based in Scripture and can remind us of God's ever-loving presence when we are low. "Let go and let God." "Abide in God's spirit." "Release this negativity to God."

Keep a lookout for good slogans, mottoes, or maxims and write them in a small notebook so you won't forget them. Be creative and devise your own. The sheer pleasure of creativity will, itself, boost your happy messengers.

FINDING A PURPOSE FOR YOUR LIFE

In the previous section, I mentioned my friend Rick Warren and his "purpose-driven" ministry approach. He also has a unique way of understanding how people need to relate to God and the church. He believes, and I concur entirely, that what people want most these days is a sense of purpose for their lives. Most people have no sense of destiny. They don't know where they've come from, and they don't know where they are going. And I just don't mean secular people, but Christians as well.

Robert Louis Stevenson believed that "to be what we are and to become what we are capable of becoming is the only end of life." The greatest burden of our life, once we have resolved our sin problem by coming to Christ, is to find a real purpose for our existence. Many grow old and never feel any sense of personal fulfillment. They go through each day, week, month, and year, feeling that they have missed out on life. And anyone with such a feeling of "falling short" will inevitably be unhappy the rest of his or her life.

Many feel that their everyday humdrum existence could never provide them with a meaningful sense of existence. Not everyone can find an exciting or fulfilling career, so they must settle for second-best careers. They may not have the financial resources to accomplish what they want or lack the intellectual or other skills to achieve it. If they jump from job to job seeking more fulfillment, sooner or later they discover that *all* jobs eventually become routine and lose their luster.

Early in my life, I knew a wonderful Christian man who was a house painter. He hated his job. It was exhausting and didn't give him the pleasure that other house painters seemed to enjoy. His hobby was electronics, and he became extremely skilled at repairing radios. When he got an offer to be a repair technician, he jumped at it, believing that now he would have really exciting work to do. But in a matter of months, the hobby he enjoyed became the work he hated. He was confined to a repair bench with little freedom to move about. Those who think that if only they could change careers or jobs they would be happier are dead wrong. Work, by its very nature, will sooner or later become routine and less fulfilling, with few exceptions. And the exceptions come *not* from finding the "right" job, but from making the right sort of adjustments to the job you already have.

Rick Warren understands this. So in his ministry approach he tries to help people find a sense of purpose in their otherwise humdrum or demanding lives by discovering the gifts they can use in God's service.

What has this got to do with enhancing our happy messengers and warding off anxiety and depression? A lot. I am not talking about "fulfilling your potential" in your career, or even in your role as a parent, which is itself a very important job. I am assuming that you are already exploring all options and uncovering all the potential that resides in you. Henry Emerson Fosdick suggested that we should all have the daring to accept ourselves as a bundle of possibilities and undertake the game of making the most of our best. Most of us, if we are not careful, will end up in a restricted circle of our potential being. We will fail to have achieved our full potential. But what if you do achieve that potential? Does it guarantee that your happy messengers will abound? No, it doesn't. If anything, most people who achieve their full potential dream will be so stressed out and panic prone that they can't live to enjoy it.

Let me put it more bluntly. Fulfilling all the potential you have does not, of itself, guarantee a happy life. *It takes something else.* It takes the more difficult task of finding a real sense of purpose for your life, whether you achieve no more than a first-grade level of education or earn twenty Ph.D.'s in every discipline imaginable. Or, to put it in financial terms, you need a sense of purpose whether you just eke out an existence or spend your nights worrying about how you can avoid death taxes because your estate is so large that most of it could end up in government coffers and relieve the likes of me from a tax burden.

A sense of purpose, of destiny, is what life is all about. By all means, fix the "lesser" problem of fulfilling your potential. Don't sell yourself short in seeking to maximize your potential. Don't settle for a less-demanding job if you know you can do better. I didn't. I changed from engineering to psychology, not because I wasn't a good engineer. I was and could have lived a very successful life as an engineer. But some "higher" purpose was calling me. Yes, God, I believe, had a big hand in my call to change professions, ultimately bringing me to a seminary as a professor of psychology to help Christians, especially pastors, become healthier in their emotions and personhood. But even in doing what I am doing, I have to pay attention to the main point I am making here: Whatever your calling in life, make sure that you steep it in a sense of purpose.

This sense of purpose is particularly important because of the aging of America. Due to medical advances, most of us will live long enough to have a second life after our working life is over. Without a well-established sense of purpose outside of our work, retirement can be a daunting endeavor. Not everyone adjusts to it successfully. Their happy messengers go south for the winter and sometimes never return. Sadly, I have seen too many patients trying to adjust to the loss of status and purpose when their working life ends. Few have given careful thought to how they should prepare for it.

Finding a deep sense of purpose, not just achieving your full potential, does not lend itself to easy steps in a self-help book, especially for Christians. There are a few guidelines, however, that I can suggest as you seek to put this side of your life in order:

DON'T HESITATE TO FIND A GOOD COUNSELOR TO HELP YOU EXPLORE YOUR NEED FOR A SENSE OF PURPOSE. Sometimes you can't think yourself through these issues alone. You need a sensitive and empathic listening ear to share it with.

REMEMBER THAT GOD IS PARTICULARLY INTERESTED IN HELPING YOU DISCOVER YOUR PURPOSE. So make it a matter of concerted prayer.

DON'T NEGLECT THE "SMALLER" THINGS OF LIFE. While finding an outlet for Christian service is vitally important, don't overlook the small things that can bring great pleasure and satisfaction.

FOCUS ON THE NEEDS OF OTHERS. If there is one domain of life that I believe gives us a greater level of satisfaction than any other, it is being oriented to the needs of others, instead of putting too much focus on our own needs. I have never met a person who is genuinely focused on helping others who is unhappy or dissatisfied with life. Their happy messengers abound. They seem more tranquil and at peace with themselves.

I put this question to you: Which comes first, being happy or being focused on others? Are happy people merely more altruistic, or are they happy because they are focused on others? I can assure you with a high degree of confidence that they are happy *because* they are directing their attention away from themselves.

Let me end this chapter with two short stories that, hopefully, make my point. The first concerns a man and his wife we met shortly after my wife and I married and moved to the city of Pietermaritzburg in South Africa. He was nearing retirement and worked as a clerk in a public agency. But he and his wife had one remarkable ability—befriending and encouraging young people who were passing through the city either as university students or nurses in training. Every weekend they would open their small home to scores of young people, mostly (but not exclusively) Christian, and provide treats, games, and fellowship, the likes of which I have never seen since. Needless to say, we relished that comfort as a young married couple. They remained wonderful friends for many years and have now both passed on.

But what I remember most about the man, in particular, was his extremely positive outlook on life, his generous outward-looking stance, and his great joy at living despite his unassuming work life. He taught my wife and me the importance of looking outside of ourselves.

The second story concerns a woman who lost her sight and hearing when she was only nineteen months old. She became a wild, rebellious, uncontrollable youngster until a nearly blind teacher was attracted to the challenge of teaching her. She went on to study French and Greek, and she learned to type assignments on a Braille-keyed typewriter. She became excited about life and compassionate toward others, without even a hint of self-pity. Soon she was an activist for change, promoting peace and helping brighten the spirits of soldiers during the Second World War, despite the fact that she lived in a world of silence and darkness.

Never did she try to be like anyone else. Always, she was focused on others, and this focus gave her a sense of purpose for her life. And it is these two characteristics that make the story of Helen Keller's remarkable life, against such odds, so remarkable and inspiring. In God's strength, such a life is possible for all of us. All it takes is a willingness to be used by God in the way of His choosing.

CHAPTER 16

ANXIETY IN CHILDREN AND ADOLESCENTS

—⊸∞⊷—

But Jesus said, Suffer little children,
and forbid them not, to come unto me:
for of such is the kingdom of heaven.

MATTHEW 19:14

D o children experience anxiety? Very much so. If anything, the groundwork for anxiety problems is laid for most sufferers during their childhood years, with boogeymen behind curtains, monsters under the bed, and scary things in the dark. Parents know very well how children's fears can be extreme.

More children suffer from anxiety disorders than any other psychological problem. Sometimes their environment causes the anxiety. Sometimes a child simply has an anxious temperament. The topic of anxiety in children is a vast one and deserves its own book. But this book would not be complete without even a brief discussion of how anxiety affects children.

Childhood anxiety can take many forms. Because a child has not yet developed the verbal skills to explain his or her anxieties, he or she will use nonverbal behaviors. Excessive crying, nightmares, misbehavior, temper tantrums, and the like can all be screams for help arising from too much anxiety.

COMPULSIVE HAIR PULLING

Samuel is a good example of how anxiety can manifest itself in children. His Chinese parents came to the United States from Hong Kong to run a family restaurant business shortly after they married. The father's mother, a widow, came to live with them to help raise their kids. Some weeknights, one of the parents would also stay home with their son and his younger sister.

For the first six or seven years of Samuel's life, everything seemed to be going along fine despite his parents' long and awkward hours of managing a restaurant. But as he entered the fourth grade, something changed. Samuel started pulling out chunks of his hair. All over his head there were bald spots. It didn't take much effort because the hair was almost ready to fall out—a condition called trichotillomania (compulsive hair pulling). All it needed was a little rubbing and out it came. Samuel did more than just rub his head. He would grab at his hair until large patches of scalp showed through his beautiful black hair.

As we evaluated Samuel's condition (the parents were seeing a graduate student I was supervising), it became clear that his parents were pushing him to do better at his school than he was able. Partly they were trying to compensate for the guilt they felt at having to leave him at home so much, and partly because they were determined that their children must succeed in the U.S. Since they couldn't be there all the time to ensure Samuel was doing his work, they would scold and threaten him to do well whenever they got the opportunity.

Samuel had started compulsively pulling his hair as early as five years of age, but the parents thought nothing of it. Yet in children, tactile stimulation, such as feeling, rubbing, biting, or sucking on the hair, can be important components of anxiety that provide sensory stimulation which is self-quieting, like thumb sucking, rubbing a favorite blanket, or stroking a stuffed animal.

Trained to be compliant, Samuel never rebelled against his parents' pressure. He never spoke back, threw temper tantrums, or made excuses. The poor boy just pulled out his hair, little by little. Sitting there in the counseling room, Samuel was a pathetic sight.

As is often the case with a child suffering from extreme anxiety, the problem has more to do with the parents than the child. So we began the tedious process of reeducating Samuel's parents. They couldn't understand what was going on. Like so many parents, they only wanted the best for their child. They wanted to leave him there to be "fixed." Finally, we convinced them that this was a "system" problem, and they were an important part of the family system. They were the authority figures. They ran the roost. They couldn't do all the crowing and then ignore their role in the chicken's panic. They *had* to be part of the therapy. Reluctantly they agreed.

So what can parents do when they discover that their young child is pulling out his or her hair, biting his or her nails, clinging to a comfort object, or showing some other sign of high anxiety? Don't panic. Many parents can be quite sensitive about their children's behaviors.

Remember that, for some children, anxiety symptoms can be a brief and passing phase associated with self-exploration and self-quieting, and it will not develop into a problem. However, if the behavior persists beyond the preschool years, then some action may be necessary.

THE ANXIOUS CHILD

All children experience anxiety. Anxiety in children is expected and perfectly normal at certain developmental stages. For example, from approximately one year of age through the preschool years, healthy youngsters may show temporary periods of intense anxiety at times of separation from their parents or siblings. This is a necessary experience that helps them to gradually become less dependent on their parents and prepare them for school.

Through this period, young children may also have short-lived fears (such as fear of the dark, storms, animals, strangers, going to school, or making friends), as part of learning to adjust to necessary life changes. First-time experiences like thunder, lightning, or—as is our case in California—an earthquake create fear and feed anxiety. As the child realizes that the danger is past or not likely, the anxiety subsides.

These are all perfectly normal experiences of anxiety that help the child's development. However, when children experience anxieties that are severe enough to interfere with their daily activities, parents should consider seeking the evaluation and advice of a child or adolescent specialist. A sure sign that you may need to get help, or at least an evaluation to determine whether your child is overreacting, is whether the anxiety is interfering with your life. For instance, if your ability to work is being hampered or you cannot leave the house because your child kicks up a fuss, then your child's problem needs to be evaluated even though he or she isn't complaining. A child psychiatrist, psychologist, or family counselor can carry out the evaluation.

SEPARATION ANXIETY

A very common form of childhood anxiety is called "separation anxiety," for obvious reasons. I know all about this problem, having experienced a mild form of it earlier in my life. Its origin clearly is in early childhood experiences, in which a lot of anxiety was created around issues of abandonment or insecurity. It can follow you well into adulthood, when the focus of the separation moves away from parents to your new spouse or family.

It is normal for toddlers and preschool children to show a degree of anxiety over real or threatened separation from people to whom they are attached. But the seriousness of the anxiety is not discovered until a child starts preschool or a parent takes a job outside of the home. Some problems must be expected with every child. It is only a serious problem when fear over separation constitutes the focus of the anxiety and when such anxiety persists.

The key diagnostic feature of a true separation problem is a focused, excessive anxiety concerning separation from those individuals to whom the child is attached (usually parents or other family members). The anxiety may take the form of any of the following:

- an unrealistic, preoccupying worry about possible harm befalling major attachment figures or a fear that they will leave and not return
- an unrealistic, preoccupying worry that some untoward event, such as being lost, kidnapped, admitted to a hospital, or killed, will separate the child from a major attachment figure
- persistent reluctance or refusal to go to school because of fear about separation (rather than for other reasons such as fear about events at school)
- persistent reluctance or refusal to go to sleep without being near or next to a major attachment figure
- persistent, inappropriate fear of being alone or apart from the major attachment figure during the day
- repeated nightmares about separation

- repeated occurrence of physical symptoms (nausea, stomachache, headache, vomiting, etc.) on occasions that involve separation from a major attachment figure, such as leaving home to go to school

Some children are afraid to meet or talk to new people. Children with this difficulty may have few friends outside the family.

What can a parent do to help a child with separation anxiety? If the symptoms are persistent and severe, then you must get professional help. If you are in doubt, play it safe and at least get a consultation with a child psychotherapist or psychologist.

If the signs of separation anxiety are present but not severe, then the following may be helpful:

DO NOT GIVE IN TO YOUR CHILD'S DEMANDS TO BE WITH YOU ALL THE TIME. Reassure your child that all is okay, and help him or her settle down at school or whatever the place is. Invariably, once you leave the scene, the child settles down.

ENCOURAGE YOUR CHILD TO "BE BRAVE." Show that you value your child's courage; don't belittle his or her fears.

REMIND YOUR CHILD THAT THE LAST TIME WORKED OUT OKAY, AND IT WILL BE OKAY THIS TIME TOO. Children have short memories and quickly forget.

MAKE SURE YOUR CHILD KNOWS WHAT'S GOING TO HAPPEN. If your child is starting preschool, arrange a short trip to the facility before school starts in order to familiarize your child with all that is going to happen. Having no surprises will help.

BE POSITIVE. Show that you are not concerned about leaving your child. Don't communicate anxiety by, say, telling a teacher that your child may be anxious. Your child will hear it and then become anxious, because you communicated some reason to be.

PHOBIAS IN CHILDREN

Since most phobias originate in childhood, it is not surprising to find lots of them in children. Some apparent phobias, however, are not yet fully developed into true phobias. That will take time, which is why the fears need to be dealt with as early in a child's life as possible. The longer the fears are left untreated, the more likely they will become entrenched and resist treatment later.

In the early stages, fears become exaggerated and appear as phobias, but many of these fears are quite normal, even necessary, for a child's development. A fear of high places, for example, helps to prevent a child from climbing high walls or other dangerous obstacles. A fear of fire prevents a child from burning himself. Phobias can develop out of a violation of such fears precisely because a child was not aware of the danger in the first place.

True phobias are extreme anxiety reactions over unreasonable fears or even something that has no danger attached to it at all. The more unreasonable, the greater the phobia. A fear of snakes is normal. But to break out in a sweat and panic at seeing a snake exhibit where the snakes are behind thick glass and you are well protected is unreasonable and phobic.

Common childhood fears that may become phobic if experienced to an extreme include:

- fear of the dark

- fear of animals

- fear of going on a bus, airplane, or amusement-park ride

- fear of the dentist or doctor

- fear of strangers

- fear of water or learning to swim

If these fears are not too extreme, you can try the systematic desensitization approach I described in chapter 13 for treating adult phobias. Be extremely careful not to proceed in exposing a child to the feared place or object too fast. Slow is always safer.

To give an example, let me describe how we set about desensitizing one of our very young grandchildren recently, after we had acquired a new and boisterous puppy of the not-too-small variety. For the first few days, we merely let him observe the puppy from a distance. We intentionally kept the exuberant canine at a safe distance from him but played with him as if he were just another member of the family. I laid down on the carpet and had the puppy lick me, climb all over me, and try to get under me. Everyone laughed at the antics, and my grandson began to grin.

Slowly he began to move closer very cautiously. When the puppy suddenly moved, he pulled back, but then came closer again. Finally, he reached out his hand and the dog licked it and wagged his tail. Battle won. They became the best of pals. Of course, you shouldn't do this with a grown dog you don't absolutely trust. Rather to be safe than sorry. But *very gradual* exposure to feared situations, with the child setting the pace, can help to eliminate many common fears. Your impatience could turn them into phobias.

CHILDHOOD NAIL BITING

Another anxiety-related problem that can drive parents nuts is nail biting. Many adults can remember their own problem with it, emphasizing how important it is to deal with the problem early. As Denise, a habitual nail biter, recalls, "I've bitten my nails for as long as I can remember. It is a very nervous habit and, obviously, made worse by stress. After college I really tried to stop, but couldn't. My nails are hopelessly soft and thin, so just letting them grow doesn't help much because they break so easily. I'm afraid to go to a manicurist and wish there were resources especially for nail biters."

Dealing with nail biting can be frustrating to a parent. For starters, you should not badger your child. The less attention you draw to it overtly, the better. By all means, gently pull your child's hand away from his or her mouth, and then divert attention elsewhere.

Whatever you do, keep the problem in perspective. Early nail biting can be harmless and can go away spontaneously, so try to ignore it. School-age kids, and even preschoolers, often chew their nails. Neither the habit nor the fingernails are very attractive, but once kids get old enough to become concerned with their appearance (usually about age ten), nail biting usually starts to taper off.

Teach your child basic nail care, such as how to file, clean, and be proud of his or her nails. If your child is a girl, take her regularly to a manicurist so that she develops a sense of the importance of her nails. Often, the real problem is that the nails are too soft. Get a nail hardener (available in pharmacies) and, if the problem is severe, also a nail varnish that tastes bad. This should not be seen as "punishment," but rather as a "reminder" to the help the child be aware when he or she is biting.

If the child is such a serious nail biter that her fingertips get raw and painful, the biting may be how she's releasing tension or stress. As with any nervous habit, try not to fix the child's attention on the mannerism. Don't talk about the nail biting, but see if there are pressures or stresses in her life that you can help alleviate.

You may wish to consider why your child bites his or her nails. Is he anxious? Are there specific situations that may be anxiety producing in which she routinely bites her nails? For the normal anxieties that are part of every child's life, some parents have even substituted "worry beads" for nail biting. These are beads a child plays with when nervous or tense. While this might help, I see a risk that it will maintain the worry, rather than address it.

For anxiety that seems excessive, consult a pediatrician or child psychologist about additional help that may be appropriate. In the meantime, use positive reinforcement (even small rewards) for those occasions when your child is not biting his nails. The key to good behavior modification is learning to catch your child being good, then rewarding that, rather than catching them doing something wrong and scolding.

GENERALIZED ANXIETY IN CHILDREN

Many children do not have specific anxiety problems but develop a "generalized" anxiety akin to that seen in adults where the anxiety is pervasive, broad based, and debilitating. Symptoms include:

- multiple worries about things before they happen;
- constant worries or concern about school, friends, or sports;
- excessive tension and uptightness;
- constant attempts to seek reassurance;
- excessive worries that interfere with normal childhood activities.

Because anxious children may also be quiet, compliant, and eager to please, their anxious difficulties may easily be missed.

Parents should be alert to the signs of severe anxiety so they can intervene early to prevent complications. Early treatment can prevent future difficulties, such as loss of friendships, failure to reach social and academic potential, and feelings of low self-esteem.

Unfortunately, generalized anxiety is not something you can treat yourself as a parent. The risk of making matters worse is very high. Sometimes it requires using antianxiety medications. If this proves to be so, make sure that the doctor prescribing them is experienced in treating anxiety disorders in children. Also, it is probably a good idea to get your child a thorough physical examination because many physical conditions, including problems in the endocrine system, can cause childhood anxiety as well.

TEST ANXIETY

A very special form of anxiety that, though not serious, is worthy of mention here, is test anxiety. Test anxiety can also be a part of a more general problem surrounding performance of any sort. It can be a real problem for a child because excessive anxiety interferes with the child's ability to perform at his or her best.

Generally, we all experience some level of nervousness or tension before tests or other important events in our lives. A little nervousness can actually help motivate us; however, too much of it can become a problem—especially if it interferes with our ability to prepare for and perform well on tests.

The first step is to distinguish between two types of test anxiety. The first is normal "rational" anxiety, and the second, problematic "irrational" anxiety. In rational anxiety, there is a reason to be concerned. You may not have prepared sufficiently or the stakes may be extremely high. In the second and often more common test anxiety, you are prepared, but your anxiety is irrational, almost phobic.

If your child's test anxiety is a direct result of his or her lack of preparation, consider it normal. We are designed to feel anxious when we don't prepare well. The anxiety helps us the next time to apply ourselves more seriously. The solution is to encourage your child to prepare better.

However, if your child is adequately prepared for the exam but still panics or overreacts, the reaction is *not* rational and needs further help than better preparation can provide.

DEALING WITH TEST ANXIETY

Preparation is the best way to minimize normal anxiety. Make sure your child understands this principle: If you don't prepare well, you will pay for it in more anxiety.

If your child has irrational test anxiety, even though he or she is well prepared, then the anxiety will interfere with performance. Here are some effective ways to reduce this anxiety:

MAKE SURE YOUR CHILD PRACTICES DEEP MUSCLE RELAXATION. The relaxation tape offered in Appendix A will give you the general idea, so adapt the principles to your child. Relaxation is always the best antidote for test anxiety. Your child should know how to relax before and during the test. The anxious feelings may not go away, but relaxing breaks the fight-or-flight response so that at least your child's performance won't be disrupted by the anxiety.

PROVIDE YOUR CHILD WITH DISTRACTIONS DURING THE PERIOD LEADING UP TO THE TEST. Too much thinking about the test ahead of time only causes further anxiety. Let your child go to a movie, or take him or her on an outing. The night before, see to it that he or she is kept busy with other activities besides preparing for the exam.

MAKE SURE YOUR CHILD GETS A GOOD NIGHT'S SLEEP BEFORE THE TEST. Good sleep is an antidote for a lot of anxieties, and test anxiety is no exception. If your child has a problem with sleep, as many anxious children do, then follow some of the suggestions I give in chapter 14. The most important principle is *always* put your child to bed at the same time. Childhood sleeping difficulties are due more to variable bedtimes than anything else. This plays havoc with their body's natural clock.

HELP FOR TEST ANXIETY IN OLDER CHILDREN AND ADOLESCENTS

Older children and adolescents have a few additional problems to contend with. Here are some ways to help them:

DISCOURAGE CRAMMING FOR THE TEST. Trying to master a semester's material the day before a test is counterproductive and will guarantee failure on *all* of the material. This tends to raise your anxiety because your body interprets this as an emergency and tries to trigger the fight-or-flight response. Cramming produces anxiety interference, not better grades. The night before a test is not the best time to learn a great deal of material.

ASK YOUR CHILD TO THINK ABOUT WHAT QUESTIONS ARE LIKELY TO BE ASKED ON THE TEST. Then, as you help him or her study for the test, try to answer these questions by integrating ideas from lectures, notes, texts, and supplementary readings. This is "focused" study and more effective than "shotgun" study, in which you try to master everything.

SELECT A PORTION OF THE TEST MATERIAL THAT YOUR CHILD CAN COVER WELL. If your child is unable to cover all the material given throughout the semester, focus on the material he or she is most likely to understand. Help your child set a goal of presenting this knowledge on the test. Getting some of the test right is better than getting none of it right.

HELP YOUR CHILD IMPROVE HIS OR HER PERSPECTIVE OF THE TEST-TAKING EXPERIENCE. This can actually help your child to enjoy studying and may improve his or her performance. Don't overplay the importance of the grade. It is not a reflection of your child's self-worth nor does it predict his or her future success. Remind your child that a test is only a test, and there will be others. Give him a reward after the test, such as taking him to a movie, going out to eat, or visiting with friends.

PLAN WAYS TO IMPROVE YOUR CHILD'S WORK NEXT SEMESTER. Better planning, clear study times, etc., can help to relieve test anxiety.

DON'T FORGET THE BASICS. Students preparing for tests often neglect basic biological, emotional, and social needs. Encourage them to continue the habits of good nutrition, exercise, recreational pursuits, and social activities. These all contribute to their emotional and physical well-being and help to lower anxiety.

TREATMENT OF SEVERE CHILDHOOD ANXIETY DISORDERS

Let me reassure parents right at the outset: Severe anxiety problems in children *can be treated*. Often the anxiety is transitory and needs a relatively short intervention. Treatments may include a combination of the following: individual psychotherapy, family therapy, medications, behavioral treatments, as well as consultation with a school counselor (because anxieties not only affect schoolwork, but often originate in conflicts at school).

No matter what the manifestation of the anxiety, always adopt a nonpunitive, noncritical attitude and give first priority to observing your child's habits and sources of anxiety. When is your child most likely to be anxious? Often, children can be helped to establish alternative, nondamaging routines while involved in activities that would typically trigger a pulling or biting episode. You may want to explore with the child a variety of distracting items such as stuffed animals, velvet, nerf balls, etc.

Throughout treatment, provide lots of praise, be encouraging, be patient, and do not nag when anxious behavior occurs. You might even stop paying any attention to the anxiety problem for a time to see if it is an attention-getting device. Remember also to pray with your child over his or her anxieties. Scripture commands you to do this: "Cast all your anxiety on him because he cares for you" (1 Pet. 5:7 NIV). This command is not to be interpreted as condemnation for our anxieties, since many of them are more the consequence of stress than worry. But God offers comfort and relief for our anxieties in times of trouble. Of this I have no doubt.

Also remember that all manifestations of childhood anxiety are complex behavior patterns, the causes of which are not all known. Some treatments are still experimental, which is why you need the support or guidance of a qualified therapist even if a specialist in anxiety disorders is treating your child. For some school-age children, early intervention can help to ensure that they are protected from the potentially devastating problems associated with adult anxiety disorders.

A comprehensive overview of the treatment of childhood anxiety disorders is neither appropriate nor possible here. Still, I would like to leave parents with a brief overview of the medications used.

Antianxiety medications are usually only resorted to in children when other interventions fail. So always try to get good psychological help first, unless the disorder is really incapacitating. Self-mutilating behaviors like head banging, cutting, biting, and even severe hair pulling are considered to be part of the obsessive-compulsive spectrum of disorders. Because it is suspected that these involve abnormalities in brain serotonin, treatment is with selective serotonin reuptake inhibitors (SSRIs), such as Prozac and Luvox. Sometimes a TCA like Anafranil is used.

For true anxiety and fear symptoms, your child's treatment should include school counseling; psychodynamic, cognitive, and behavioral therapies; family therapy; and medication. *Many children need these treatments in combination simultaneously or successively.*

Some of the medications used in treating adult anxiety disorders are also helpful to children. One study has found that the antidepressant imipramine (used to treat panic attacks and agoraphobia in adults) is more effective than a placebo in children who refuse to go to school. Forty-five children participated in the experiment; after six weeks, 70 percent of those taking imipramine and 44 percent of those taking a placebo were able to return to school. Antianxiety drugs, such as buspirone and the benzodiazepines, have occasionally been successful with overanxious children, but research is limited.[1]

The beta blockers (propranolol or Inderal and others) have been used safely in children; they relieve physical symptoms of anxiety by suppressing activity in the sympathetic nervous system. All these drugs, of course, have side effects and dangers. Prescribing them for children requires even more caution than prescribing them for adults.

Drugs are usually not the first choice in treating children and should never be the only treatment. No doubt that in the not-too-distant future we will see more effective and less problematic medications available for treating childhood anxiety. As stress continues to grow, our children will become more and more prone to developing anxiety disorders. Children today already have to master more information and make more adjustments than at any time in history. The information highway is not going away, and the competition to succeed is not decreasing. Their needs are too precious for us to ignore, so we need to provide the best help we can. Appropriate antianxiety agents will help tremendously.

CHAPTER 17

MASTERING CHRISTIAN MEDITATION

———— ⚬⚬⚬ ————

Till I come, give attendance to reading, to exhortation, to doctrine. . . .
Meditate upon these things; give thyself wholly to them;
that thy profiting may appear to all.

1 TIMOTHY 4:13, 15

The New Age's emphasis on meditation in its various forms like yoga and transcendental meditation (known simply as TM), has put the fear of life into Christians, many of whom have rejected the very idea as unchristian. This is a pity, for I fear that we have thrown the baby out with the bath water. New Age, or any eastern or other so-called religious system, doesn't own meditation. And we Christians need to rediscover the value of meditation by putting Christ at the center of it.

Christian meditation has been a spiritual discipline from the inception of the gospel. In fact, it was there before Christ came. For instance, the psalms are full of references to meditating on God. Psalm 1:1–2 says, "Blessed is the man . . . [whose] delight is in the law of the LORD, and on his law he meditates day and night" (NIV) Another psalm declares, "May the words of my mouth and the meditation of my heart be pleasing in your sight, O LORD, my Rock and my Redeemer" (Ps. 19:14 NIV).

Jesus Himself withdrew regularly from His disciples and the throng following Him to go into the hills and be alone with God. These were times of spiritual and physical refreshment after which He returned to His ministry with renewed energy and vigor.

The very act of prayer, as the meeting with God, is a form of meditation. The study of Scripture and reflection of its truth, meaning, and application to our lives is a form of meditation. Even the act of worship is a form of meditation. Whichever way we turn, we encounter meditation in one form or another. It is inescapable.

For the Christian, meditation takes on a very special meaning. It is *not* the same as yoga or TM or Zen Buddhism, and it should never be reduced to just this level of experience. I say this because the whole notion of meditation has been secularized in modern times. Contemporary psychology has adapted it for therapy and relaxation. And that is all it is for the majority of people.

Yes, it's true. Meditation can be totally nonreligious. You can meditate on your navel if you like and probably still find it helpful in lowering your stress and relieving your anxiety. You can stare at the stars and find that you have stopped obsessing for a while as you contemplate the vastness of the universe and the smallness of your problems. But for the Christian, meditation is more than this. It is a spiritual discipline. And it just so happens that, as a discipline, it also works wonders in relieving the pain of anxiety.

So, read me out here. Meditation, even just for meditation's sake, is a powerful and natural anxiety reliever. And as a spiritual discipline, it also has eternal benefits. You win on both fronts.

WHAT IS MEDITATION?

Since the word *meditation* now has so many different meanings, we need to be sure about what it really means.

Psychologically, there are two types of meditation—concentrative meditation and external awareness meditation. In concentrative meditation, a person seeks to restrict awareness of the outside world by focusing attention on an object or thought. Here, you try to restrict each of the senses in turn until you have them all shut out. Visually, you may concentrate on a picture. Auditorily, you could focus on a distant sound. Physically, you restrict your movement. Together, this deprives your senses and you become highly focused.

Concentrative meditation is the foundation for yoga, TM, tai chi, Zen Buddhism, and so forth.

Don't misunderstand me. Such a practice can powerfully reduce stress. It stands to reason that if you train yourself in such a high level of focus and concentration, your stress levels *will* diminish. My objection, however, is that those who practice concentrative meditation don't attribute the benefits to the simple and natural value of restricting the senses. They attribute it to their particular religious or New Age practice. In other words, they legitimize their beliefs through it.

Or let me put it another way. If you practice any of these concentrative meditation techniques without accepting the quasi-religious underpinnings, you will clearly benefit. In fact, some of the things we do in our Christian forms of meditation incorporate concentration, simply because concentration helps us to assimilate Scripture and pray more effectively. Clearly, *there is nothing wrong or unchristian with concentration.* Some of our praying could benefit from a whole lot more of it.

The second form of meditation, understood psychologically, is external awareness meditation. Here, the practice is the opposite of the former—you meditate in order to open up your awareness of the outside world. For instance, the Benedictine monks have a discipline of "listening" to the world. They believe God speaks through nature and history, that God is manifest in *all* of His creation. For example, when you peel and eat an orange, you pay attention to all its attributes: its fragrance, its texture, its taste. Even tragedy must be listened to for its message from God.

Similarly, the Quakers have a practice of "listening with the heart." Silence is used extensively to aid in "hearing" what God has to say to your heart.

I must confess that I find the external awareness approach more appealing, but this may well just be my personality. But, here again, the stress-lowering value of the meditation doesn't necessarily come from the content of the meditation, but from the process of meditation. It slows you down, for one thing. In addition, it helps you to control your thoughts. Christians who meditate on a personal and knowable God have the added benefit of coming closer to the real, living God, and having Him draw closer to you. For the Christian, then, meditation is a very special experience.

If we can conceive of *adding* a truly Christian emphasis and focus to meditation, we come closer to a discipline that is helpful both physically *and* spiritually. I realize that in saying this I am diminishing the spiritual importance of other religious systems, but that is my position.

IS THERE A CHRISTIAN FORM OF MEDITATION?

From my remarks thus far, you will no doubt have discerned that I strongly believe that there is a Christian form of meditation. This may not be such a startling statement in some circles, but for many conservative Christians it might be revolutionary. Not only is meditation valid, but I would go a step further and say that it is *essential* to the Christian's life.

Those Christians who suffer from severe forms of anxiety are depriving themselves of a rich and powerful resource for recovery. Research indicates that the benefits of meditation are overwhelmingly positive. From Olympic athletes to business executives, meditation has been found to be very beneficial.

True, a lot of the research that has examined the benefits of meditation has only looked at secular forms of meditation, but my feeling is that if secular meditation ("navel gazing," if you like) helps to relieve anxiety, how much more will a Christ-centered and purposeful Christian meditation be of help? Besides, Christian anxiety sufferers deserve to know how to develop a Christian form of meditation.

To be Christian, meditation must depend for its results not just on the physical value of meditating, but on the very action of God's grace as well. It is the action of the Holy Spirit within the soul of the believer, releasing the presence of God to be felt and experienced down to the very marrow of every bone that brings healing. It is this form of meditation that I would like to outline briefly now.

To begin with, think of Christian meditation as a form of "spiritual resting" and a time to listen to God. It can be a form of prayer, praise, or reflection on Scripture. It is not the use of a mantra or any other such device. In other words, do not mimic TM or other secular form of meditation. Do not adopt their language or phrases. This only confuses what you are trying to do. I am trying to define what is a truly acceptable Christian form of meditation, not mimic the popular variants.

Webster's Dictionary defines *meditation* as: "Deep reflection on sacred matters as a devotional act; study; ponder; to think deeply and continuously." I love this definition because it guides us exactly into what Christian meditation is and is not. It is not some mystical, esoteric, or strange operation. You do not leave your body or visit strange planets, inside or outside your inner or outer universe. Meditation is simply a devotional act of deep reflection. Some branches of the Christian church have a long history of such meditational practices. Most conservative Christians have neglected it. So I think that we Christians could do with a lot more deep reflection on matters to do with our faith and Christian experience.

There are, therefore, two essential ingredients you need to focus on as you develop your ability to practice Christian meditation. First, you must develop some ability to focus on something specific. Type A minds, like my own, are all over the place. Thoughts flood my thinking and jump from pillar to post. Clinically, we call this "polyphasic" thinking. Some of us will require disciplined practice to enable us to become "monophasic" thinkers—one thought at a time. Then, and only then, is *deep reflection* possible.

Second, you have to get into the habit of worshiping beyond attendance at church. This seems obvious, but my experience with many Christians is that they seriously think that worship is what you do in church and only in church. They have never stood on the edge of a canyon, marveled at the grandeur of nature, and felt compelled to fall on their knees in an act of worship. They have never looked into the face of a newborn baby and wanted to cry out in worship. It never even dawns on them that worship is for every moment of any day. And this is where Christian meditation can be helpful. It is all about worship, a *devotional act.* And if you learn to meditate regularly, you will also come to worship regularly.

Christian meditation, therefore, not only has the advantage of providing us with a powerful antidote for stress and anxiety, but at the same time helps us to develop a worshipful lifestyle. So let me make myself clear: Christian meditation, designed to help your mind and body to become more tranquil, is a spiritual discipline that can enhance your experience of God. It is a form of worship—not the jubilant, celebrative form in which you experience peak mountaintop or high emotions, but the peaceful, tranquil form in which you remain quiet and at rest, coming to know the peacefulness of the presence of God. Christian meditation is the literal embodiment of Psalm 46:10, "Be still, and know that I am God" (NIV). It is not a substitute for your prayer or Bible study time, but a supplement to it. It is not a substitute for corporate worship time when you join with others in community, but an extension of it.

HOW TO DEVELOP A CHRISTIAN WAY OF MEDITATING

There are many ways you can meditate. Here I want to suggest five ways of Christian meditation that can, at least, serve as a starting point. Obviously, you may have a form or style of your own or one you've learned from someone else. If so, please feel free to substitute your own. There are no absolutes here. Some people prefer to sing hymns to break up their meditation time into segments. Others prefer to remain silent the whole time. Some prefer to pray out loud, others silently.

The relaxation tape I am offering in Appendix A includes a guided tour through these ways, and some readers may prefer to listen to the tape while they practice their meditation, rather than try to read a book. I would suggest, however, that you read through the guidelines I provide here and then set the book aside during meditation and adapt my suggestions to the best of your memory. This will be more effective than trying to follow along in the book as you try to meditate.

IMAGINATION AND CONCENTRATION

There are two essential skills you will need to draw on as you meditate: imagination and concentration. These are abilities that God has given to us, in part so that we might be able to experience and enjoy Him. When these capacities are lost, as in a major brain disorder like Alzheimer's disease, we suffer a serious loss in our capacity to worship. God knows and allows for this. But those of us who have healthy minds need to use each of these capacities in our meditation. Allow me to briefly suggest some ways we can enhance these capacities.

Imagination is the way we create a mental image of something. But we don't all "imagine" in quite the same way. Some people are fortunate in that they can visualize in their imagination. They can actually conjure up images that are like real pictures, even moving pictures, in their minds. These are the people who usually become artists or architects. If they are redecorating their bedrooms, they can actually "see" what they imagine. If this is how you imagine, then you are very fortunate and already have a running start on your ability to meditate.

For years, as a child, I thought there was something wrong with me because I could not "see" pictures quite so clearly when a teacher asked me to imagine something. I could only see glimpses that were too fleeting and changeable to be of any value. Then I discovered that a lot of my friends were like I was—not having a clue about what you were supposed to do with your imagination. (We all became engineers.)

If you can imagine in a visual way, you will have no difficulty here. More of us, however, don't imagine visually but descriptively. By this, I mean that we use words to describe what we are imagining, rather than fixed pictures. We carry on a self-conversation describing what we imagine. If you ask me to imagine a river, I will describe the banks, the ripples, the overhanging trees, etc. It will not be a complete picture in my mind. If you are like this, then continue to develop this ability. Describe to yourself what it is you are imagining. Paint in the little pieces bit by bit, and even if they vanish as soon as you paint in the next bits, that's quite okay. Just exercise your imagination, and, like any muscle, it gets stronger.

Now what about concentration? Concentration is the ability to fix your thoughts or attend to something particular. It is a focusing down on something special. Here, our brains have a phenomenal ability. The brain is designed to selectively shut out what it doesn't need. For instance, sitting here at my computer typing, I didn't notice at first that an ambulance had come into our street, a cul-de-sac, with siren howling. I was concentrating so hard on what I was writing that I didn't notice it. (Having a home with good sound-proofing helps a little.) Finally, I realized that there was a noise bugging me, recognized it as a nearby ambulance, and went to investigate.

We have the capacity to focus and concentrate in such a way that we can shut out the outside world for a short period of time. This capacity to concentrate is essential to meditation. It increases the strength or intensity of the experience. It fixes our attention for a while on the focus of our attention.

Here again, practice makes perfect. You have to do it over and over again until you learn to concentrate your concentration. Oswald Chambers, the author of the stunningly impactful daily devotional I mentioned earlier, *My Utmost for His Highest,* has a lot to say about the importance of concentration as a spiritual discipline. He believes that the "test" of spiritual concentration is "bringing the imagination into captivity."[1] We can easily become starved in our imagination of God if we cannot concentrate. Where is your imagination looking now? On an idol? Money? Success? Prestige? Yourself? Your work? Don't starve your imagination, but free it by deliberately turning it over to God.

Chambers also goes on to say that one of the reasons why our prayers are stultified is that "there is no imagination, no power or ability to put ourselves deliberately before God."[2] Christian meditation is a way to correct this deficiency. It demands a lot of imagination and concentration.

WAYS TO MEDITATE

Before you begin to meditate, think about the *setting* in which you will meditate. As with your personal prayer life, meditation should be private and at a place where you will not be disturbed. This may be difficult for a young mother, so use the time when your baby is sleeping (and the rest of the family as well). Some may want to try meditating on a commuter train or bus, and, while you can meditate almost anywhere you choose, privacy is preferred.

Then think about your *posture.* You may feel comfortable kneeling on a cushion, lying on a bed, or sitting in a chair. The important consideration here is that your posture must not be distracting. You are not doing penance, but meditating, so pain or discomfort will not be an aid to your meditation. In fact, it may be too distracting. I have no idea where the idea comes from, but I do remember earlier in my own devotional life that I somehow got the idea that praying or any Christian act of worship shouldn't be too comfortable. Phrases like "No pain, no gain" and "God will not look favorably on me if I am too comfortable when I pray" were stuck in my mind. It took me a long time to figure out that physical discomfort was of no value to the soul. For penance, yes, if you're into punishing yourself, but for spiritual growth, no.

Finally, think about the *time* you want to meditate and for how long. Some prefer early mornings; I think evenings are better. At first, you may not be able to tolerate too long a session. So begin with five minutes and then gradually extend the time until you are spending thirty or forty-five minutes in meditation, which is about the ideal amount of time for busy people. Set an alarm to alert you when your time is up so that you don't have to keep looking at the clock or counting the seconds.

Now choose which *form* of meditation you want to engage in today. You may stay with one form for the whole period or move from one to the other as you desire or feel comfortable. At first, you may benefit by trying all the forms I will suggest within the same meditation period. Then later, you can be more selective, depending on your needs.

Here are the five ways for meditating that I recommend:

SURRENDERING YOUR WILL TO GOD

- Be deliberate in "letting go" or surrendering your life to God. Imagine that Jesus is standing in front of you, beckoning you to hand over all that bothers you.

- Be still; be quiet. Try to concentrate on the words you have read in Scripture.

- Practice focusing on God. Imagine Him inviting you to hand over your tensions and worries. Your thoughts may wander, so keep bringing them back to the main thought on your mind. Don't give up easily.

- Keep reminding yourself that God is with you. Feel His presence welcoming you, comforting you, and smiling on you.

- Jesus said: "Look unto me." Oswald Chambers, commenting on this invitation, reminds us that we lose power if we do not concentrate on the right thing. We have to concentrate on Jesus.

- Use your imagination to enhance your act of surrender. The wonderful thing about surrendering to God is that you get your life back again, magnified by His power.

- Select one attribute of God and focus on it. His love, compassion, grace, long-suffering, forgiveness, and holiness can all be rich resources for your imagination. Think about how you have experienced these attributes in your own life.

MEDITATIONAL PRAYER

The act of meditational prayer should be *listening more than speaking* and *receiving more than giving.* This is not the time to present God with your spiritual shopping list for the day. Since most of us have spent our lives speaking to God, rather than listening to Him, this will be a tough exercise to follow, but it is possible. Its purpose is to help you discover your need for God as a person, not the provider of all your needs. While you could combine meditational prayer with a relaxation exercise, I would strongly recommend that you separate the two. In other words, set aside a time each day for deep muscle relaxation and a separate time for meditation. The one could follow the other, but since each requires its own form of concentration, it is difficult to combine them without one suffering.

- Scripture tells us: "Ye ask, and receive not, because ye ask amiss" (James 4:3). Reflect on these words for a few minutes. What would God want to say to you? What, above everything else, would He want you to ask for? Is it not to be present with you as the living God, entering into all of your being? Since He already dwells within you, inviting Him to be present is more an invitation to be more aware of His presence.

- Personal contact with God alters everything. It helps you to let go of that which is, after all, not that important. Listen for God's prompting. Remain silent in your mind and try to receive what He has to say to you.

- Be God-centered. Ponder His great plan of salvation as it has come down to us through the ages.

- Periodically pray a meditational prayer that praises God and expresses your thankfulness to Him, then silence yourself. Invite God to speak to you. How does He speak? With thoughts, feelings, and reminders.

- Don't avoid long periods of absolute silence. In fact, the more silence you can tolerate the better. Try to lengthen the time between when you find your mind active.

- Jan Johnson, in a wonderful book, *Enjoying the Presence of God*, writes about rediscovering intimacy with God in the daily rhythms of your life. Johnson introduces the idea of "breath prayers," a habit many Quakers developed. Breath prayers are simple, whispered words of just a few phrases. "Into Thy hands." "Lord, have mercy." "Hold me, Jesus." "Thee I adore." "Let go and let God." The number of breath prayers you can create are endless. Repeat them over and over again as a way of focusing on God. Then stop and listen again.

MEDITATING ON SCRIPTURE

Meditating on Scripture can be a very beneficial form of meditation. Here the purpose is to focus all your concentration on portions of Scripture. Your goal is not to enhance your study or understanding of Scripture. This is also important, but study time is usually more active and arousing. It should be undertaken sitting at a desk with pen and paper, so you can make notes like you do when you study in school. Here it is meditating on Scripture and finding out what God wants to say to you through His Word.

- Begin by selecting a portion of Scripture you want to meditate on. Don't take too long a passage—a verse or two is sufficient. You could select the text from last Sunday's sermon, something you read in your daily devotional, or you could work through a book that is special to you. I am particularly fond of 2 Corinthians, so I often find myself being drawn there.

- Read the passage in several translations until you know its real meaning. Memorize whichever version you prefer, then put away your Bible and begin meditating. Take each word in turn and ponder it. Think about what it means to you. How does it fit together with the whole?

- Keep concentrating and reflecting on each part of the verse and then begin to put it all together.

- Try to discern what it is you believe God would like to say to you there and then about that verse.

- Then close your meditation time with a brief time of prayer, thanking God for His revealed Word and for giving you the wisdom to understand it.

- If your meditation causes you to be confused about the passage you have been meditating on, or if you think you may need to understand it better, consult a study resource or talk to a friend or your pastor.

- After you have finished, write down the verse you have used on a card and keep it in a place where you can be reminded of it often. My wife has Bible verses on cards all around the house. Not only is this a comforting reminder, but you will retain the memory of these verses more easily.

CONTEMPLATING WHO GOD IS

At several points, I have emphasized the importance of concentration in these meditation exercises. I am indebted to Oswald Chambers for this emphasis, and that is why I mention him often. *My Utmost for His Highest* has blessed many generations and is still as fresh today as it was when it first appeared. He strongly emphasizes the value of concentration in devotional life; it is equally as important in other areas of our life as well.

We can never take a holiday from concentration. When life becomes slipshod, we make disastrous mistakes in judgment or action. We need to keep ourselves as fit in our concentration as we do physically. And just as you cannot take a moral holiday and expect to remain moral, you cannot take a spiritual holiday and remain spiritual. Concentration fitness is the key to keeping yourself spiritually fit.

Here I want to suggest that you concentrate on who God is. Everything in our spiritual life depends on it. People don't get into emotional turmoil because they forget who they are; they get into turmoil because they forget who God is. So contemplating who God is can be a pwerful antidote for spiritual and emotional turmoil, as well as a great meditational exercise.

- Ponder His love, grace, and mercy for you. Try to recall portions or stories from Scripture that show God's love, grace, and mercy. Read the story of the woman taken in adultery (John 8:2–11).

- Ponder God's compassion. Read Matthew 9:36; 14:14; and 15:32.

EXPERIENCING GOD'S PRESENCE

Perhaps the most powerful of all meditational exercises is to practice experiencing the presence of God. Jan Johnson's *Enjoying the Presence of God* provides many practical suggestions on how to do this, and many of these can be incorporated into a meditational exercise. If you prefer something more classical, try Thomas à Kempis's *The Imitation of Christ*, or Brother Lawrence's *The Practice of the Presence of God*. Practicing the presence of God not only helps us learn more about who God is, but also more about who we are. Time spent with God always leads to a better understanding of ourselves.

It is difficult to experience God in the busy, irritating, angry, anguished moments of life. Charging down the fast lane, which many of us do daily, is not conducive to connecting with God. We are too distracted, too unfocused, too hassled, too self-preoccupied, too hurting, too bewildered to be able to make any connection. The best resource for making God's presence felt in your life is meditation.

The purpose of this exercise is to focus on increasing your awareness of God. Begin with a short, personal, worship time. Read a portion of Scripture of your choosing, and then pray for a few minutes, asking God to quiet your mind and increase your awareness of His presence.

- Remind yourself that God is closer to you than you are to yourself. It is not that He needs to be closer because He is already there with you, but that your awareness and sensitivity to His presence needs to be developed.

- Try to focus away from your world with its demands and problems. It will be there when you are done. Worry—or as Scripture calls it, "the cares of this world"—can easily distract us from God.

- Concentrate on God. Become increasingly aware of His presence. You can't see Him in your imagination because He has no physical image to conjure up. The many paintings of the face of Jesus may or may not be helpful. After all, they are only products of someone else's imagination. Try to find an image that helps you to imagine or visualize God. Both my wife and I find the image of a shepherd meaningful—not the young man you might see tending modern sheep on your travels, but a caring, wise, and compassionate shepherd tending the sheep as they lie down, fetching the stray lambs, and leading them on to newer and richer pastures. These images are very meaningful for us. Try to find an image that you find meaningful.

- Write down and keep close to you verses of Scripture that remind you of who God is, like Hebrews 13:5, in which He says, "I will never leave thee, nor forsake thee."

- Believe He is with you. Receive His presence and enjoy it. Bathe in it, as you would in warm water or the warm sun. Images of warmth, comfort, protection, refuge, etc., can be helpful in your meditation.

- Practice the presence of God so that it becomes a way of life with you. Soon you will be able to experience God's presence on a busy bus or in a crowded restaurant. God doesn't hide Himself when we get crowded. We lose the sense of His presence; He doesn't hide from us. So practice His presence in every situation.

God wants us to be totally consumed with Him. It is not a consumption that restricts, but frees. It doesn't distract us from the demands of life, but empowers us to live more fully. This is the paradox of the Christian life: The more we give of ourselves to God, the more He gives us a meaningful life back. But our responsibility is to keep ourselves in tune with God, and Christian meditation is just one way of doing this. We can take no spiritual holidays and expect to remain spiritual. We can take no shortcuts to a deeply spiritual life and expect to be effective. Keep God at the center of your life, and you will remain at the center of the power you need to live. And you will also achieve freedom from the anxiety that destroys your tranquillity.

CHAPTER 18

A SPIRITUALITY FOR
TRANQUILLITY

———— ⌾⌾⌾ ————

Abide in me, and I in you.
As the branch cannot bear fruit of itself, except it abide in the vine;
no more can ye, except ye abide in me.

JOHN 15:4

This book has been all about bringing healing to people who are wracked by anxiety. As we come to this last chapter, we need to put this healing in a larger context, that of the spiritual resources that God has given us for coping with life.

The word *heal* comes from the root Old English word *haelen*, which means "to make whole." No healing, or cure, is complete unless it contributes to making us "whole" or complete, and we can only be complete if the body, mind, and spirit are brought together. Socrates, commenting on the medical theory of healing in his day, said: "As it is not proper to cure the eyes without the head, nor the head without the body; so neither is it proper to cure the body without the soul."[1]

For Christians, this means that we need to redefine healing in the sense that it is used in Scripture, the healing of the whole person. For a long time, medical and psychological science tended to compartmentalize healing. If your body was full of infection, the infection was cured without regard to anything else. If your mind was depressed, then all you needed was for the depression to be removed.

One writer whom I have admired very much over the years is Jewish social anthropologist Ernest Becker. While not a Christian, he was about as honest a commentator on the human condition as I have ever encountered. In his book, *Denial of Death,* Becker examines the work of psychotherapy. He concedes that while it can do many good things for troubled people, relieving their fears and giving them a little hope, there are many things it can't do. He says that what psychotherapy, and other medical treatments, can't do hasn't been aired honestly enough. "Not everyone was as honest as Freud was when he said that he cured the miseries of the neurotic only to open him up to the normal miseries of life," he wrote.[2]

If ever there was a message we need to hear today it is this one: Healing is not complete until that healing restores our wholeness. The implication here is that we cannot expect to be healed from our anxiety problems without healing our "larger" selves. The anxiety will return as certainly as the sun will rise tomorrow.

PSYCHOLOGY'S REVOLUTION

It is in this context that something profound is happening at the core of psychology today. It is becoming more spiritual—not necessarily Christian, but definitely more open to spiritual matters. And this change is producing a product that is very much more in harmony with what Christians believe and practice. Psychology is finally moving away from focusing on fixing just what is broken in the human psyche to looking at the larger picture—nurturing strength and resilience. In other words, it is focusing less on what is destructive and more on what is constructive in psychology.

This means that the central point in contemporary psychology is shifting from a disease model that fosters a "victim mentality," toward "positive" psychology that explores how we can develop strengths and emotional health as the antidotes for our emotional problems. Leading this change, as we will see, is the president of the American Psychological Association, Martin Seligman. He has undergone precisely such a change in his own career, starting with his development of the concept of "helplessness" and ending with the concept of "optimism." It is a move that is both long overdue and extremely exciting.

This shift is very compatible with our Christian gospel. It is a positive gospel about growth and mastery, not about weakness and disease. While it points up sin and its consequences, it offers forgiveness for sin.

In keeping with this transformation, I have explored the positive side to our anxiety and stress problems and examined the antidote for these problems—namely, tranquillity. Rather than just focusing on the negative aspects of what produces stress disease and anxiety problems, I looked at what positive strengths will prevent these debilitating problems. This is surprisingly revolutionary but, as you will see, in keeping with our latest scientific discoveries.

Tranquillity, therefore, is the goal of this book. Put simply, tranquillity is the antidote for anxiety. Its presence prevents the development of anxiety disorders and heals anxiety when it is out of control. As we have seen, tranquillity requires biological harmony in the brain. Upon this foundation of biological harmony, we must build emotional and spiritual tranquillity. One cannot survive without the other, and each serves to strengthen the other.

Why do we need such a book at this time? I wrote *Adrenaline and Stress* for hurried people—for normal people who live busy but hectic and overextended lives, for those who strive for excellence but just don't have enough time in each day to accomplish all they set out to do. If you are one of these people, then you are likely to be at risk for both stress *and* anxiety and lack one very important antidote for either stress disease or anxiety disease—*tranquillity.* So this book is about the tranquillity that can counteract the effects of a hurried life. It has to be a natural tranquillity if it is going to work for us, not the tranquillity we can create with a tranquilizer, though for a temporary period we may need to use a tranquilizer to get us through a rough period. For the long haul, we must learn how to create within us a deep calmness and peacefulness that is the product of a balanced life. In this book, I have focused on the biology, psychology, and spirituality of this tranquillity.

Why do we need this message today? Because we all drive ourselves too hard. We don't take enough time off for rest. We push ourselves to achieve excellence and to live life to the fullest. Do we reach our goal? Seldom. We end up robbing ourselves of real peace, that deep, inner calmness and serenity that are best summed up in the word *tranquillity.* Pastors, business executives, professionals, artisans, teachers, doctors—you name it—we are all pretty much at risk here for eventually needing to depend on an artificial tranquilizer to get rid of the stress and anxiety of living.

Adrenaline and Stress addressed the misunderstandings of the nature of stress. But we also misunderstand the nature of anxiety. We look for the source of our anxieties in the wrong places and fail to see it staring out at us from the exciting, mostly enjoyable rush of adrenaline that accompanies the challenges of life. We also fail to realize that science has made some fantastic discoveries over the last few years about how the brain achieves its own natural tranquillity. In this book, I have shared these discoveries in practical ways and showed how tranquillity of mind and spirit *is* attainable.

My message here is also important to us spiritually. Stress and anxiety can play havoc with our spiritual aspirations. When our body and mind are fighting for basic survival, they don't have the energy or time to connect with God. If there is one sad aspect to modern-day spirituality it is that it is hurried; it prays and meditates "on the run." There is no time for reflection or any other spiritual contemplation. And if history teaches us anything here, it is that spiritual formation and hurriedness are not compatible companions. In fact, they don't mix at all. Proverbs 19:2 tells us that "he that hasteth with his feet sinneth." He (or she) also suffers from a lot of stress and anxiety.

Never give up. Jesus didn't. He was tempted to, but He resisted. You must also resist the temptation to give up.

Several times in this book, I have referred to Winston Churchill's "never-give-up" tenacity. The most famous moment of this attitude came when he was speaking to the boys at Harrow School, his alma mater. Even as a boy, Churchill was tempted to give up many times. Disliked by his father, he was sent away to boarding school at the age of seven. Teased because of his ungainliness, he would hide in the woods. Needless to say, he got the lowest scores of any boy in his school. He seemed destined to be a total failure.

All his life Churchill suffered spells of depression and had a morbid fear of some insects that today would be classified as a phobia. We are told that no man wept more easily, whether over some gallantry in battle, observing the victims of anti-Semitism, or seeing a ladybug trampled on. But deep within was a genius waiting to be discovered. Among his many traits was a kind of built-in shock absorber that gave him the courage to survive. If he was knocked down, he bounced back on the rebound. His suffering built his resiliency.

And so it was that on that bleak day in October 1941, the Harrow School honored Winston Churchill, a day when all looked hopeless for the British people suffering under the onslaught of Hitler's air force. And he made a speech that would go down in history: "Never give in, never give in, never, never, never, never—in nothing great or small, large or petty—never give in except to convictions of honor and good sense."

This sounds very much like the words of the apostle Paul in Romans 5:3–4: "We also rejoice in our sufferings, because we know that suffering produces perseverance; perseverance, character; and character, hope" (NIV).

If I know anything about winning over anxiety, it is that you come out of the battle with a lot more integrity, humility, and perseverance than when you started.

SPIRITUAL ANTIDOTES FOR STRESS

Most of my discussions thus far about how we can deal with stress has focused on psychological and biological principles. But there are also important spiritual antidotes for stress that we need to consider. Unfortunately, some people's religious beliefs and behaviors can be more stress-producing than relieving. Obviously, this is not a healthy expression of your religious faith.

So what are some principles we can follow to ensure that our experience as Christian believers is positive and wholesome? I happen to believe that good stress management is as much a matter of spirituality as it is of self-discipline and mastery over our bodies. Faith can play a major role in determining how chaotic our lives become.

How can we develop a healthy faith that fosters protection from stress? I think we should begin by briefly reviewing the life of Jesus. His example can teach us a lot about the spiritual antidotes for stress.

Even a cursory reading of the Gospels will show that Jesus was a model of calmness and composure. What He demonstrated was the very opposite of what most of us experience in our hassled and hurried existences. In Mark 4:38, we see Him asleep at the back of a ship. A great storm comes up; waves beat on the ship so that it is swamped with water. But Jesus goes on sleeping. Was He oblivious to the storm? I doubt it, but He wasn't afraid of the storm. When the disciples woke Him and asked, "Master, carest thou not that we perish?" He not only calmed the sea but asked them, "Why are ye so fearful? how is it that ye have no faith?"

So the life of Jesus was a model of unhurriedness. Yes, it's true that in New Testament times life didn't move very fast anyway, but I don't think that is an adequate excuse. *We need to learn the spirit of unhurriedness.* It is the essential foundation for the tranquillity we need to protect us from the ravishes of anxiety.

The life of Jesus was also a model of balanced priorities. We see this in the story of Martha and Mary, sisters who had received Jesus into their home, recorded in Luke 10:38–42. Martha, who was probably older, was so caught up with the importance of her visitor that she went into quite a dither about getting things just right for Jesus. I can just imagine the questions that were bothering her: *Where's the wine? Who knocked the jug over? Why do you have to make extra work for me? What should I cook for dinner?* Finally, after she could take no more, Martha accused Jesus of not caring about how hard she was working and of allowing Mary, her irresponsible sister, to just sit at His feet and soak up all His teaching. Jesus in His patient and perspective restoring reply says, "Martha, Martha, thou art careful and troubled about many things: But one thing is needful; and Mary hath chosen that good part, which shall not be taken away from her" (vv. 41–42).

We're not told how Martha took these words of admonishment from Jesus. Perhaps she threw down her dishcloth and stormed out of the house in anger. Perhaps she had a passive-anger response and went into a silent sulk hiding in the corner. Who knows? But I like to think that she did the mature thing and calmly put down the pot she was holding, took off her apron, pulled up a pillow, and sat down next to Mary at the feet of Jesus. Perhaps they didn't even bother to eat that day; perhaps they gave the food prepared for Jesus to the poor. After all, food cannot be all that important when you have an opportunity to sit before the Messiah and hear the words of God. So keeping this moral from Jesus' life of unhurriedness and balanced priorities can go a long way toward minimizing the stress in your busy life. He is never impatient, so learn tolerance from Him. Keep regular devotional times with Him, and you will never be tempted to run ahead of Him.

I have a closing assignment for you. Treat this assignment with all the sincerity and seriousness that you have treated the rest of this book, and it might just give you more freedom from anxiety than the rest.

CLOSING ASSIGNMENT

Take your Bible, a pen, and a sheet of paper and review again the story as it appears in Luke 10:38–42. Imagine that you are sitting at the feet of Jesus with Mary and Martha. Also imagine that Jesus asks you to make a list of everything you are trying to accomplish at this time in your life. Take five minutes or so to do this.

Then, on a second sheet of paper, list all the disappointments you have experienced thus far in your life. Also list all your uncompleted projects and unrealized dreams.

Go down the list, review each one in turn, and ask yourself: Is this really all that important as a disappointment, an unrealized dream, or incomplete project? If it is not important, cross it off your list and forget about it.

When you are done, review those remaining items on the list and prioritize some new goals for the next month or two that might help you attain these goals. Write these goals down on a third sheet of paper.

Now, with this revised set of important goals, ask yourself: What would Jesus want you to do first? What would He want you to forget? Whom would He like you to forgive? Try to increase your awareness of what is urgent and what can wait. More importantly, try to be clear about what really matters.

This is equivalent to what Jesus asked Martha to do. Put down your pots and pans and sit at the feet of Jesus for a while to do some deep, soul-searching evaluations about your priorities. Perhaps much won't change in your priorities, but the exercise will go a long way in helping you build a peaceful, anxiety-free life.

The Mary and Martha story is in the Bible for a reason. Perhaps *you* are that reason.

HOW TO ORDER DR. HART'S RELAXATION TRAINING TAPE

⊸∘∘⊷

This relaxation tape is designed to do four things:

1. It will help you develop the ability to rapidly produce a deep state of muscle relaxation, called the "relaxation response." This response minimizes your body's arousal systems, including your adrenaline, cortisol, and other "sad messengers" and maximizes your "happy messengers."

2. It will also teach you how to warm your hands as a way of particularly switching off your fight-or-flight response. The "cold hands" phenomenon is particularly prevalent in those who easily trigger their adrenaline response or who are under high stress.

3. It will teach you how to take control of your thoughts and redirect them, in times of worry or high anxiety, into more constructive channels. Included in this section will be training in how to cut off your worrying.

4. It will provide you with a way you can enhance your sensory awareness of what is going on around you and participate in Christian-based meditation exercises. Not only will these exercises help you to become more focused on God and His Word, but they will assist you in becoming more prayerful and conscious of God's presence.

The tape is available directly from Dr. Hart for a cost of $7.50, including postage. Please put your name and mailing address on a three-by-five piece of paper and send, along with your check, to:

> Dr. Archibald Hart
> 1042 Cyrus Lane
> Arcadia, CA 91006

ADDITIONAL READING RESOURCES

————— ∞∞∞ —————

Benson, Herbert. *The Relaxation Response.* Mass Market Paperback, 1990.

Chambers, Oswald. *My Utmost for His Highest.* Westwood, NJ: Barbour, 1963.

Hart, Archibald D. *Adrenaline and Stress.* Dallas, TX: Word, 1995.

Hart, Archibald D. *Habits of the Mind.* Dallas, TX: Word, 1996.

Hart, Archibald D., Catherine Hart Weber and Debra L.Taylor, *Secrets of Eve.* Nashville, TN: Word, 1998.

Johnson, Jan. *Enjoying the Presence of God.* Colorado Springs, CO: NavPress, 1996.

Kempis, Thomas à. *The Imitation of Christ.* London: Samuel Bagster.

Lawrence, Brother. *The Practice of the Presence of God.* Grand Rapids, MI: Spire, 1958.

Nouwen, Henri J. M. *Making All Things New.* San Francisco, CA: Harper-Collins, 1981.

Nouwen, Henri J. M. *The Road to Daybreak.*New York: Doubleday, 1988.

ENDNOTES

---∞∞∞---

CHAPTER 3

1. Jasmine Arthur-Jones and Julian Hafner, "Panic Anxiety Management Workshop," reported on the Internet at <http://www.paems.com. au/research>.

CHAPTER 4

1. K. B. Schmalling and J. Bell, "Asthma and Panic Disorder," *Archives of Family Medicine* 6, no. 1 (1997): 20–23.

2. T. J. Lessmeier, et al. "Unrecognized Paroxysmal Supraventricular Tachycardia: Potential for Misdiagnosis as Panic Disorder," *Archives of Internal Medicine* 157, no. 5 (1997): 537–543.

3. D. H. Barlow, "Cognitive-Behavioral Therapy for Panic Disorder: Current Status," *Journal of Clinical Psychiatry* 58, suppl 2:32–36.

CHAPTER 5

1. Mark Rapaport, M.D., "Zoloft As an Effective Treatment of Panic Anxiety," *American Journal of Psychiatry*, 155 (1998).

CHAPTER 8

1. Jasmine Arthur-Jones, "Panic Anxiety Disorder Treatment Needs Research Project," reported on the Internet at <http://www. paems.com. au/research>.

CHAPTER 10

1. Edmund J. Bourne, *The Anxiety and Phobia Workbook* (Oakland, Calif.: New Harbinger Publications, 1995), 351.

CHAPTER 12

1. J. M. Zajecka and J. S. Ross, "Treatment of Depression Complicated by Anxiety," *Journal of Clinical Psychiatry* 56, suppl. 2 (1995): 10–13.

2. R. Reid Wilson, *Don't Panic* (New York: Harper and Row, 1986), 81.

CHAPTER 14

1. A. C. King et al., "Moderate-Intensity Exercise and Self-Rated Quality of Sleep in Older Adults," *Journal of the American Medical Association* 277 (1997): 33–37.

CHAPTER 15

1. Dr. William F. Fry, "Medical Perspectives on Humor," *Humor and Health Journal* 2, no. 1 (1993).

2. Rabbi Noah Weinberg, reported on the Internet at <http://www.aish.edu/learning>.

3. Rick Warren, *The Purpose Driven Church* (Grand Rapids: Zondervan, 1995), 113.

CHAPTER 16

1. Barbara J. Coffey, *The Harvard Mental Health Letter* 9, no. 9 (1993).

CHAPTER 17

1. Oswald Chambers, *My Utmost for His Highest* (Westwood, N.J.: Barbour and Company, 1963), 26 November reading.

2. Ibid.

CHAPTER 18

1. Quoted in R. Moody, *Laugh after Laugh* (Jacksonville, Fla.: Headwaters Press, 1978).

2. Ernest Becker, *Denial of Death* (New York: McMillan, 1973), 270.